D1366666

LBW
Laughter Before Wicket!
100 Years of Humorous Cricket Short Stories

LBW
Laughter Before Wicket!
100 Years of Humorous Cricket Short Stories

Edited by
PETER HAINING

London
ALLEN & UNWIN
Boston   Sydney

First published 1986

**Allen & Unwin (Publishers) Ltd,
40 Museum Street, London WC1A 1LU, UK**

Allen & Unwin (Publishers) Ltd,
Park Lane, Hemel Hempstead, Herts HP2 4TE, UK

Allen & Unwin Australia Pty Ltd,
8 Napier Street, North Sydney, NSW 2060, Australia

Allen & Unwin with the Port Nicholson Press,
PO Box 11-838 Wellington, New Zealand

British Library Cataloguing in Publication Data

LBW: laughter before wicket.
1. Cricket—Anecdotes, facetiae, satire, etc.
I. Haining, Peter
796.35'8'0207   GV919
ISBN 0-04-827152-7

Set in 10 on 12 point Plantin by Fotographics (Bedford) Ltd
and printed in Great Britain by
Billing and Sons, London and Worcester

For

JOHN ARLOTT

*To recall that
year of '59*

Contents

Introduction   *page*   xiii

The Feelings of a Bowler *by J. M. Barrie*   3

The Great Britannula Game *by Anthony Trollope*   9

The Rustic Heroes *by Horace Hutchinson*   21

The Talisman *by Alfred Cochrane*   27

The Story of Spedegue's Dropper *by Sir Arthur Conan Doyle*   35

A Bowler's Innings *by E. W. Hornung*   55

Playing the Game *by P. G. Wodehouse*   67

An Indian Cricket Tutor *by E. V. Lucas*   79

A West Indian Cricket Match *by Eden Phillpotts*   85

A Scratch Lot *by A. A. Milne*   99

The Umpire's Remorse *by E. B. V. Christian*   117

The Match *by Stacy Aumonier*   125

A Buffer's Wicket *by Ben Travers*   137

Biffin on Acquaintances *by Harry Graham*   147

Some Record Catches *by Herbert Farjeon*   159

How Our Village Beat the Australians *by Hugh de Selincourt*   165

The Guardian Angel *by W. A. Darlington*   187

How Jembu Played for Cambridge *by Lord Dunsany*   203

Cricket in the Caucasus *by A. P. Herbert*   217

Dingley Dell v. All-Muggleton *by A. G. Macdonell*   229

French Cricket *by Ian Hay*   241

Cricket for Americans *by Stephen Leacock*   247

The Seasonable Twinge *by Bernard Hollowood*   255

Tripping O'Er the Greensward *by Michael Parkinson*   263

Ain't Half a Bloody Game *by John Arlott*   271

Daffodil Summer *by Leslie Thomas*   295

The Test in Witney Scrotum *by Peter Tinniswood*   309

The Wizzerd of Oz *by Ian Wooldridge*   313

Acknowledgements

The Editor is grateful to the following authors, their agents and publishers for permission to include copyright material in this collection: the Executors of the Estate of J. M. Barrie for 'The Feelings of a Bowler'; the Estate of Alfred Cochrane for 'The Talisman'; A. P. Watt Literary Agency for 'Playing The Game' by P. G. Wodehouse and 'Cricket In The Caucasus' by A. P. Herbert from *Mild And Bitter*; Methuen & Co. Ltd for 'An Indian Cricket Tutor' by E. V. Lucas from *Giving & Receiving*; the Executors of the Estate of Eden Phillpotts for 'A West Indian Cricket Match'; Curtis Brown Literary Agency for 'A Scratch Lot' by A. A. Milne from *The Day's Play* and 'How Jembu Played For Cambridge' by Lord Dunsany from *The Travel Tales of Mr Joseph Jorkens*; the Estate of E. B. V. Christian for 'The Umpire's Remorse'; the Executors of Ben Travers for 'A Buffer's Wicket'; Century Hutchinson Publishers Ltd for 'Some Record Catches' by Herbert Farjeon from *Herbert Farjeon's Cricket Bag*; Jonathan Cape Ltd for 'How Our Village Beat the Australians' by Hugh de Selincourt from *The Game of the Season*; Longmans Publishing Group for 'The Guardian Angel' by W. A. Darlington; Chapman & Hall Ltd for 'Dingley Dell *v.* All-Muggleton' by A. G. Macdonell from *A Pickwick Celebration*; the Estate of Ian Hay for 'French Cricket'; the Bodley Head Ltd for 'Cricket For Americans' by Stephen Leacock, from *My Remarkable Uncle*; *Punch* magazine for 'The Seasonable Twinge' by Bernard Hollowood; Express Newspapers for 'Tripping O'Er The Greensward' by Michael Parkinson and 'The Test in Witney Scrotum' by Peter Tinniswood; John Arlott for 'Ain't Half a Bloody Game'; Heinemann Publishing Group for 'Daffodil Summer' by Leslie Thomas; Associated Newspapers Ltd for 'The Wizzerd of Oz' by Ian Wooldridge.

While every care has been taken to clear permissions for use of the stories in this book, in the case of any accidental infringement, copyright holders are asked to contact the Editor in care of the publishers.

Introduction

The idea for this book had its origins in the spring of 1959. I was a young journalist working in Essex, and was devoting my spare time to helping John Arlott in what was to prove his sadly unsuccessful second attempt to win the Epping parliamentary seat for the Liberal Party. (So now you know *my* political persuasions!)

As anyone who has ever met John will tell you, cricket is as much a part of his life as breathing and good wines, and although he was a dedicated and hardworking candidate in that stoutly Tory stronghold, the subject of the 'Sovran King of Sport' – as H. S. Vere Hodge called it – did have a habit of slipping into our conversations. It came up, I recall most vividly, after one particularly frustrating period of canvassing in a well-heeled section of the community. At most of the houses there was no-one in (or else the occupants wouldn't come to the door) and at the rest we got sympathetic, though hardly what you would call committed, support for the Party. At only one were we greeted with anything approaching real enthusiasm.

At this house, John introduced himself politely and talked – most convincingly, I thought – about what he believed the future held for Britain and what he hoped to be able to achieve for the constituency *if* he were elected the MP. When he had finished, he paused to see what effect he had had on his listener, a man in his sixties.

'I know you,' the chap said after a short pause and with a slight narrowing of his eyes, 'you're on the radio, aren't you?'

John smiled and agreed he was.

'Ah, I thought so,' the man said, turning sharply and closing the door in our surprised faces, 'Can't stand *football!*'

Despite the rebuff, John chuckled as we walked back up the garden path. 'Life's funny, isn't it?' he finally interrupted our silence. 'Just like cricket!'

For a moment I was taken aback at what seemed like an almost sacrilegious remark from one of the sport's leading personalities. John smiled at my quizzical look.

'Well, it does seem to contrive to make a man look silly,' he explained. 'Think of what happens when a catch is dropped, or a batsman falls on his bottom after having a bouncer hurled at him! And see what it's just done for *me* – I'm supposed to be a cricket commentator, yet there was someone who thought I was on about football!'

I took his point. *Of course* cricket can be funny, for after all humour often develops out of the most serious situations, and there's nothing much more serious than being several wickets down with a single figure still on the scoreboard! I know because I've gone out to face it myself a time or two.

But don't get the impression I'm anything other than a rabbit at the game. I'd rather draw a veil over that part of my life, in fact, and get to the point of this preamble by saying that during those days in 1959 John substantiated his claim by telling me a host of amusing true stories about cricket, all within his own knowledge, as well as recommending a number of short stories which had greatly amused him over the years.

Some of those stories were to become the basis of the book now in your hands. I say some, because as the idea crystallised, I decided on a collection of humour in which all the authors were – or had been – cricketers, though the standard of their play was not important. If the men were humorous writers into the bargain, so much the better, for they would see the funny side of things even more vividly. But again this was not vital, for it appears that even the most serious writer can sometimes be moved to laughter on the cricket field! My research has also shown that cricket is a game which has always appealed to men of letters, and though some were quite evidently more accomplished with the pen than they ever were with bat and ball, their love of the game shines through in their work.

Although literature can boast accounts of cricket matches for at least two centuries and more, humour does not appear to have become a regular feature until just one hundred years ago – in particular when the great J. M. Barrie (he of Allahakbarries CC fame) began a series of light-hearted cricket essays which he signed as 'Gavin Ogilvy'. One such item, then, I chose as my starting point, and you will find following on from Barrie a most distinguished team of cricket-loving writers. His friend, the redoubtable all-rounder, Sir Arthur Conan Doyle, for instance; the opening bowler, P. G. Wodehouse, the stylish batsman, A. A. Milne; the eccentric Lord Dunsany; as well as some of today's village green men like Michael Parkinson and Ian Wooldridge. There could have been more – many more – but the dictates of space and a desire to avoid similar themes as much as possible have imposed their own restrictions.

The best of the contributors, as you will read in my introductory notes, have the talent to form a most impressive and potentially successful XI. And as for the rest – what other editor would not give his cherished seat at Lords to include such famous contributors between the covers of a single volume. *What* a game cricket is to unite such people in a common interest. What a FUNNY game!

Peter Haining,
Suffolk, 1985.

LBW
Laughter Before Wicket!
100 Years of Humorous Cricket Short Stories

Just one hundred years ago in May 1885 a journalist who signed himself 'Gavin Ogilvy' began a series of humorous pieces in the popular St. James's Gazette. *These essays were not only the first of their kind, but also something of a departure for the paper, for cricket was not generally regarded as a suitable topic for humour. And indeed the laughter which the columns produced might well have been somewhat stifled if readers had known that 'Ogilvy' was not only an exiled Scot but actually had plans to run his own cricket team! For behind that pen-name lurked James Matthew Barrie (1860–1937), later to create the immortal character, Peter Pan, and write a string of good-humoured social satires for the theatre such as 'Quality Street' and 'The Admirable Crichton'. Today, of course, his memory is cherished in cricketing circles, and his admirers therein are legion. The great Don Bradman, for example, in his twenties remembered listening to Barrie telling stories. 'My favourite,' he was later to recall, 'was the one in which, describing his bowling, he told how, after delivering the ball, he would go and sit on the turf at mid-off, and wait for it to reach the other end – "which it sometimes did".' Although he was small and rather frail, Barrie had an enormous enthusiasm for cricket and though he was never as good at the game as he would have liked, turned his pleasure to fun and founded and captained his own side, Allahakbarries CC, which he later commemorated in a small booklet published in 1899 and several times reprinted. In the side (which got its name, Barrie explained, from the Moorish expression for 'God Help Us!') were several literary friends including Owen Seaman, the editor of* Punch, *and the great Sir Arthur Conan Doyle. The matches were all spirited mixtures of keen competition and high farce. That same sense of humour and admiration which Sir James had for the game is just as evident in his writing, as what follows will amply demonstrate. And there is surely no-one more suited to opening our innings . . .*

1

The Feelings of a Bowler

(By a Poet)

The feelings of a Bowler, how seldom are they considered! The sorrows of a Poet are respected, and Lord Tennyson has particularly requested the public not to trouble the Poet's mind. But what are they to the feelings of a Bowler (like Lord Byron)? I am a Poet myself, and a Bowler; and I have no hesitation in saying that the chords which vibrate in the bosom of the latter are infinitely more sensitive than those which thrill the breast of the former. For, at worst, a Poet is merely neglected, or sniffed at by the gents who write the Minor Notices without cutting the pages of the books sent to them. But the Bowler hears with his ears the cry of "Take him off!" and sees, occasionally, the lack of appreciation shown in the faces of the fields. What is a literary "slating" compared to being hit for four fours in an over? Not that I blame the batsman – he acts after his kind; but the fielders, and the captain, and

3

the public, occasionally – them I do blame. Besides, poetry is a mere pastime of the intellect; to bowl head balls – to bowl them well – requires a very different sort of mind and body. I lately read advice to batsmen, in which they were counselled to wait for a fast bowler's attempt at a low head-ball (which is nearly certain to be bad) and then to let him have it! It may have been Dr. Grace or Mr. A. G. Steel who wrote these unfeeling words; I am sure it was no fast bowler.

The sensitive genius in other walks of art may not always "come off." If I were a painter, for example, I should hardly joy when the work of months was skied, and that in the New Gallery. But it is worse when one's pet head-ball is either not skied at all, but crumped along the ground for six; or is skied, and then dropped by a fellow who misjudges it, though it was hit into his hands in the very place you set him. I have a pet head-ball. The reflection of my waking hours was given to it for weeks, and I could nearly always bring it off – in practice. You begin your over with a good length ball, then you send in one rather short, but high in the curve, just good enough for the batter to find it is a trap and play back. The next looks the same, and is as high in the curve, but it is pitched almost a half-volley. The batsman (in practice) thinks this is the same ball as the one before and plays back again. Hence "a row in his timber-yard," as Mr. Bouncer said. But in a match he "yanks" it round to broad field for as many as the nature of the boundary will permit him to score. Then think of the feelings of the bowler, especially if his captain comes up and suggests the need of a change!

It is a horrid thing to be taken off. Nobody likes it; and some bowlers, when captains, never take themselves off at all. "An obvious instance," as the crib to the Ethics says, "will readily occur": you feel as I fancy the author of "Treasure Island" may when everybody asks him if he has read "Robert Elsmere" – at least, that is how I feel. You can hardly take pleasure in the success of your side when the new man gets the wickets. An amateur once told me a horrid but credible instance of these sentiments. He was playing in a country match, and the professional bowler on his side failed to dislodge a sturdy opponent. The professional was taken off, my friend went on, and lowered the wickets in his first over. The professional then went stark staring mad on the spot (he had been a little off the spot before), and never recovered from the shock. Did any one ever hear of the feelings of a poet carrying him so far?

4

I was present (an unworthy guest) at the dinner of the Royal Academy when Mr. Lecky, that eminent authority on verse, praised Mr. Robert Buchanan's new poems and said they were—— I don't quite remember what, but I *think* he said as good as the classical pictures exhibited in the gallery. More than one poet was there besides myself – two other poets at least; and yet none of us had to be put in strait-waistcoats. We merely remarked that we shouldn't wonder. Yes; that poor untutored ground-bowler had far finer feelings, a far more frantic sense of envy, and less self-control than quite a choir of poets. But who cares, who ever dreams of sparing the feelings of a bowler? You may say, How could a captain win matches if he did? and there is something in that. Besides, of course, there are the other men yearning to be put on. I have not enumerated – who could? – the trials of a bowler. What a thing it is to have catches missed off one! My extreme Radical opinions I trace to the day when a batsman was missed off me four times in one over by a titled wicket-keeper, and several times at cover-point by a belted earl. But is that much worse than over-throws? A batsman makes a feeble push to short-leg. The field lets it go for one, buzzes it in frantically, wicket-keeper lets it go for four; and that four is against *you*, the bowler, in the analysis. They complain of bowlers trundling to keep down the runs; they say Mr. Spofforth is the only man who bowls (like a cricketing General Grant) for wickets purely, at any cost of runs. Then Mr. Spofforth must be a fellow of no delicacy, though his technical skill is undeniable. Perhaps the roughest thing for a bowler is when singles are made, nearly every ball, to short-leg and third man. These detestable fellows are *never* in the right place. Somehow the wonder is that Bowlers are not misanthropes. For my part I attribute the spleen of Lord Byron to no other causes. What else had he to complain of? He bowled for Harrow; Eton beat them; and I dare say catches were missed off him. Cowper, too, was a poet and a cricketer – probably a bowler. *Hinc illæ lacrymæ.* Swift, as all the world knows, attributed his bad humour to losing a big trout when he was a boy and had nearly landed him. That, also, might well embitter a disposition for life; but it is less trying than getting the best Cambridge bat notoriously l-b-w in the first over, and having the umpire give him "Not out," and then seeing him put on a century. But if a bowler once begins to talk about umpires! Enough has been said to show that the fine and subtle temperament of the Bowler is subjected to sorrows far exceeding those

5

which make the Poet teach in song what he learned in suffering. And we, Bowlers I mean, are mute! We do not turn the agonies of our hearts into metrical copy, and revel in dozens of editions at a royalty. These consolations, which a successful Poet rejoices in – these pecuniary rewards of his regrets, his moans for dead friends and faithless young women – a Bowler would scorn to receive. *He* does not coin his heart-drops: he suffers and is still. That is why you never, hardly, meet elegant little volumes, named "Heart's Sorrows," by Lohmann, or Briggs, or Mr. Whitby, or Mr. Christopherson. They are too manly to weep in public. My own "Elegies" (still in their first edition) are about agonies I never felt half so much as I feel being "collared." "Collared!" the very word is like a knell!

There had been the occasional isolated piece of humorous writing about cricket before J. M. Barrie's series, usually in novels, and most notably in Charles Dickens' Pickwick Papers (1836) with its hilarious and frequently anthologised account of the match between Dingley Dell and All Muggleton, and Anthony Trollope's futuristic story of The Fixed Period, published in 1882. Trollope (1815–82), author of the famous Barchester Chronicles *and regarded as one of England's greatest novelists, seems at first glance to be an unlikely author to have written on matters futuristic or even on cricket. Yet investigation into his life provides clues to the reasons for the writing of* The Fixed Period. *It is a story set a hundred years on, in the year 1980, and concerns a British colony called Britannula, located somewhere near New Zealand, where a new law – 'The Fixed Period' of the title – has been instituted with decrees that the elderly are no longer of use to society once they reach the age of 68 and must therefore be executed. Trollope had himself visited New Zealand and Australia in 1871 and returned home deeply pessimistic about what he saw as the* laissez-faire *attitude of the people there. A chapter of the book also describes a most bizarre game of cricket played at 'Gladstonopolis' between the Britannulans and a visiting team of amateurs and professionals from England captained by two noblemen, Sir Lords Longstop and Sir Kennington Oval. I say bizarre because Trollope's futuristic version of cricket is played between teams consisting of sixteen men a side, with the bowlers aided by steam driven machinery and the batsmen not surprisingly covered from head to foot in protective gear looking for all the world like diving suits! (Indeed, the 'Pallas helmets' which protect the batsmens' heads might well be seen as a forerunner of the modern cricketer's helmet!) Some of the savagery of the story is evidently Trollope's revenge on the boys who so mercilessly teased him when, awkward and uncouth, he was made the butt of the jokes of the young aristocrats and plutocrats who were his contemporaries at Harrow School. Despite this ragging, Trollope enjoyed cricket and was undeniably a fair batsman and bowler when*

7

given a chance by his fellows. His knowledge of the game is evident in the extract I have selected from The Fixed Period *describing the match between the Britannulans and their visitors. The story is narrated by the President of Britannula whose son, Jack Neverbend, is captain of the home side, and is somewhat distracted in his task by knowing that Eva Crasweller, the girl he loves and whose father has just reached the fatal age of 68, has fallen for the handsome visiting captain, Sir Kennington Oval. The job of both sides to achieve a victory has not been helped by the fact that during strenuous training both sides have lost men seriously injured by the steam-driven equipment, and take to the field with fifteen men each. Now read on . . .*

The Great Britannula Game

by Anthony Trollope

The day for the match had come. It was all England against Britannula!
The two captains tossed for the first innings, and the English club won
it. Think of the population of the two countries. We had, however, been
taught to believe that no community ever played cricket as did the
Britannulans. The English went in first, with the two baronets, Sir
Kennington and Sir Lords, at the wickets. They looked like two stout
Minervas with huge wicker helmets. I know a picture of the goddess, all
helmet, spear and petticoats, carrying her spear over her shoulder as
she flies through the air over the cities of the earth. Sir Kennington did
not fly, but in other respects he was very like the goddess, so completely
enveloped was he in his india-rubber guards, and so wonderful was the

9

machine upon his head, by which his brain and features were to be protected.

As he took his place upon the ground there was great cheering. Then the steam-bowler was ridden into its place by the attendant engineer, and Jack began his work. I could see the colour come and go in his face as he carefully placed the ball and peeped down to get its bearing. It seemed to me as though he were taking infinite care to level it straight and even at Sir Kennington's head. I was told afterwards that he never looked at Sir Kennington, but that, having calculated his distance by means of a quicksilver levelling-glass, his object was to throw the ball on a certain inch of turf, from which it might shoot into the wicket at such a degree as to make it very difficult for Sir Kennington to know what to do with it. It seemed to me to take a long time, during which the fourteen men around all looked as though each man were intending to hop off to some other spot than that on which he was standing. There used, I am told, to be only eleven of these men; but now, in a great match, the long-offs, and the long-ons, and the rest of them, are all doubled. The double long-off was at such a distance that, he being a small man, I could only just see him through the field-glass which I kept in my waistcoat-pocket. When I had been looking hard at them for what seemed to be a quarter of an hour, and the men were apparently becoming tired of their continual hop, and when Jack had stooped and kneeled and sprawled, with one eye shut, in every conceivable attitude, on a sudden there came a sharp snap, a little smoke, and lo, Sir Kennington Oval was——out!

There was no doubt about it. I myself saw the two bails fly away into infinite space, and at once there was a sound of kettle-drums, trumpets, fifes, and clarionets. It seemed as though all the loud music of the town band had struck up at the moment with their shrillest notes. And a huge gun was let off.

> "And let the kettle to the trumpet speak,
> The trumpet to the cannoneer without,
> The cannons to the heavens, the heavens to earth.
> Now drinks the king to Hamlet."

I could not but fancy, at these great signs of success, that I was Hamlet's father.

Sir Kennington Oval was out,—out at the very first ball. There could be no doubt about it, and Jack's triumph was complete. It was melancholy to see the English Minerva, as he again shouldered his spear and walked back to his tent. In spite of Jack's good play, and the success on the part of my own countrymen, I could not but be sorry to think that the young baronet had come half round the world to be put out at the first ball. There was a cruelty in it,—an inhospitality,— which, in spite of the exigencies of the game, went against the grain. Then, when the shouting, and the holloaing, and the flinging up of the ball were still going on, I remembered that, after it, he would have his consolation with Eva. And poor Jack, when his short triumph was over, would have to reflect that, though fortunate in his cricket, he was unhappy in his love. As this occurred to me, I looked back towards the house, and there, from a little lattice window at the end of the verandah, I saw a lady's handkerchief waving. Could it be that Eva was waving it so as to comfort her vanquished British lover? In the meantime Minerva went to his tent, and hid himself among sympathetic friends; and I was told afterwards that he was allowed half a pint of bitter beer by Dr MacNuffery.

After twenty minutes spent in what seemed to me the very ostentation of success, another man was got to the wickets. This was Stumps, one of the professionals, who was not quite so much like a Minerva, though he, too, was prodigiously greaved. Jack again set his ball, snap went the machine, and Stumps wriggled his bat. He touched the ball, and away it flew behind the wicket. Five republican Minervas ran after it as fast as their legs could carry them; and I was told by a gentleman who sat next to me scoring, that a dozen runs had been made. He spent a great deal of time in explaining how, in the old times, more than six at a time were never scored. Now all this was altered. A slight tip counted ever so much more than a good forward blow, because the ball went behind the wicket. Up flew on all sides of the ground figures to show that Stumps had made a dozen, and two British clarionets were blown with a great deal of vigour. Stumps was a thick-set, solid, solemn-looking man, who had been ridiculed by our side as being much too old for the game; but he seemed to think very little of Jack's precise machine. He kept chopping at the ball, which always went behind, till he had made a great score. It was two hours before Jack had sorely lamed him in the hip, and the umpire had given it leg-before-wicket. Indeed it was leg-before-wicket, as the poor man felt when he was assisted back

11

to his tent. However, he had scored 150. Sir Lords Longstop, too, had run up a good score before he was caught out by the middle long-off,—a marvellous catch they all said it was,—and our trumpets were blown for fully five minutes. But the big gun was only fired when a ball was hurled from the machine directly into the wicket.

At the end of three days the Britishers were all out, and the runs were numbered in four figures. I had my doubts, as I looked at the contest, whether any of them would be left to play out the match. I was informed that I was expected to take the President's seat every day; but when I heard that there were to be two innings for each set, I positively declined. But Crasweller took my place; and I was told that a gleam of joy shot across his worn, sorrowful face when Sir Kennington began the second innings with ten runs. Could he really wish, in his condition, to send his daughter away to England simply that she might be a baronet's wife?

When the Britannulists went in for the second time, they had 1500 runs to get; and it was said afterwards that Grundle had bet four to one against his own side. This was thought to be very shabby on his part, though if such was the betting, I don't see why he should lose his money by backing his friends. Jack declared in my hearing that he would not put a shilling on. He did not wish either to lose his money or to bet against himself. But he was considerably disheartened when he told me that he was not going in on the first day of their second innings. He had not done much when the Britannulists were in before,—had only made some thirty or forty runs; and, worse than that, Sir Kennington Oval had scored up to 300. They told me that his Pallas helmet was shaken with tremendous energy as he made his running. And again, that man Stumps had seemed to be invincible, though still lame, and had carried out his bat with a tremendous score. He trudged away without any sign of triumph; but Jack said that the professional was the best man they had.

On the second day of our party's second innings,—the last day but one of the match,—Jack went in. They had only made 150 runs on the previous day, and three wickets were down. Our kettle-drums had had but little opportunity for making themselves heard. Jack was very despondent, and had had some tiff with Eva. He had asked Eva whether she were not going to England, and Eva had said that perhaps she might do so if some Britannulists did not do their duty. Jack had chosen to take

12

this as a bit of genuine impertinence, and had been very sore about it. Stumps was bowling from the British catapult, and very nearly gave Jack his quietus during the first over. He hit wildly, and four balls passed him without touching his wicket. Then came his turn again, and he caught the first ball with his Neverbend spring-bat,—for he had invented it himself,—such a swipe, as he called it, that nobody has ever yet been able to find the ball. The story goes that it went right up to the verandah, and that Eva picked it up, and has treasured it ever since.

Be that as it may, during the whole of that day, and the next, nobody was able to get him out. There was a continual banging of the kettle-drum, which seemed to give him renewed spirits. Every ball as it came to him was sent away into infinite space. All the Englishmen were made to retire to further distances from the wickets, and to stand about almost at the extremity of the ground. The management of the catapults was intrusted to one man after another,—but in vain. Then they sent the catapults away, and tried the old-fashioned slow bowling. It was all the same to Jack. He would not be tempted out of his ground, but stood there awaiting the ball, let it come ever so slowly. Through the first of the two days he stood before his wicket, hitting to the right and the left, till hope seemed to spring up again in the bosom of the Britannulists. And I could see that the Englishmen were becoming nervous and uneasy, although the odds were still much in their favour.

At the end of the first day Jack had scored above 500;—but eleven wickets had gone down, and only three of the most inferior players were left to stand up with him. It was considered that Jack must still make another 500 before the game would be won. This would allow only twenty each to the other three players. "But," said Eva to me that evening, "they'll never get the twenty each."

"And on which side are you, Eva?" I inquired with a smile. For in truth I did believe at that moment that she was engaged to the baronet.

"How dare you ask, Mr Neverbend?" she demanded, with indignation. "Am not I a Britannulist as well as you?" And as she walked away I could see that there was a tear in her eye.

On the last day feelings were carried to a pitch which was more befitting the last battle of a great war,—some Waterloo of other ages,—than the finishing of a prolonged game of cricket. Men looked, and moved, and talked as though their all were at stake. I canot say that the Englishmen seemed to hate us, or we them; but that the affair was too serious to admit of playful words between the parties. And those unfortunates who had to stand up with Jack were so afraid of themselves that they were like young country orators about to make their first speeches. Jack was silent, determined, and yet inwardly proud of himself, feeling that the whole future success of the republic was on his shoulders. He ordered himself to be called at a certain hour, and the assistants in our household listened to his words as though feeling that everything depended on their obedience. He would not go out on his bicycle, as fearing that some accident might occur. "Although, ought I not to wish that I might be struck dead?" he said; "as then all the world would know that though beaten, it had been by the hand of God, and not by our default." It astonished me to find that the boy was quite as eager about his cricket as I was about my Fixed Period.

At eleven o'clock I was in my seat, and on looking round, I could see that all the rank and fashion of Britannula were at the ground. But all the rank and fashion were there for nothing, unless they had come armed with glasses. The spaces required by the cricketers were so enormous that otherwise they could not see anything of the play. Under my canopy there was room for five, of which I was supposed to be able to fill the middle thrones. On the two others sat those who officially scored the game. One seat had been demanded for Mrs Neverbend. "I will see his fate,—whether it be his glory of his fall,"—said his mother, with true Roman feeling. For the other Eva had asked, and of course it had been awarded to her. When the play began, Sir Kennington was at the catapult and Jack at the opposite wicket, and I could hardly say for which she felt the extreme interest which she certainly did exhibit. I, as the day went on, found myself worked up to such excitement that I could hardly keep my hat on my head or behave myself with becoming presidential dignity. At one period, as I shall have to tell, I altogether disgraced myself.

There seemed to be an opinion that Jack would either show himself at once unequal to the occasion, and immediately be put out,—which opinion I think that all Gladstonopolis was inclined to hold,—or else that he would get his "eye in" as he called it, and go on as long as the three others could keep their bats. I know that his own opinion was the same as that general in the city, and I feared that his very caution at the outset would be detrimental to him. The great object on our side was that Jack should, as nearly as possible, be always opposite to the bowler.

14

He was to take the four first balls, making but one run off the last, and then beginning another over at the opposite end do the same thing again. It was impossible to manage this exactly; but something might be done towards effecting it. There were the three men with whom to work during the day. The first unfortunately was soon made to retire; but Jack, who had walked up to my chair during the time allowed for fetching down the next man, told me that he had "got his eye", and I could see a settled look of fixed purpose in his face. He bowed most gracefully to Eva, who was so stirred by emotion that she could not allow herself to speak a word. "Oh Jack, I pray for you; I pray for you," said his mother. Jack, I fancy, thought more of Eva's silence than of his mother's prayer.

Jack went back to his place, and hit the first ball with such energy that he drove it into the other stumps and smashed them to pieces. Everybody declared that such a thing had never been before achieved at cricket,—and the ball passed on, and eight or ten runs were scored. After that Jack seemed to be mad with cricketing power. He took off his greaves, declaring that they impeded his running, and threw away altogether his helmet. "Oh, Eva, is he not handsome?" said his mother, in ecstasy, hanging across my chair. Eva sat quite without a sign. It did not become me to say a word, but I did think that he was very handsome;—and I thought also how uncommonly hard it would be to hold him if he should chance to win the game. Let him make what orations he might against the Fixed Period, all Gladstonopolis would follow him if he won this game of cricket for them.

I cannot pretend to describe all the scenes of that day, nor the growing anxiety of the Englishmen as Jack went on with one hundred after another. He had already scored nearly 1000 when young Grabbe was caught out. Young Grabbe was very popular, because he was so altogether unlike his partner Grundle. He was a fine frank fellow, and was Jack's great friend. "I don't mean to say that he can really play cricket," Jack had said that morning, speaking with great authority; "but he is the best fellow in the world, and will do exactly what you ask him." But he was out now; and Jack, with over 200 still to make, declared that he gave up the battle almost as lost.

"Don't say that, Mr Neverbend," whispered Eva.

"Ah yes; we're gone coons. Even your sympathy cannot bring us round now. If anything could do it that would!"

"In my opinion," continued Eva, "Britannula will never be beaten as long as Mr Neverbend is at the wicket."

"Sir Kennington has been too much for us, I fear," said Jack, with a forced smile, as he retired.

There was now but the one hope left. Mr Brittlereed remained, but he was all. Mr Brittlereed was a gentleman who had advanced nearer to his Fixed Period than any other of the cricketers. He was nearly thirty-five years of age, and was regarded by them all as quite an old man. He was supposed to know all the rules of the game, and to be rather quick in keeping the wicket. But Jack had declared that morning that he could not hit a ball in a week of Sundays. "He oughtn't to be here," Jack had whispered; "but you know how those things are managed." I did not know how those things were managed, but I was sorry that he should be there, as Jack did not seem to want him.

Mr Brittlereed now went to his wicket, and was bound to receive the first ball. This he did; made one run, whereas he might have made two, and then had to begin the war over. It certainly seemed as though he had done it on purpose. Jack in his passion broke the handle of his spring-bat, and then had half-a-dozen brought to him in order that he might choose another. "It was his favourite bat," said his mother, and buried her face in her handkerchief.

I never understood how it was that Mr Brittlereed lived through that over; but he did live, although he never once touched the ball. Then it came to be Jack's turn; and he at once scored thirty-nine during the over, leaving himself at the proper wicket for recommencing the operation. I think that this gave him new life. It added, at any rate, new fire to every Britannulist on the ground, and I must say that after that Mr Brittlereed managed the matter altogether to Jack's satisfaction. Over after over Jack went on, and received every ball that was bowled. They tried their catapult with single, double, and even treble action. Sir Kennington did his best, flinging the ball with his most tremendous impetus, and then just rolling it up with what seemed to me the most provoking languor. It was all the same to Jack. He had in truth got his "eye in," and as surely as the ball came to him, it was sent away to some most distant part of the ground. The Britishers were mad with dismay as Jack worked his way on through the last hundred. It was piteous to see the exertions which poor Mr Brittlereed made in running backwards and forwards across the ground. They tried, I think, to bustle him by the rapid succession of their bowling. But the only result was that the ball was sent still further off when it reached Jack's wicket. At last, just as every clock upon the ground struck six with that wonderful unanimity which our clocks have attained since they were all regulated by wires from Greenwich, Jack sent a ball flying up into the air, perfectly regardless whether it might be caught or not, knowing well that the one now needed would be scored before it could come down from the heavens into the hands of any Englishman. It did come down , and was caught by Stumps, but by that time Britannula had won her victory. Jack's total score during that innings was 1275. I doubt whether in the annals of cricket any record is made of a better innings that that. Then it was that, with an absence of that presence of mind which the President of a republic should always remember, I took off my hat and flung it into the air.

Jack's triumph would have been complete, only that it was ludicrous to those who could not but think, as I did, of the very little matter as to which the contest had been raised;—just a game of cricket which two sets of boys had been playing, and which should have been regarded as no more than an amusement,—as a pastime, by which to refresh them- selves between their work. But they regarded it as though a great national combat had been fought, and the Britannulists looked upon themselves as though they had been victorious against England. It was absurd to see Jack as he was carried back to Gladstonopolis as the hero of the occasion, and to hear him, as he made his speeches at the dinner which was given on the day, and at which he was called upon to take the chair. I was glad to see, however, that he was not quite so glib with his tongue as he had been when addressing the people. He hesitated a good deal, nay, almost broke down, when he gave the health of Sir Kennington Oval and the British sixteen; and I was quite pleased to hear Lord Marylebone declare to his mother that he was "a wonderfully nice boy." I think the English did try to turn it off a little, as though they had only come out there just for the amusement of the voyage. But Grundle, who had now become quite proud of his country, and who lamented loudly that he should have received so severe an injury in preparing for the game, would not let this pass. "My lord," he said, "what is your population?" Lord Marylebone named sixty million. "We are but two hundred and fifty thousand," said Grundle, "and see what we have done." "We are cocks fighting on our own dunghill," said Jack, "and that does make a deal of difference."

But I was told that Jack had spoken a word to Eva in quite a different spirit before he had left Little Christchurch. "After all, Eva, Sir Kennington has not quite trampled us under his feet," he said.

"Who thought that he would?" said Eva. "My heart has never fainted, whatever some others may have done."

Another of J. M. Barrie's contemporaries who took to writing about the funny side of cricket was Horace (Horatio) Hutchinson (1859–1932), the great all-round sportsman, who also penned the very first cricketing novel, Peter Steele, the Cricketer, *published in Bristol in 1896, and which tells the story of the rise of a child prodigy to become a national hero. The book is redolent with details of university cricket (Hutchinson himself was educated at Oxford) as well as the delights of the village green matches deep in the heart of the English countryside to which Hutchinson took himself each summer in between the more solemn county affairs. He used the intimate knowledge of the game and its personalities which he garnered to compile the first cricket anthology,* Cricketing Saws and Stories, *published at the turn of the century and now one of the most sought-after pieces of memorabilia. Cricket was also the subject of his novel,* Creatures of Circumstances, *written in 1891, and containing what I think is one of the most amusing early accounts of a village green match, 'Little Pipkin* v. *White-Cross'. It is this story which follows hereunder.*

The Rustic Heroes

by Horace Hutchinson

Of latter years the cricket in the annual match, Little Pipkin against White-Cross, had not been going at all as Mr. Slocombe could have wished. It was not merely that Little Pipkin had been beaten, but a custom had crept in of asking foreign cricketers—men not in the county even—to take part in the match. The innovation had been commenced by White-Cross, and Mr. Slocombe was liberal enough to admit that White-Cross had had some reason for the step—in fact, that it was rendered necessary, if the match were to be a match at all, by the over-mastering genius of Robert Burscough. So far he even approved of it as a just recognition on the part of White-Cross of Little Pipkin's superiority.

But now Robert was gone. This was the third year that he had been unable to come to the match, for the year before he went abroad an even greater fixture had hindered him, and by the help of foreign allies—men whose names were of note even at Lord's—White-Cross had given

21

Little Pipkin two parlous beatings. This year Colonel Burscough, on the part of Little Pipkin, had written to Lord Morningham as representing White-Cross, proposing, as Robert was abroad, that they should return to the good old ways, and that the match should again become one of village teams pure and simple.

But Lord Morningham could not agree to this, because, as he said, his guests were already invited. So Colonel Burscough devised a scheme almost Cheadleian in its subtilty, and laid it before the cricket committee of Little Pipkin, in whose eyes it found favour, and they were all sworn to secrecy respecting it.

On the day of the great match Lord Morningham drove over in his dogcart with two of his friends, betimes, and another friend, and the rest of the eleven of White-Cross, in a drag, were not long behind him. When they came out of the dressing-tent the eleven of White-Cross presented a splendour that charmed the eye with the colours of the I. Zingari, Free Foresters, and M. C. C. adorning the persons of the three imported cricketers; while the appearance of the eleven of Little Pipkin was of pure, unrelieved rusticity. But some of the men of White-Cross began to ask one another who was that rustic with the long legs and the hat pulled over his eyes; and who that one with the stout legs? There was also a third who was a stranger to them, but he escaped general notice because he was of little stature. They asked the men of Little Pipkin who these men were, and some said, quite truly, that they did not know, and others that the strangers had but lately come to the village; and this again was true, for they had come to it but the night before.

White-Cross won the toss, and Lord Morningham sat in the pavilion and watched the first of his friends, who was a mighty swiper, go in, and settled himself to see him swipe.

The long-legged stranger rustic began to bowl. At the first ball Lord Morningham whistled after a manner he had when in the pavilion at Lord's; for he affected cricket, as being a popular game, and because he had been the coolest slow bowler for an Eton boy that had ever trundled out a Harrow eleven. But he whistled because the ball went so fearfully near the wicket. To the second ball the batsman played forward carefully, and met it. But the third pitched a trifle shorter, and the batsman, playing forward as before, returned it to the hands of the bowler, where it remained.

22

The most terrible catastrophes are those that happen most suddenly, and in quick succession the wickets fell of the other two whose names were great at Lord's, and they were together in the pavilion explaining to each other the causes of their several downfalls, which they agreed in attributing to luck, and expressed every confidence that, given another trial, they could go on playing that sort of bowling all day long. For the other bowler was the stranger rustic who had escaped general notice by his shortness of stature.

Disheartened by the defeat of their best and brightest, the eleven of White-Cross were all out for twenty-seven, and byes had contributed the most of these.

Then it was the turn of Little Pipkin to go in, and the short stranger rustic and the stout-legged stranger rustic went to the wickets. And despite all the efforts of the friends of Lord Morningham, whose names were so great at Lords', they were at the wickets still when the luncheon bell rang; and most of this time had been spent by the eleven of White-Cross, assisted by the entire village of Little Pipkin, in hunting for the ball in the hedge of the vicarage glebe, into which these stranger rustics repeatedly hit it. And the telegraph read 137, and that only, for of wickets fallen there was no tale to tell. At the beginning of luncheon the strangers were conspicuous by their absence, but after a short time they came in, no longer in their rustic garb, but in the unclouded majesty of white flannel. And Lord Morningham and his friends at once recognized them, and gave a shout, for the long rustic was a very famous bowler of the Surrey eleven, and the stout-legged rustic was the best batsman on a mud-wicket in all England (the champion not excepted), and the rustic of short stature was the most brilliant fieldsman of the eleven of Lancashire, and good with bat and ball alike.

Thus had Colonel Burscough schemed Cheadleianly, and accomplished the overthrow of the men of White-Cross and their famous allies; and when they saw by whom they had been defeated they felt no shame and bore no malice, but joined in the laugh against themselves.

23

Alfred Cochrane (1865–1948) was one of Oxford University's most outstanding cricketers between 1885 and 1888 and while there developed a passion for the game which never diminished even long after he had had to give up playing – a fact which was made evident in the large number of articles and essays on cricket he subsequently wrote for various magazines and journals. He also compiled the well-regarded volume, Told In The Pavilion *published in 1896. From time to time I have come across items by Cochrane which I have thought deserved republication, but none more so than the next hilarious story which he wrote for* Cornhill Magazine *in 1896. I am sure a great many cricketers have harboured superstitions which they believed affected their game, but surely none quite like those of Cresswell . . .*

The Talisman

by Alfred Cochrane

Cresswell was one of those absurd cricketers who are very superstitious, though I must say he made a power of runs. Whenever he got out he had always some thundering good reason to account for it. Either, it was that a baby had been brought on the ground in a perambulator, which was a most unlucky thing to happen, or the end of his trouser-leg had slipped out of the lower strap of his pad, or something like that. He had a batting cap, and a bowling cap, and a fielding cap, and nothing would induce him to do anything unless he had the right cap on. There were also a number of other things about his attire and his outfit which either brought him good or bad luck, and he always had to go in in a particular place or else he was a certain duck. One of his ideas was that he never could get a run if he was in with Biggs. When Biggs came in, Cresswell invariably got out. He did not tell Biggs so, but he told everyone else. Not that he much fancied Biggs anyhow, apart from the evil influence he believed him to have over his batting.

27

They were neither of them bad chaps, but at opposite poles altogether. Cresswell was neat and slim and precise, a bit touchy, perhaps, but kindhearted. Biggs was fat and massive; thick-skinned and noisily good-humoured. He had a loud voice which usually said the wrong thing, and which put Cresswell's back up; but Biggs never noticed it, for he was that kind of person who cannot believe himself unappreciated by anybody.

Well, one Bluebottle tour a year or so ago, Cresswell had a dreadful run of bad luck. He could not get a double figure to save his life, and it upset him very much. We finished up that year with four days at Potash Hall, which is one of the very best places to stop at that I know. There was a large house-party for the cricket matches and everyone was very cheerful except Cresswell, who sat moodily apart wondering how he had offended Fortune.

"I think I shall chuck something away," he said to Stockley, as they sat on a bench waiting to go in.

"Not your wicket, I hope," Stockley answered, "we want all the runs we can get."

"No, I mean like that old Greek king who threw a ring into the sea."

"Yes, but if I remember right, that was because he was so happy, and you are down in the mouth, so that doesn't fit."

"No more it does," assented Cresswell, gloomily. "I must think of something else. Come on, they are taking the roller off."

"Before we go," said Stockley, "I hope you've got everything right. You've got the right number of folds in your sleeve, the right knots to your bootlaces, and your bat that makes runs on Wednesdays. I see they've got a wooden-legged umpire which may or may not be a good omen."

It must have been a bad one, for that very umpire gave poor old Cresswell caught at the wicket in the second over. He admitted he was out but ruefully added, that with any luck he ought to have been given in, for it was a "deuced light tip," he said.

The same evening there was a dance and Cresswell found Miss May Carrington very sympathetic about his sorrows. He waltzes uncommonly well and is liked by ladies, I think. Anyhow, Miss May showed no sign of being bored as Cresswell in the billiard-room window-seat during No. 16 (Lancers), for which she was engaged to Biggs, asked her if she could not suggest some new fetish that would effectively defy all abnormally difficult balls and astonishing catches, and inhumanly acute umpires. They must have got on pretty good terms before the end of the programme, for as they parted she gave him something wrapped up in tissue paper.

"It's not your lady's sleeve," she said in a delightful whisper, "but it is the next best thing. You'll take it in with you, won't you?"

"Of course I will."

"And don't open it or you will break the charm. I'm sure you will do well to-morrow."

"Coming to smoke, Cressy, old man?" shouted Biggs from the foot of the stairs. He had a habit of shortening Cresswell's name in this affectionate manner, which was painful to a degree.

Cresswell hastily went down to the hall where his cricket bag was and secreted his precious little parcel under his pads, until the following morning, after getting rid of Biggs by saying he wanted to get a pipe.

Next day we had 130 to get and Cresswell, as usual, went in first with his last and newest talisman tied about his neck, invisible, of course, and still wrapped in its tissue paper. He was rather shaky at starting, and we were horrified when three wickets fell so quickly that Biggs had to go in, for we knew how disastrously his company affected Cresswell.

Sure enough in about three minutes the latter skied one on the leg side, but it was a very windy day and mid-on could not quite get to it. Then Biggs nearly ran him out: in fact mid-off had a shot at the sticks and only missed them by inches. Presently there was a tremendous appeal for leg-before against him.

"How's *that*?" screamed the bowler, jumping and tossing his arms about.

"*Not* out;" stolidly replied the wooden-legged umpire, and I remember wondering why Miss Carrington, who understands the game, rubbed her hands together so cheerily and laughed so gaily.

After these escapes Cresswell settled down and gave the other side a taste of his best quality. He never looked like getting out again, and the baneful presence of Biggs seemed rather to improve his game. In fact, they knocked the runs off between them, and Cresswell was not out 84, when the match ended in our favour by seven wickets.

"Now wasn't that extraordinary?" said Miss May Carrington to Cresswell, whom everybody was congratulating.

"Yes, it was," Cresswell answered, and as the other people went off

29

to tea, and the two found themselves more or less alone, he pulled out the little parcel and laid it on her knee. "Your favour has had a first-rate effect on my innings."

"And with Mr Biggs at the other end, too?"

"Yes, wasn't it queer? Did you see the fellow miss me at mid-on?"

"Of course I did. Do you know what is wrapped up in this paper?"

"No," he said, "but I'm dying to find out."

"It's my glove," said Miss Carrington, blushing a little. "You may open it if you like."

Cresswell, lingering over the pleasant task and dallying with the sweet pleasure of anticipation, slowly unrolled the paper. Within was an old white kid glove of the most enormous size: it looked, as it lay spread out before them, almost big enough for Miss Carrington to wear as an opera cloak.

She stared at him blankly and then she laughed, while he mentally compared this vast gauntlet with her small hand.

"It's like a conjuring trick," she exclaimed. "How it has altered in the night."

"I'm afraid you would stretch it a bit," Cresswell said, "if you tried to put it on."

She pointed to a rent in the glove close to the thumb. "Huge as it is," she said, "the hand inside was huger. Just try and imagine it."

"It must be——" began Cresswell, and then he stopped.

"It can only belong to——" said Miss Carrington, and then she, too, checked herself.

"Cressy," cried a cheerful voice, as Biggs, hot and crimson in the face, drew near, while Cresswell hastily concealed the glove and stood up.

"I took a glove from your bag this morning old chap," continued Biggs, easily. "I wanted something to shove inside the knee of my left pad. It's a bit groggy, you know, with a knock I got on it last week. So I looked in your bag and found a long kid glove which was just the thing."

"Oh!" was all Cresswell could think of saying.

"Yes," said Biggs, and then went on with the air of one reluctantly advertising his own thoughtful unselfishness, "but it occurred to me afterwards that you might want a kid glove for blisters or something of that sort, so as I happened to have one of my own with me I shoved it in your bag. I wrapped it up in the paper so that you might know where to find it."

"Thanks very much," stuttered Cresswell.

"Ripping things for blisters, Miss Carrington, are kid gloves," Biggs said, "they save your hands, you know."

"So I should suppose, Mr Biggs," replied the young lady, taking a demure interest in the point.

After a few more heavy remarks Biggs passed on, and the guilty couple went into fits of laughter.

"It serves me right," admitted Cresswell, "for being so nonsensical."

"And me," put in his companion, "for being so shockingly forward as to give you my glove."

"No, no," he said, "I can't allow that. It was charming of you."

Cresswell has not been nearly so superstitious since, nor dealt anything like so largely in fetishes and charms. But then he has had other things to think of. He couldn't play on tour this year, confound him. The idea of having a honeymoon in August!

As I mentioned earlier, a member of J. M. Barrie's Allah-akbarries CC was Sir Arthur Conan Doyle (1859–1930), creator of the immortal Sherlock Holmes and a cricketer – according to Barrie at the time – 'good enough to go into second-class cricket'. Which, of course, he was and did – making some memorable scores with the bat and once taking seven wickets for 61 runs for the MCC against Cambridgeshire at Lord's. Doyle's love of the game is a well-known factor of his life, and it remains a mystery why such a versatile man did not write more about it – there are references to be found in his biography, Memories and Adventures, an essay on W. G. Grace for the Strand in July 1927, and three short stories, 'About Cricket' in which a father tries to explain the subtleties of the game to his three small children until they are interrupted for bedtime by an unsympathetic mother; 'The Story of Spedegue's Dropper' included here and of which more anon; and the very brief Sherlock Holmes excursion into the cricket arena, 'The Field Bazaar' written to help raise funds for his old university at Edinburgh in 1896.

Interestingly, it has been suggested that because of his fascination with cricket, Doyle actually derived the name for his famous detective from those of two county cricketers of the time. However, a search of the records of first-class players has failed to locate any men of these names who played before 1887 when the first Holmes adventure, A Study in Scarlet, was written. It is possible, though, that Sherlock was derived from a combination of Mordecai Sherwin and T. F. Shacklock who both played for Nottinghamshire during the 1880s. Shacklock was a bowler and Sherwin kept wicket, so there are frequent references to be found to dismissals 'c Sherwin, b. Shacklock'. It seems probable, too, that Holmes's brother, Mycroft, was named after two half-brothers of that surname who played for Derbyshire at this same time. Be this as it may, Conan Doyle's best cricket tale is undoubtedly the one which follows about Tom Spedegue and his amazing bowling action which defeats the Australians in 'the greatest joke in the history of cricket'. I won't spoil a moment of your enjoyment by adding anything further.

The Story of Spedegue's Dropper

by Sir Arthur Conan Doyle

The name of Walter Scougall needs no introduction to the cricketing public. In the 'nineties he played for his University. Early in the century he began that long career in the county team which carried him up to the War. That great tragedy broke his heart for games, but he still served on his county Club Committee and was reckoned one of the best judges of the game in the United Kingdom.

Scougall, after his abandonment of active sport, was wont to take his exercise by long walks through the New Forest, upon the borders of which he was living. Like all wise men, he walked very silently through that wonderful waste, and in that way he was often privileged to see sights which are lost to the average heavy-stepping wayfarer. Once, late in the evening, it was a badger blundering towards its hole under a hollow bank. Often a little group of deer would be glimpsed in the open rides. Occasionally a fox would steal across the path and then dart off at the sight of the noiseless wayfarer. Then one day he saw a human sight which was more strange than any in the animal world.

In a narrow glade there stood two great oaks. They were thirty or forty feet apart, and the glade was spanned by a cord which connected them up. This cord was at least fifty feet above the ground, and it must have entailed no small effort to get it there. At each side of the cord a cricket stump had been placed at the usual distance from each other. A tall, thin young man in spectacles was lobbing balls, of which he seemed to have a good supply, from one end, while at the other end a lad of sixteen, wearing wicket-keeper's gloves, was catching those which missed the wicket. "Catching" is the right word, for no ball struck the ground. Each was projected high up into the air and passed over the cord, descending at a very sharp angle on to the stumps.

Scougall stood for some minutes behind a holly bush watching this curious performance. At first it seemed pure lunacy, and then gradually he began to perceive a method in it. It was no easy matter to hurl a ball up over that cord and bring it down near the wicket. It needed a very correct trajectory. And yet this singular young man, using what the observer's practised eye recognized as a leg-break action which would entail a swerve in the air, lobbed up ball after ball either right on to the bails or into the wicket-keeper's hands just beyond them. Great practice was surely needed before he had attained such a degree of accuracy as this.

Finally his curiosity became so great that Scougall moved out into the glade, to the obvious surprise and embarrassment of the two performers. Had they been caught in some guilty action they could not have looked more unhappy. However, Scougall was a man of the world with a pleasant manner, and he soon put them at their ease.

"Excuse my butting in," said he. "I happened to be passing and I could not help being interested. I am an old cricketer, you see, and it appealed to me. Might I ask what you were trying to do?"

"Oh, I am just tossing up a few balls," said the elder, modestly. "You see, there is no decent ground about here, so my brother and I come out into the Forest."

"Are you a bowler, then?"

"Well, of sorts."

"What club do you play for?"

"It is only Wednesday and Saturday cricket. Bishops Bramley is our village."

"But do you always bowl like that?"

"Oh, no. This is a new idea that I have been trying out."

"Well, you seem to get it pretty accurately."

"I am improving. I was all over the place at first. I didn't know what parish they would drop in. But now they are usually there or about it."

"So I observe."

"You said you were an old cricketer. May I ask your name?"

"Walter Scougall."

The young man looked at him as a young pupil looks at the world-famed master.

"You remember the name, I see."

"Walter Scougall. Oxford and Hampshire. Last played in 1913. Batting average for that season, twenty-seven point five. Bowling average, sixteen for seventy-two wickets."

"Good Lord!"

The younger man, who had come across, burst out laughing.

"Tom is like that," said he. "He is Wisden and Lillywhite rolled into one. He could tell you anyone's record, and every county's record for this century."

"Well, well! What a memory you must have!"

"Well, my heart is in the game," said the young man, becoming amazingly confidential, as shy men will when they find a really sympathetic listener. "But it's my heart that won't let me play it as I should wish to do. You see, I get asthma if I do too much—and palpitations. But they play me at Bishops Bramley for my slow bowling, and so long as I field slip I don't have too much running to do."

"You say you have not tried these lobs, or whatever you may call them, in a match?"

"No, not yet. I want to get them perfect first. You see, it was my ambition to invent an entirely new ball. I am sure it can be done. Look at Bosanquet and the googlie. Just by using his brain he thought of and worked out the idea of concealed screw on the ball. I said to myself that Nature had handicapped me with a weak heart, but not with a weak brain, and that I might think out some new thing which was within the compass of my strength. Droppers, I call them. Spedegue's droppers—that's the name they may have some day."

Scougall laughed. "I don't want to discourage you, but I wouldn't bank on it too much," said he. "A quick-eyed batsman would simply treat them as he would any other full toss and every ball would be a boundary."

Spedegue's face fell. The words of Scougall were to him as the verdict of the High Court judge. Never had he spoken before with a first-class cricketer, and he had hardly the nerve to defend his own theory. It was the younger one who spoke.

"Perhaps, Mr. Scougall, you have hardly thought it all out yet," said he. "Tom has given it a lot of consideration. You see, if the ball is tossed high enough it has a great pace as it falls. It's really like having a fast bowler from above. That's his idea. Then, of course, there's the field."

"Ah, how would you place your field?"

"All on the on side bar one or two at the most," cried Tom Spedegue, taking up the argument. "I've nine to dispose of. I should have mid-off well up. That's all. Then I should have eight men to leg, three on the boundary, one mid-on, two square, one fine, and one a rover, so that the batsman would never quite know where he was. That's the idea."

Scougall began to be serious. It was clear that this young fellow really had plotted the thing out. He walked across to the wicket.

"Chuck up one or two," said he. "Let me see how they look." He brandished his walking-stick and waited expectant. The ball soared in the air and came down with unexpected speed just over the stump. Scougal looked more serious still. He had seen many cricket balls, but never quite from that angle, and it gave him food for thought.

"Have you ever tried it in public?"

"Never."

"Don't you think it is about time?"

"Yes, I think I might."

"When?"

"Well, I'm not generally on as a first bowler. I am second change as a rule. But if the skipper will let me have a go——"

"I'll see to that," said Scougall. "Do you play at Bishops Bramley?"

"Yes; it is our match of the year—against Mudford, you know."

"Well, I think on Saturday I'd like to be there and see how it works."

Sure enough Scougall turned up at the village match, to the great

38

excitement of the two rural teams. He had a serious talk with the home captain, with the result that for the first time in his life Tom Spedegue was first bowler for his native village. What the other village thought of his remarkable droppers need not influence us much, since they would probably have been got out pretty cheaply by any sort of bowling. None the less, Scougall watched the procession to and from the cow-shed which served as a pavilion with an appreciative eye, and his views as to the possibilities lying in the dropper became clearer than before. At the end of the innings he touched the bowler upon the shoulder.

"That seems all right," he said.

"No, I couldn't quite get the length—and, of course, they did drop catches."

"Yes, I agree that you could do better. Now look here! you are second master at a school, are you not?"

"That is right."

"You could get a day's leave if I wangled with the chief?"

"It might be done."

"Well, I want you next Tuesday. Sir George Sanderson's house-party team is playing the Free Foresters at Ringwood. You must bowl for Sir George."

Tom Spedegue flushed with pleasure.

"Oh, I say!" was all he could stammer out.

"I'll work it somehow or other. I suppose you don't bat?"

"Average nine," said Spedegue, proudly.

Scougall laughed. "Well, I noticed that you were not a bad fielder near the wicket."

"I usually hold them."

"Well, I'll see your boss, and you will hear from me again."

Scougall was really taking a great deal of trouble in this small affair, for he went down to Totton and saw the rather grim head master. It chanced, however, that the old man had been a bit of a sport in his day, and he relaxed when Scougall explained the inner meaning of it all. He laughed incredulously, however, and shook his head when Scougall whispered some aspiration.

"Nonsense!" was his comment.

"Well, there is a chance."

"Nonsense!" said the old man once again.

"It would be the making of your school."

"It certainly would," the headmaster replied. "But it is nonsense all the same."

Scougall saw the head master again on the morning after the Free Foresters match.

"You see it works all right," he said.

"Yes, against third-class men."

"Oh, I don't know. Donaldson was playing, and Murphy. They were not so bad. I tell you they are the most amazed set of men in Hampshire. I have bound them all over to silence."

"Why?"

"Surprise is the essence of the matter. Now I'll take it a stage farther. By Jove, what a joke it would be!" The old cricketer and the sporting schoolmaster roared with laughter as they thought of the chances of the future.

All England was absorbed in one question at that moment. Politics, business, even taxation had passed from people's minds. The one engrossing subject was the fifth Test Match. Twice England had won by a narrow margin, and twice Australia had barely struggled to victory. Now in a week Lord's was to be the scene of the final and crucial battle of giants. What were the chances, and how was the English team to be made up?

It was an anxious time for the Selection Committee, and three more harassed men than Sir James Gilpin, Mr. Tarding and Dr. Sloper were not to be found in London. They sat now in the committee-room of the great pavilion, and they moodily scanned the long list of possibles which lay before them, weighing the claims of this man or that, closely inspecting the latest returns from the county matches, and arguing how far a good all-rounder was a better bargain than a man who was supremely good in one department but weak in another—such men, for example, as Worsley of Lancashire, whose average was seventy-one, but who was a sluggard in the field, or Scott of Leicestershire, who was near the top of the bowling and quite at the foot of the batting averages. A week of such work had turned the committee into three jaded old men.

"There is the question of endurance," said Sir James, the man of many years and much experience. 'A three days' match is bad enough, but this is to be played out and may last a week. Some of these top average men are getting on in years."

40

"Exactly," said Tarding, who had himself captained England again and again. "I am all for young blood and new methods. The trouble is that we know their bowling pretty well, and as for them on a marled wicket they can play ours with their eyes shut. Each side is likely to make five hundred per innings, and a very little will make the difference between us and them."

"It's just that very little that we have got to find," said solemn old Dr. Sloper, who had the reputation of being the greatest living authority upon the game. "If we could give them something new! But, of course, they have played every county and sampled everything we have got."

"What can we ever have that is new?" cried Tarding. "It is all played out."

"Well, I don't know," said Sir James. "Both the swerve and the googlie have come along in our time. But Bosanquets don't appear every day. We want brain as well as muscle behind the ball."

"Funny we should talk like this," said Dr. Sloper, taking a letter from his pocket. "This is from old Scougall, down in Hampshire. He says he is at the end of a wire and is ready to come up if we want him. His whole argument is on the very lines we have been discussing. New blood, and a complete surprise—that is his slogan."

"Does he suggest where we are to find it?"

"Well, as a matter of fact he does. He has dug up some unknown fellow from the back of beyond who plays for the second eleven of the Mudtown Blackbeetles or the Hinton Chawbacons or some such team, and he wants to put him straight in to play for England. Poor old Scougie has been out in the sun."

"At the same time there is no better captain than Scougall used to be. I don't think we should put his opinion aside too easily. What does he say?"

"Well, he is simply red-hot about it. 'A revelation to me.' That is one phrase. 'Could not have believed it if I had not seen it.' 'May find it out afterwards, but it is bound to upset them the first time.' That is his view."

"And where is this wonder man?"

"He has sent him up so that we can see him if we wish. Telephone the Thackeray Hotel, Blooomsbury."

"Well, what do you say?"

41

"Oh, it's pure waste of time," said Tarding. "Such things don't happen, you know. Even if we approved of him, what would the country think and what would the Press say?"

Sir James stuck out his grizzled jaw.

"Damn the country and the Press, too!" said he. "We are here to follow our own judgment, and I jolly well mean to do so."

"Exactly," said Dr. Sloper.

Tarding shrugged his broad shoulders.

"We have enough to do without turning down a side-street like that," said he. "However, if you both think so, I won't stand in the way. Have him up by all means and let us see what we make of him."

Half an hour later a very embarrassed young man was standing in front of the famous trio and listening to a series of very searching questions, to which he was giving such replies as he was able. Much of the ground which Scougall had covered in the Forest was explored by them once more.

"It boils down to this, Mr. Spedegue. You've once in your life played in good company. That is the only criterion. What exactly did you do?"

Spedegue pulled a slip of paper, which was already frayed from much use, out of his waistcoat pocket.

"This is *The Hampshire Telegraph* account, sir."

Sir James ran his eye over it and read snatches aloud. "Much amusement was caused by the bowling of Mr. T. E. Spedegue." "Hum! That's rather two-edged. Bowling should not be a comic turn. After all, cricket is a serious game. Seven wickets for thirty-four. Well, that's better. Donaldson is a good man. You got him, I see. And Murphy, too! Well, now, would you mind going into the pavilion and waiting? You will find some pictures there that will amuse you if you value the history of the game. We'll send for you presently."

When the youth had gone the Selection Committee looked at each other in puzzled silence.

"You simply can't do it!" said Tarding at last. "You can't face it. To play a bumpkin like that because he once got seven wickets for thirty-four in country-house cricket is sheer madness. I won't be a party to it."

"Wait a bit, though! Wait a bit!" cried Sir James. "Let us thresh it out a little before we decide."

So they threshed it out, and in half an hour they sent for Tom Spedegue once more. Sir James sat with his elbows on the table and his finger-tips touching while he held forth in his best judicial maner. His conclusion was a remarkable one.

"So it comes to this, Mr. Spedegue, that we all three want to be on surer ground before we take a step which would rightly expose us to the most tremendous public criticism. You will therefore remain in London, and at three-forty-five to-morrow morning, which is just after dawn, you will come down in your flannels to the side entrance of Lord's. We will, under pledge of secrecy, assemble twelve or thirteen groundmen whom we can trust, including half-a-dozen first-class bats. We will have a wicket prepared on the practice ground, and we will try you out under proper conditions with your ten fielders and all. If you fail, there is an end. If you make good, we may consider your claim."

"Good gracious, sir, I made no claim."

"Well, your friend Scougall did for you. But anyhow, that's how we have fixed it. We shall be there, of course, and a few others whose opinion we can trust. If you care to wire Scougall he can come too. But the whole thing is secret, for we quite see the point that it must be a complete surprise or a wash-out. So you will keep your mouth shut and we shall do the same."

Thus it came about that one of the most curious games in the history of cricket was played on the Lord's ground next morning. There is a high wall round that part, but early wayfarers as they passed were amazed to hear the voices of the players, and the occasional crack of the ball at such an hour. The superstitious might almost have imagined that the spirits of the great departed were once again at work, and that the adventurous explorer might get a peep at the bushy black beard of the old giant or Billie Murdoch leading his Cornstalks once more to victory. At six o'clock the impromptu match was over, and the Selection Committee had taken the bravest and most sensational decision that had ever been hazarded since first a team was chosen. Tom Spedegue should play next week for England.

"Mind you," said Tarding, "if the beggar lets us down I simply won't face the music. I warn you of that. I'll have a taxi waiting at the gate and a passport in my pocket. Poste restante, Paris. That's me for the rest of the summer."

"Cheer up, old chap," said Sir James. "Our conscience is clear. We have acted for the best. Dash it all, we have ten good men, anyhow. If the worst came to the worst, it only means one passenger in the team."

"But it won't come to the worst," said Dr. Sloper, stoutly. "Hang it, we have seen with our own eyes. What more can we do? All the same, for the first time in my life I'll have a whisky-and-soda before breakfast."

Next day the list was published and the buzz began. Ten of the men might have been expected. These were Challen and Jones, as fast bowlers, and Widley, the slow left-hander. Then Peters, Moir, Jackson, Wilson, and Grieve were at the head of the batting averages, none of them under fifty, which was pretty good near the close of a wet season. Hanwell and Gordon were two all-rounders who were always sure of their places, dangerous bats, good change bowlers, and as active as cats in the field. So far so good. But who the Evil One was Thomas E. Spedegue? Never was there such a ferment in Fleet Street and such blank ignorance upon the part of "our well-informed correspondent." Special Commissioners darted here and there, questioning well-known cricketers, only to find that they were as much in the dark as themselves. Nobody knew—or if anyone did know, he was bound by oath not to tell. The wildest tales flew abroad. "We are able to assure the public that Spedegue is a 'nom de jeu' and conceals the identity of a world-famed cricketer who for family reasons is not permitted to reveal his true self." "Thomas E. Spedegue will surprise the crowd at Lord's by appearing as a coal-black gentleman from Jamaica. He came over with the last West Indian team, settled in Derbyshire, and is now eligible to play for England, though why he should be asked to do so is still a mystery." "Spedegue, as is now generally known, is a half-caste Malay who exhibited extraordinary cricket proficiency some years ago in Rangoon. It is said that he plays in a loincloth and can catch as well with his feet as with his hands. The question of whether he is qualified for England is a most debatable one." "Spedegue, Thomas E., is the head-master of a famous northern school whose wonderful talents in the cricket field have been concealed by his devotion to his academic duties. Those who know him best are assured," etc., etc. The Committee also began to get it in the neck. "Why, with the wealth of talent available, these three elderly gentlemen, whose ideas of selection seem to be to pick names out of a bag, should choose one who, whatever his hidden virtues, is certainly unused to first-class cricket, far less to Test Matches, is one of those things which make one realize that the lunacy laws are not sufficiently comprehensive." These were fair samples of the comments.

And then the inevitable came to pass. When Fleet Street is out for something it invariably gets it. No one quite knows how *The Daily Sportsman* succeeded in getting at Thomas Spedegue, but it was a great scoop and the incredible secret was revealed. There was a leader and there was an interview with the village patriarch which set London roaring with laughter. "No, we ain't surprised nohow," said Gaffer Hobbs. "Maister Spedegue do be turble clever with them slow balls of his'n. He sure was too much for them chaps what came in the char-à-bancs from Mudford. Artful, I call 'im. You'll see." The leader was scathing. "The Committee certainly seem to have taken leave of their senses. Perhaps there is time even now to alter their absurd decision. It is almost an insult to our Australian visitors. It is obvious that the true place for Mr. Thomas Spedegue, however artful he may be, is the village green and not Lord's, and that his competence to deal with the char-à-bancers of Mudford is a small guarantee that he can play first-class cricket. The whole thing is a deplorable mistake, and it is time that pressure was put upon the Selection Board to make them reconsider their decision."

"We have examined the score-book of the Bishops Bramley village club," wrote another critic. "It is kept in the tap-room of The Spotted Cow, and makes amusing reading. Our Test Match aspirant is hard to trace, as he played usually for the second eleven, and in any case there was no one capable of keeping an analysis. However, we must take such comfort as we can from his batting averages. This year he has actually amassed a hundred runs in nine recorded innings. Best in an innings, fifteen. Average, eleven. Last year he was less fortunate and came out with an average of nine. The youth is second master at the Totton High School and is in indifferent health, suffering from occasional attacks of asthma. And he is chosen to play for England! Is it a joke or what? We think that the public will hardly see the humour of it, nor will the Selection Committee find it a laughing matter if they persist in their preposterous action." So spoke the Press, but there were, it is only fair to say, other journals which took a more charitable view. "After all," said the sporting correspondent of *The Times*, "Sir James and his two colleagues are old and experienced players with a unique knowledge of the game. Since we have placed our affairs in their hands we must be content to leave them there. They have their own knowledge and their own private information of which we are ignorant. We can but trust them and await the event."

As to the three, they refused in any way to compromise or to bend to the storm. They gave no explanations, made no excuses, and simply dug in and lay quiet. So the world waited till the day came round.

We all remember what glorious weather it was. The heat and the perfect Bulli-earth wicket, so far as England could supply that commodity, reminded our visitors of their native conditions. It was England, however, who got the best of that ironed shirt-front wicket, for in their first knock even Cotsmore, the Australian giant, who was said to be faster than Gregory and more wily than Spofforth, could seldom get the ball bail-high. He bowled with splendid vim and courage, but his analysis at the end of the day only showed three wickets for a hundred and forty-two. Storr, the googlie merchant had a better showing with four for ninety-six. Cade's mediums accounted for two wickets, and Moir, the English captain, was run out. He had made seventy-three first, and Peters, Grieve, and Hanwell raked up sixty-four, fifty-seven, and fifty-one respectively, while nearly everyone was in double figures. The only exception was "Thomas E. Spedegue, Esq.," to quote the score card, which recorded a blank after his name. He was caught in the slips off the fast bowler, and, as he admitted afterwards that he had never for an instant seen the ball, and could hardly in his nervousness see the bowler, it is remarkable that his wicket was intact. The English total was four hundred and thirty-two, and the making of it consumed the whole of the first day. It was fast scoring in the time, and the crowd were fully satisfied with the result.

And now came the turn of Australia. An hour before play began forty thousand people had assembled, and by the time that the umpires came out the gates had to be closed, for there was not standing room within those classic precincts. Then came the English team, strolling out to the wickets and tossing the ball from hand to hand in time-honoured fashion. Finally appeared the two batsmen, Morland, the famous Victorian, the man of the quick feet and the supple wrists, whom many looked upon as the premier batsman of the world, and the stonewaller, Donahue, who had broken the hearts of so many bowlers with his obdurate defence. It was he who took the first over, which was delivered by Challen of Yorkshire, the raging, tearing fast bowler of the North. He sent down six beauties, but each of them came back to him down the pitch from that impenetrable half-cock shot which was characteristic of the famous Queenslander. It was a maiden over.

And now Moir tossed the ball to Spedegue and motioned him to begin at the pavilion end. The English captain had been present at the surreptitious trial and he had an idea of the general programme, but it took him some time and some consultation with the nervous, twitching bowler before he could set the field. When it was finally arranged the huge audience gasped with surprise and the batsmen gazed round them as if they could hardly believe their eyes. One poor little figure, alone upon a prairie, broke the solitude of the off-side. He stood as a deep point or as a silly mid-off. The on-side looked like a mass meeting. The fielders were in each other's way, and kept shuffling about to open up separate lines. It too some time to arrange, while Spedegue stood at the crease with a nervous smile, fingering the ball and waiting for orders. The Selection Board were grouped in the open window of the committee-room, and their faces were drawn and haggard.

"My God! This is awful!" muttered Tarding.

"Got that cab?" asked Dr. Sloper, with a ghastly smile.

"Got it! It is my one stand-by."

"Room for three in it?" said Sir James. "Gracious, he has got five short-legs and no slip. Well, well, get to it! Anything is better than waiting."

There was a deadly hush as Spedegue delivered his first ball. It was an ordinary slow full pitch straight on the wicket. At any other time Morland would have slammed it to the boundary, but he was puzzled and cautious after all this mysterious setting of the field. Some unknown trap seemed to have been set for him. Therefore he played the ball quietly back to the bowler and set himself for the next one, which was similar and treated the same way.

Spedegue had lost his nerve. He simply could not, before this vast multitude of critics, send up the grotesque ball which he had invented. Therefore he compromised, which was the most fatal of all courses. He lobbed up balls which were high but not high enough. They were simply ordinary overpitched, full-toss deliveries such as a batsman sees when he has happy dreams and smiles in his sleep. Such was the third ball, which was a little to the off. Morland sent it like a bullet past the head of the lonely mid-off and it crashed against the distant rails. The three men in the window looked at each other and the sweat was on their brows. The next ball was again a juicy full toss on the level of the batsman's ribs. He banged it through the crowd of fielders on the on with a deft turn of the wrist which insured that it should be upon the ground. Then,

47

gaining confidence, he waited for the next of those wonderful dream balls, and steadying himself for a mighty fast-footed swipe he knocked it clean over the ring and on to the roof of the hotel to square-leg. There were roars of applause, for a British crowd loves a lofty hit, whoever may deliver it. The scoreboard marked fourteen made off five balls. Such an opening to a Test Match had never be seen.

"We thought he might break a record, and by Jove he has!" said Tarding, bitterly. Sir James chewed his ragged moustache and Sloper twisted his fingers together in agony. Moir, who was fielding at mid-on, stepped across to the unhappy bowler.

"Chuck 'em up, as you did on Tuesday morning. Buck up, man! Don't funk it! You'll do them yet."

Spedegue grasped the ball convulsively and nerved himself to send it high into the air. For a moment he picture the New Forest glade, the white line of cord, and his young brother waiting behind the stump. But his nerve was gone, and with it his accuracy. There were roars of laughter as the ball went fifty feet into the air, which were redoubled when the wicket-keeper had to sprint back in order to catch it and the umpire stretched his arms out to signal a wide.

For the last ball, as he realized, that he was likely to bowl in the match, Spedegue approached the crease. The field was swimming round him. That yell of laughter which had greeted his effort had been the last straw. His nerve was broken. But there is a point when pure despair and desperation come to a man's aid—when he says to himself, "Nothing matters now. All is lost. It can't be worse than it is. Therefore I may as well let myself go." Never in all his practice had he bowled a ball as high as the one which now, to the amused delight of the crowd, went soaring into the air. Up it went and up—the most absurd ball ever delivered in a cricket match. The umpire broke down and shrieked with laughter, while even the amazed fielders joined in the general yell. The ball, after its huge parabola, descended well over the wicket, but as it was still within reach Morland, with a broad grin on his sunburned face, turned round and tapped it past the wicket-keeper's ear to the boundary. Spedegue's face drooped towards the ground. The bitterness of death was on him. It was all over. He had let down the Committee, he had let down the side, he had let down England. He wished the ground would open and swallow him so that his only memorial should be a scar upon the pitch of Lord's.

And then suddenly the derisive laughter of the crowd was stilled, for it was seen that an incredible thing had happened. Morland was walking towards the pavilion. As he passed Spedegue he made a good-humoured flourish of his bat as if he would hit him over the head with it. At the same time the wicket-keeper stooped and picked something off the ground. It was a bail. Forgetful of his position and with all his thoughts upon this extraordinary ball which was soaring over his head, the great batsman had touched the wicket with his toe. Spedegue had a respite. The laughter was changing to applause. Moir came over and clapped him jovially upon the back. The scoring board showed total fifteen, last man fourteen, wickets one.

Challen sent down another over of fizzers to the impenetrable Donahue which resulted in a snick for two and a boundary off his legs. And then off the last ball a miracle occurred. Spedegue was field at fine slip, when he saw a red flash come towards him low on the right. He thrust out a clutching hand and there was the beautiful new ball right in the middle of his tingling palm. How it got there he had no idea, but what odds so long as the stonewaller would stonewall no more? Spedegue, from being the butt, was becoming the hero of the crowd. They cheered rapturously when he approached the crease for his second over. The board was twenty-one, six, two.

But now it was a different Spedegue. His fears had fallen from him. His confidence had returned. If he did nothing more he had at least done his share. But he would do much more. It had all come back to him, his sense of distance, his delicacy of delivery, his appreciation of curves. He had found his length and he meant to keep it.

The splendid Australian batsmen, those active, clear-eyed men who could smile at our fast bowling and make the best of our slow bowlers seem simple, were absolutely at sea. Here was something of which they had never heard, for which they had never prepared, and which was unlike anything in the history of cricket. Spedegue had got his fifty-foot trajectory to a nicety, bowling over the wicket with a marked curve from the leg. Every ball fell on or near the top of the stumps. He was as accurate as a human howitzer pitching shells. Batten, who followed Morland, hit across one of them and was clean bowled. Staker tried to cut one off his wicket, and knocked down his own off-stump, broke his bat, and finally saw the ball descend amid the general *débris*. Here and there one was turned to leg and once a short one was hit out of the

49

ground. The fast bowler sent the fifth batsman's leg-stump flying and the score was five for thirty-seven. Then in successive balls Spedegue got Bollard and Whitelaw, the one caught at the wicket and the other at short square-leg. There was a stand between Moon and Carter, who put on twenty runs between them with a succession of narrow escapes from the droppers. Then each of them became victims, one getting his body in front, and the other being splendidly caught by Hanwell on the ropes. The last man was run out and the innings closed for seventy-four.

The crowd had begun by cheering and laughing, but now they had got beyond it and sat in a sort of awed silence as people might who were contemplating a miracle. Half-way through the innings Tarding had leaned forward and had grasped the hand of each of his colleagues. Sir James leaned back in his deck-chair and lit a large cigar. Dr. Sloper mopped his brow with his famous red handkerchief. "It's all right, but, by George! I wouldn't go through it again," he murmured. The effect upon the players themselves was curious. The English seemed apologetic, as though not sure themselves that such novel means could be justified. The Australians were dazed and a little resentful. "What price quoits?" said Batten, the captain, as he passed into the pavilion. Spedegue's figures were seven wickets for thirty-one.

And now the question arose whether the miracle would be repeated. Once more Donahue and Morland were at the wicket. As to the poor stonewaller, it was speedily apparent that he was helpless. How can you stonewall a ball which drops perpendicularly upon your bails? He held his bat flat before it as it fell in order to guard his wicket, and it simply popped up three feet into the air and was held by the wicket-keeper. One for nothing. Batten and Staker both hit lustily to leg and each was caught by the mass meeting who waited for them. Soon, however, it became apparent that the new attack was not invincible, and that a quick, adaptive batsman could find his own methods. Morland again and again brought off what is now called the back drive—a stroke unheard of before—when he turned and tapped the ball over the wicket-keeper's head to the boundary. Now that a crash helmet has been added to the stumper's equipment he is safer than he used to be, but Grieve has admitted that he was glad that he had a weekly paper with an insurance coupon in his cricket bag that day. A fielder was placed on the boundary in line with the stumps, and then the versatile Morland proceeded to elaborate those fine tips to slip and tips to fine

50

leg which are admitted now to be the only proper treatment of the dropper. At the same time Whitelaw took a pace back so as to be level with his wicket and topped the droppers down to the off so that Spedegue had to bring two of his legs across and so disarrange his whole plan of campaign. The pair put on ninety for the fifth wicket, and when Whitelaw at last got out, bowled by Hanwell, the score stood at one hundred and thirty.

But from then onwards the case was hopeless. It is all very well for a quick-eyed active genius like Morland to adapt himself in a moment to a new game, but it is too much to ask of the average first-class cricketer, who, of all men, is most accustomed to routine methods. The slogging bumpkin from the village green would have made a better job of Spedegue than did these great cricketers, to whom the orthodox method was the only way. Every rule learned, every experience endured, had in a moment become useless. How could you play with a straight bat at a ball that fell from the clouds? They did their best—as well, probably, as the English team would have done in their place—but their best made a poor show upon a scoring card. Morland remained a great master to the end and carried out his bat for a superb seventy-seven. The second innings came to a close at six o'clock on the second day of the match, the score being one hundred and seventy-four. Spedegue eight for sixty-one. England had won by an innings and one hundred and eighty-four runs.

Well, it was a wonderful day and it came to a wonderful close. It is a matter of history how the crowd broke the ropes, how they flooded the field, and how Spedegue, protesting loudly, was carried shoulder-high into the pavilion. Then came the cheering and the speeches. The hero of the day had to appear again and again. When they were weary of cheering him they cheered for Bishops Bramley. Then the English captain had to make a speech. "Rather stand up to Cotsmore bowling on a ploughed field," said he. Then it was the turn of Batten the Australian. "You've beat us at something," he said ruefully; "don't quite know yet what it is. It's not what we call cricket down under." Then the Selection Board were called for and they had the heartiest and best deserved cheer of them all. Tarding told them about the waiting cab. "It's waiting yet," he said, "but I think I can now dismiss it."

Spedegue played no more cricket. His heart would not stand it. His doctor declared that this one match had been one too many and that he must stand out in the future. But for good or for bad—for bad, as many think—he has left his mark upon the game for ever. The English were more amused than exultant over their surprise victory. The Australian papers were at first inclined to be resentful, but then the absurdity that a man from the second eleven of an unknown club should win a Test Match began to soak into them, and finally Sydney and Melbourne had joined London in its appreciation of the greatest joke in the history of cricket.

Conan Doyle's great enthusiasm for cricket was shared by another member of his family, his brother-in-law, E. W. Hornung, creator of the famous 'Gentleman Cracksman' Raffles. It has been said that writing first brought these two men together (both were contributors to the Cornhill Magazine and Temple Bar), but it was cricket that sealed their friendship – a bond which was further strengthened when Hornung met, fell in love with and married Conan Doyle's sister, Constance. There are even parallels to be found in their work, for more than one authority has suggested that Hornung deliberately took his brother-in-law's characters, Holmes and Watson, and 'reincarnated' them on the wrong side of the law as Raffles and his faithful assistant in crime, Bunny Manders. True or not, Hornung created a literary figure almost as famous as the great detective, and certainly every bit as fascinating. For, apart from being a master burglar able to pull off the most audacious robberies, wasn't he also a dangerous batsman, a brilliant fielder and 'perhaps the very finest slow bowler of his decade'? It was, in truth, a brilliant stroke by Hornung to provide his master cracksman with the day-to-day persona of a great county and test cricketer, thereby allowing him to move unsuspected among the great and the wealthy as he plotted his daring burglaries. This fact has been commented on by George Orwell who wrote, 'In making Raffles a cricketer as well as a burglar, Hornung was not merely providing him with a plausible disguise; he was also drawing the sharpest moral contrast that he was able to imagine.'

The fact he should have made him a cricketer becomes, though, less surprising when one learns of Hornung's skill as well as fascination with the game. Ernest William Hornung (1866–1921) was a small, rather frail boy affected by asthma, but during his education at Uppingham School proved himself an accurate slow bowler and good middle-order batsman. Because of this poor health, however, he was sent to Australia where he travelled widely and eventually returned to England somewhat stronger and healthier. (It is interesting to note, incidentally, that Raffles makes his first

53

appearance in Australia with a touring party.) Back home, Hornung took up writing, and following a string of short stories and several novels, at last achieved fame with The Amateur Cracksman *published in 1899. Raffles later appeared in two more collections of stories,* The Black Mask *(1901) and* A Thief In The Night *(1905) as well as a full-length novel,* Mr Justice Raffles *(1909). The success of these books made Hornung financially secure, and also enabled him to play a little cricket as well as watching county and international matches. Despite the accolades his books earned him, Hornung most prized the invitation which was extended to him in 1907 to join the MCC. He also possessed an encyclopaedic knowledge of the game, and it is no wonder that he utilised this along with his literary skill to write a number of other stories featuring cricketers – the best of these being, I think, 'A Bowler's Innings', which is by turn both comical and poignant . . .*

A Bowler's Innings

by E. W. Hornung

I was in search of some quiet spot to work in over the Christmas holidays, and here under my handlebars was the very place: a sheltered hollow with a solitary house set close beside the frozen road. Transversely ran a Yorkshire beck, overfed with snow, and on the opposite bank the pinched trees rose intricate and brittle and black against the setting sun. But what pleased me more was the blue signboard hanging immovable in the windless frost. And the yellow legend on the same, when I had back-pedalled down the hill, and was near enough to read it, was to yield the keenest joy of all:

BLUEBELL INN

RICHARD UNTHANK

Dick Unthank! The old Yorkshire bowler! The most popular player of his day! It must be the same; the name was uncommon; and was not inn-keeping the last state of most professional cricketers? I had never spoken to Unthank in my life; but I had kept his analysis when a small enthusiast, and had seen him bowl so often that the red good-humoured face, with the crafty hook-nose and the ginger moustache, was a very present vision as I entered the inn where I made sure of finding it. A cold deserted passage led me to a taproom as empty and as cold. No sign of Dick could I discover; but in the taproom I was joined by a sour-looking slattern with a grimy baby in her arms.

"Mrs. Unthank, I presume?"

"Yes, I'm Mrs. Unthank," said the woman, with a sigh which offended me. Her voice was as peevish as her face.

"Am I right in taking your husband to be the famous old cricketer, Dick Unthank?"

"I don't know, I'm sure; he's not that old."

"But he is the cricketer?"

"Ay; he used to play."

"Used to play!" I echoed with some warmth. "Only for the County, and the Players, and England itself!"

"So I've heard tell," returned Dick's wife indifferently; "it was before my time, you see."

"Is your husband at home?" cried I, out of patience with the woman.

"Ay; he's at home!" was the meaning reply.

"Busy?"

"I wish he was! No such luck; he's bad in bed."

Dick Unthank ill in bed! I thought of that brick-red countenance and of the arm of gnarled oak which could bowl all day on a batsman's wicket, and I felt sure it could be nothing serious. Meanwhile I was looking at the woman, who was either entirely ignorant or else wilfully unappreciative of her husband's fame, and I also felt that the least indisposition would become aggravated in such hands. I said that I should like to see Mr. Unthank, if I might, and if he would see me.

"Are you a friend of his?" inquired the wife.

"I have known him for years—on the cricket-field."

"Well, t' doctor said coompany was good for him; and dear knows I can't be with him all day, with his work to do as well as my own. If you step this way, I'll show you up. Mind your head as you come upstairs. It's the ricketiest old house iver *I* was in, an' no good for trade an' all; but Mr. Unthank took a fancy to it, and he wouldn't listen to me. I doubt he's sorry now. This is the room at t' top o' t' stairs. Oh, no, he won't be asleep. Well, Unthank, here's a gentleman come to see you."

We had entered a square, low room, with no carpet upon its lumpy floor, and very little furniture within its dingy walls. There was one window, whose diamond panes scored the wintry glow across and across, and this was what first caught my eye. Then it rested on the fire, in which the coal had been allowed to cake until it gave out as little warmth as light. The bed was in the darkest corner of the room. I could make out little more than a confused mass of bedclothes, and, lying back upon the pillows, the head and shoulders of a man.

"He says he's known you for years," added Mrs. Unthank as I shut the door.

"Why, who can it be?" said a hollow voice from the corner. "Poke up the fire, missus, an' let's see each other."

"You won't know me, Mr. Unthank," I hastened to confess. "I have only seen you play, but you have given me many a happy hour, and I wanted to tell you so when I saw your name on the signboard. I am only sorry to find you like this. Nothing very serious, I hope?"

"Not it!" was the hoarse reply. "'Tis nobbut a cold I caught last spring, an' never properly throwed off. It serves me right for giving up the game! I'd have sweaten it off in half an hour at the nets. But I mean to give this up, an' get a school or club to coach next season' then I'll be myself again. That's better, missus! Now we can see to shake hands."

And he gave me the cunning member which had been a county's strength; but the Dick Unthank of old days was dead to me before I felt its slack and humid clasp. The man on the fire-lit bed seemed half Dick's size, the lusty arms were gone to skin and bone, the weather-beaten face shone whiter than the unclean pillow which was its frame. The large nose was wasted and unduly prominent, and a red stubble covered the sunken cheeks and the chin. Only the moustache was ruddy and unchanged; and it glistened with a baleful dew.

I was utterly amazed and shocked. How I looked I do not know, but Mrs. Unthank paused at the door before leaving us together.

"Ay," said she, "I thought you'd see a difference! He talks about playing next season, but he'll be lucky if he sees another. I doubt he isn't that long for this world!"

It was my first experience of the class which tells the truth to its sick and dying, and my blood was boiling; but Unthank smiled grimly as the door closed.

"Poor lass," said he, "it would be hard on her if there was owt in what she says. But trust a woman to see black, an' trust old Dick to put on flesh and muscle once he gets back into flannels. I never should ha' chucked it up; that's where I made a mistake. But spilt milk's spilt milk, and I'm right glad to see you, sir. So you've watched me bowl, have you? Not at my best, I'm afraid, sir, unless you're older than what I take you for." And Dick looked sorry for himself for the first time.

"On the contrary," said I, "you never did much better than the very first time I saw you play."

"When was that, sir?"

"Eighteen years ago last July."

"Eighteen year? Why you must have been a little lad, sir?"

"I was twelve; but I knew my *Lillywhite* off by heart, and all that season I cut the matches out of the newspapers and pasted them in a book. I have it still."

"Mebbe it wasn't a first-class match you saw me come off in?"

"It was against the Gentlemen, at Lord's."

"Eighteen—year—ago. Hold on, sir! Did I take some wickets in t' second innings?"

"Seven for forty-three."

"An' made some runs an' all?"

"Thirty-two not out. It was the fastest thing I ever saw!"

Dick shook his head.

"It wasn't good cricket, sir," said he. "But then I niver was owt of a bat. It was a bowler's innings was that—a short life but a merry one; 'twas a bowler's wicket an' all, I mind, an' I was in a hurry to make use of it. Ay, ay, I remember it now as if it was yesterday."

"So do I; it was my first sight of Lord's."

"Did you see the ball that took W. G.?"

"I did. It nearly made me cry! It was my first sight of W. G. also!"

"She came back nine inches," said the old bowler in a solemn voice. "Mr. Grace, he said eighteen inches, and the *Sportsman* it said six; but it wasn't less than nine, as sure as I lie here. Ay, t' wicket might ha' been made for me that day; there's no ground to bowl on like Lord's on the mend. I got Mr. Lucas too—and there wasn't a finer batsman living at the time—an' Mr. Webbe was caught off me at cover. Them were the days, an' no mistake, an' yon day was one o' my very best; it does me good to think about it. I may never play first-class cricket again, but mebbe I'll coach them as will."

The fire had died down again; the wintry glow was blotted out by early night, and, once more the old professional's face was invisible in the darkened room. I say "old" because he had been very long before the public, but he was little worse than forty in mere years, and now in the dark it was difficult to believe that his cricket days were altogether over. His voice was fuller and heartier than when he greeted me, and if the belief that one will recover be half the battle against sickness then Dick Unthank was already half-way to victory. But his gaunt face haunted me, and I was wondering whether such wasted limbs could ever fill out again, when there came a beating of hoofs like drumsticks on the frozen road, and wheels stopped beneath the window.

"That's the doctor," grumbled Dick. "I'm sure I don't know what he wants to come every day for. Sit still, sir, sit still."

"No; I must go. But I shall want something to eat, and a bed for the night at least, and I shall come up later without fail."

Already there were steps on the rickety stairs; and I made my escape as Mrs. Unthank, with a streaming candle, ushered in a tall old gentleman in a greatcoat and creaking boots. I was detaching my impedimenta from the bicycle when the creaking boots came down again.

"I should like one word with you, sir," said the doctor. "I gather that you are thinking of putting up here, and it will be a real charity if you do. You have done my patient more good in half an hour than I have in the last month."

"Oh, as to that," said I, "it is a treat to me to meet an old cricketer like Dick Unthank, but I hardly think I can stay beyond to-morrow. I want a quiet place to do some work in, but I must be reasonably comfortable too; and, to be frank, I doubt the comfort here."

"You may well!" exclaimed the doctor, lowering his voice. "That woman is enough to scare anybody; yet for the money's sake she would look after you in a way, and with it she might make her husband more comfortable than he is. I may frighten you away myself by saying so, but it would be an untold relief to me to feel that there was one responsible and humane person in the house."

"Is he so very ill?"

"So very ill? Have you seen him and can you ask? He is in a galloping consumption."

"But he is so full of hope. Is there no hope for him?"

"Not the shadow of a chance! They are always sanguine. That is part of the disease."

"And how long do you give him?"

The doctor shrugged.

"It may be weeks, it may be days, it *might* be months," said he. "I can only say that in this weather and with such a nurse nothing would surprise me."

"That is enough for me," I replied. "I shall give the place a trial."

And I did.

Many nights I passed in a chamber as accessible to the four winds of heaven as to the companies of mice which broke each night's sleep into so many naps. Many days I lived well enough on new-laid eggs and Yorkshire ham, and wrought at my book until for good or ill the stack of paper lay complete upon the table. And many a winter's evening I spent at Dick's bedside, chatting with him, listening to him, hearing a score of anecdotes to one that I can set down here, and admiring more and more the cheeriness and the charity of the dying man. In all our talks I cannot remember an unkind story or a word of spite, though Dick had contemporaries still in the county ranks, the thought of whom must have filled his soul with envy. Even his wife was all that was good in his eyes; in mine she was not actually bad, but merely useless, callous and indifferent from sheer want of intelligence and imagination.

In the early days I sent for my portmanteau, and had my old cricket scrap-book put into it. Dick's eyes glistened as he took up leaf after leaf. I had torn them out for his convenience, and for days they kept him amused while I was absent at my work. Towards the end I brought my work beside him, for he was weakening visibly, though unconsciously, and it was a new interest to his simple mind.

"I don't know how you do it, sir," said he one afternoon, as I gathered my papers together. "I've been watching you this half-hour—your pen's hardly stopped—and it's all out of your own head! It beats an' bowls me, sir, does that. Dear knows how you do it."

"Well," I laughed, "and it's a puzzle to me how you pitch a ball just where you like and make it break either way at will. Dear knows how you do that!"

Dick shook his head.

"Sometimes you can't," said he reflectively; "sometimes you're off the spot altogether. I've heard you say you can't write some days; and some days a man can't bowl. Ay, you *could* write, and I *could* bowl, but they'd smack me to t' boundary over after over."

"And what I wrote I should tear up next morning."

He lay looking at the window. It was soft weather now, and a watery sun shone weakly into the room, slanting almost to the bed, so that a bleached and bony hand hung glistening in the rays. I knew that it was itching to hold a ball again—that Dick's spirit was in flannels—even before he continued:

"Now to-day's a day when you could bowl. I'm glad it isn't t' season: it'd be my day, would this, wi' a wet wicket drying from t' top. By gum, but you can do summat wi' a wicket like yon. The ground fairly bites, an' the ball'll come in wi' your arm, or break back or hang, just as it's told; it's the time a ball answers its helm, sir, is that! And it's a rum thing, but it'll drop where you ask it on a bowler's wicket; but on a good 'un it seems to know that they can make a half-volley of it 'most wherever it drops, so it loses heart and pitches all over the shop. Ay, there's a deal o' human natur' in a treble-seam, sir; it don't like getting knocked about any more than we do."

So we would chat by the hour together, and the present was our favourite tense, as though his cricket days were not nearly over. Nor did I see any sense or kindness in convincing him that they were, and a little persuasion brought Mrs. Unthank to my way of thinking and acting in the matter. Clergymen, however, are bound by other considerations, and though Unthank was by no means an irreligious man, but had an open ear and mind for the manly young curate who came to see him from time to time, he did bitterly complain to me one evening when the curate was gone.

"No game's lost till it's won, sir, and t' parson has no right to shake his head till the umpire gives me out. I don't say I'm in for a long score— bowlers very seldom are, but I isn't going out just yet a bit. I'll get better set by-and-by, and you'll see me trouble the scorers yet."

It was easy to tell that Dick was proud of his metaphor, and it recurred continually in his talk. His disease was "the bowler," and each fit of coughing "a nasty one," but if he could only keep up his wicket till summer-time he felt confident of adding some years to his score. This confidence clung to him almost to the last. He would give up the inn and get back to Bramall Lane, and umpire for "t' owd team" as long as he had a leg to stand on.

I remember when he realised the truth.

In a corner of the best parlour, beneath an accumulation of old newspapers and the ruins of a glass shade, I found one day, when I had finished but was still polishing my book, a war-worn cricket-ball with a tarnished silver plate let into the bruised leather. The inscription on the plate announced that this was the actual ball with which Richard Unthank had taken nine Nottingham wickets (the tenth being run out) for a matter of fifty runs, at Bramall Lane, in his palmy days.

That was twenty years ago, but I knew from Dick that it remained the achievement of which he was proudest, and I took the ball upstairs to him after cleaning the silver plate as well as I could with soap and water.

His hot eyes glistened.

"Why, wherever did you find this, sir?" he cried, with the joy of a child in his shallow voice. "I'd forgot I had it. How canny it feels! Ay, ay, yon was the happiest day in all my life!"

And rapidly and excitedly he gave me full particulars, explaining how and why the wicket had suited him to a nicety, and how he had known before he finished an over that it was his day of days. Then he went through the Notts eleven, and told me with what ball and by what wile he had captured this wicket after that. Only one of the nine had fallen more by luck than good bowling; that was when Dick atoned for a half-volley by holding a terrific return, and son won the match for Yorkshire by the narrow margin of three runs.

"It was my slow ball, and a bit too slow, I doubt, an' he runs out of his ground an' lets drive. There was an almighty crack, and next thing I hears is a rush of air low down to the on. I goes for it wi'out seeing a thing, feels a smack on my hand, an' there's the beautiful ball stuck in it that tight that nobbut gunpowder could ha' shifted her! She looked that sweet and peaceful sticking in my hand that what do you think I did? Took an' kissed her instead of chucking her up! You see, sir, I'd forgot that if I'd lost her we should ha' lost t'match instead o' winning, for she was a dead-sure boundary; when owd Tom tell'd me it made me feel that bad, I'd got to have a big drink or faint; an' I feel bad when I think of it yet."

In his excitement he had raised himself on his left elbow. The effort had relaxed his muscles, and the historic ball had slipped from his fingers and was rolling across the floor. I picked it up, and was about to return it to him, but Dick Unthank waved me back.

"Nay, nay," said he. "Give us a catch, sir. They're runnin'!"

So I tossed it gently into his outstretched hand, but the weak fingers closed too soon, and once more the ball rolled on the floor. Dick looked at me comically, yet with a spot of colour on either cheekbone, as he shook his head.

"I doubt I'm out of practice," he said. "Come, let's try again."

"I wouldn't, Dick."

"You wouldn't? What do you mean? Do you think I'm that bad I can't catch a cricket-ball—me that's played for All England in my day? Chuck her in again and I'll show you! Get to t' boundary at t'other side o' t' room!"

He was sitting bolt upright now, with both hands ready, and in his altered tone there was such umbrage that I could not cross him. So again I threw; but two such hands were no better than one; the ball fell through them into the bed; and Dick Unthank sat looking at me with death dawning in his eyes.

"It's the light," I said gruffly, for it was the finest day of the New Year, and even now the sun was glinting on the silver-mounted ball. "Who could make catches in a light like this?"

"No, sir," whispered Dick, "it's not the light. I see what it is. Its—it's what they call the beginning o' the end."

And he burst into tears. Yet was he sanguine even then, for the end was very near. It came that night.

P. G. Wodehouse (1881–1975) is another of the great figures of English letters who was also a devotee of cricket, and indeed was an opening bowler for Dulwich College around the turn of the century and later joined the Author's XI in which Sir Arthur Conan Doyle appeared from time to time. Like Doyle, Wodehouse drew on his cricketing knowledge in the creation of his most famous character – for the real-life original of the 'gentleman's gentleman', Jeeves, was a Warwickshire fast bowler named Percy Jeaves who was tragically killed in the First World War. Wodehouse's undoubted accomplishments on the Dulwich cricket field gave him the idea for the character of Mike Jackson, the youngest of three cricketing brothers, who appeared in several public school stories he wrote in the early 1900s with titles such as Mike *and* Psmith in the City. *At this same time, Wodehouse was also starting to write for* Punch, *and in the files of that venerable humour magazine can be found essays and poems with self-explanatory titles such as 'Under M.V.C. Rules' (October 1902) and 'The Cricketer in Winter' (verse, September 1903). Wodehouse also contributed to the popular monthly magazine,* Pearson's, *and in its pages can be found several lengthy poems such as 'The Traitor' (September 1907), as well as the following short story 'Playing The Game' from July 1906. It is an amusing period piece in several respects, and though not typical of Wodehouse's later style, is a variation on our theme with a clever ending. It is also notable as one of the few uncollected Wodehouse stories, and therefore of especial interest to his admirers as well as lovers of cricket humour.*

Playing the Game

A Public School Story

by P. G. Wodehouse

Oh, woman, woman!

As somebody once said. I forget who.

Woman, always noted for serpentine snakiness, is perhaps more snakily serpentine at the age when her hair is wavering on the point of going up, and her skirts hesitating on the brink of going down than at any other moment in her career. It is then most of all that she will bear watching. Take, for example, Scott's sister. Which brings me to my story.

*   *   *   *

Charteris first made the acquaintance of Scott's sister when Scott asked him home to spend the last week of the Easter holidays with him. They were in different houses at Locksley, Scott being a member of the School House, while Charteris was in Merevale's; but as they were both in the first eleven they saw a good deal of one another. In addition, Charteris frequently put in an evening in the winter and Easter terms at those teas which Scott gave in his study, where the guests did all the work, and the host the greater part of the feeding. So that it came as no surprise when he received the invitation.

He hesitated about accepting it. He was a wary youth, and knew that scores of school friendships have died an untimely death owing to one of the pair spending part of the holidays at the other's home. Something nearly always happens to disturb the harmony. Most people are different in the home circle, and the alteration is generally for the worse. However, things being a little dull at home with illness in the house, and Scott's letter mentioning that there was a big lawn with a cricket net, where they could get into form for next term, he decided to risk it.

The shades of night were beginning to fall when the train brought Charteris to his destination.

Looking up and down the platform he could see no signs of his host. Former instances of his casualness, for which quality Scott was notorious, floated across his mind. It would be just like him to forget that his guest was to arrive that day.

The platform gradually emptied of the few passengers who had alighted. He walked out of the station, hoping to find a cab which would convey him to Scott's house.

"I say," said a voice, as he paused outside and looked round about him.

Through the gathering dusk he could see the dim outline of a dog-cart.

"Hullo," he said.

"Are you Charteris?"

"Somebody's been telling you," said he in an aggrieved voice. His spirits had risen with a bound at the prospect of getting to his destination at last.

"Jump in, then. I thought you couldn't have come. I was just going to drive off."

"Don't talk of it," said Charteris.

"Billy couldn't come to meet you. He had to get the net down. You mustn't leave it up all night. The gardener's boy is a perfect idiot and always gets it tangled up. So he sent me. Have this rug. Is the box all right? Then gee up, Peter. Good night, Mr. Brown."

"Good night, miss," said the station-master affably. Charteris examined her out of the corner of his eyes. As far as he could see through the darkness she was pretty. Her hair was in the transition stage between mane and bun. It hung over her shoulders, but it was tied round with a ribbon. He had got thus far with his inspection when she broke the silence.

"I hope you'll like our wicket," she said. "It's slow, as there's a good deal of moss on the lawn, but it plays pretty true. Billy smashed a bedroom window yesterday."

"He would," said Charteris. The School House man was the biggest hitter at Locksley.

"What do you think of Billy as a bat?" asked the lady turning to face him.

"He can hit," said Charteris.

"But his defence isn't any good at all, is it? And he's nervous before he gets started, and a man who goes in for a forcing game oughtn't to be that, ought he?"

"I didn't know he was nervous. He's not got that reputation at school. I should have thought that if there was one chap who went in without caring a bit about the bowling, it was Scott."

It surprised him in a vague sort of way that a girl should have such a firm and sensible grasp on the important problems of life. He had taken his sister to Lord's one summer to watch the Gentlemen *v.* Players match, and she had asked him if the light screens were there to keep the wind off the players. He had not felt really well since.

"Oh, no," said the girl. "He's as jumpy as a cat. He's often told me that it all depends on the first ball. If he can hit that, he's all right. If he doesn't he's nervous till he gets out or slogs a four. You remember his seventy-one against the M.C.C. last year. He managed to get Trott round past mid-on for three the first ball. After that he was as right as anything. Against Haileybury, too, when he made fifty-four. He didn't see his first ball at all. He simply slogged blindly, and got it by a fluke, and sent it clean into the pavilion."

"Did you see those games?" inquired Charteris, amazed.

"No. Oh, now I wish I had. But I make Billy promise faithfully when

69

he goes back to school that he'll write me a full account of every match. And he does it, too, though those are about the only letters he does write. He hates writing letters. But he's awfully good about mine. I love cricket. Billy says I'm not half a bad bat. Here we are."

The dog-cart swung into a long drive, at the end of which a few lighted windows broke the blackness. A dog barked inside the house as they drove up, and rushed out as the door opened and Scott's drawl made itself heard.

"That you, Charteris?"

"It looks like me, doesn't it?" said Charteris, jumping down.

"How many times has Molly spilt you on the way here?" inquired Scott.

"I drove jolly well," protested his sister with indignation. "Didn't I?"

"Ripping," said Charteris.

"It's very decent of you to hush it up," said Scott. "Come along and brush some of the mud off."

*   *   *   *

Charteris woke abruptly on the following morning at twenty-three minutes and eight seconds past seven. What woke him was a cricket ball. It hummed through the open window, crashed against the opposite wall—an inch lower and an engraving of "The Fallowfield Hunt" would have needed extensive alterations and repairs—and, after circling round the room, came to a standstill under the chest of drawers. Charteris hopped out of bed and retrieved it.

"I say," said a penetrating voice from the regions of the drive.

Charteris put on a blazer and looked out. Scott's sister was standing below. She held a bat in her hand. In the offing lurked a shirt-sleeved youth whom he took to be the gardener's boy. He was grinning sheepishly. Across the lawn stood the net and wickets.

"Hullo, are you awake?" inquired Molly.

"More or less," said Charteris.

"Did you see a ball come in just now?"

"I thought I noticed something of the sort. Is this it?"

She dropped the bat, and caught the descending ball neatly. Charteris looked on with approval.

"I'm sorry if it disturbed you," said Miss Scott.

70

"Not at all," said Charteris. "Jolly good way of calling people in the morning. You ought to take out a patent. Did you hit it?"

"Yes."

"Rather a pull," said Charteris judicially.

"I know—I can't help pulling. It runs in the family. Billy will do it, too. Are you coming out?"

"Ten minutes," said Charteris. "Shall I do some bowling for you?"

The lady expressed surprise.

"Can you bowl?" she said.

"Trumble isn't in it," replied Charteris. "It's an education to watch my off-break."

"They never put you on in first matches."

"That," said Charteris, "is because they don't know a good thing when they see one."

"All right, then. Don't be long."

"Well," said Molly half-an-hour later, as the gong sounded for breakfast and they walked round to the door, "I think your bowling's jolly good, and I don't know why they don't give you a chance for the first. Still, you couldn't get Billy out, I don't think."

"Billy!" said Charteris. "As a matter of fact, Billy is a gift to me. He can't stand up against my stuff. When he sees my slow hanging ball coming he generally chucks down his bat, hides his face in his hands, and bursts into tears."

"I'll tell him that."

"I shouldn't," said Charteris. "Don't rub it into the poor chap. We all have these skeletons in our cupboards."

Molly regarded him seriously.

"Do you know," she said, "I believe you're very conceited?"

"I've been told so," replied Charteris complacently, "by some of the best judges."

The dining-room was empty when they arrived. The Scott family was limited to Molly, her brother, and Mrs. Scott, who was a semi-invalid and generally breakfasted in bed. Colonel Scott had been dead some years.

Molly made the tea in a business-like manner, and Charteris was half-way through his second cup when his host strolled in. Scott had been known to come down in time for the beginning of breakfast, but he did not spoil a good thing by doing it too often.

71

"Slacker," said Charteris, "we've been up and out for an hour."

"What do you think of the wicket?"

"Very good. Miss Scott——"

"You can call me Molly if you like," interrupted that lady, biting a section out of a healthy slab of bread and butter.

"Thanks," said Charteris. "Molly has got that stroke of yours to the on. She pretty nearly knocked a corner off the house with it once."

"Molly is always imitating her elders and betters," replied her brother. "At a picnic last summer——"

"Billy, stop! You're not to."

"Now, I can't do the dashing host, and make the home bright and lively," said Scott complainingly, "if you go interrupting my best stories. Molly went to a picnic—grown-up affair—last summer. Wanted to be taken for about ten years older than she is."

"Be quiet, Billy."

The story became jerky from this point, for the heroine was holding the narrator by the shoulders from behind, and doing her best to shake him.

"So," continued Scott, "she turned up the collar of her jacket, and shoved—shoved her hair underneath it. See? Looked as if it was up instead of down her back. Palled up with another girl. Other girl began talking about dances and things. 'Oh,' said Molly, 'I haven't been out a great deal lately.' After a bit it got so hot that Molly had to take off her jacket, and down came the hair. 'Why,' said the other girl, 'you're only a child after all!' "

And Scott, who had been present at the massacre, howled with brotherly laughter at the recollection.

Molly looked across at Charteris with flaming cheeks. Charteris's face was grave and composed. This, he felt, was not the place to exhibit a sense of humour.

"I don't see the joke," said Charteris. "I think the other girl was a beast."

Charteris found a note on his dressing-table when he went to his room that night.

It was a model of epistolary terseness. "Thanks awfully for not laughing," it ran.

Charteris went back to Locksley at the end of the Easter holidays fit both in body and mind. In the first card match, against the local regiment, he compiled a faultless eighty-six. The wretched Scott, coming to the crease second wicket down outwardly confident but inwardly palpitating, had his usual wild swing at his first ball, and was yorked.

A long letter from Molly arrived in the course of the next week. Apparently Scott sent her details of all the matches, not only of those in which he himself had figured to advantage. One sentence in the letter amused Charteris. "I'm sorry I called you conceited about your bowling. I asked Billy after you had gone, and he said he was more afraid of you till he got set than of anyone else in the school." This was news to Charteris. Like many people who bat well he had always treated his bowling as a huge joke. He bowled for the house first change, but then Merevale's were not strong in that department. Batting was their speciality. It had never occurred to him that anyone could really be afraid of his strange deliveries. And Scott of all people, who invariably hit him off after three overs! It was good news, however, for the School House was Merevale's chief rival in the House matches, and Scott was the School House star performer. If there was a chance of his being too much for Scott, then Merevale's should win the cup.

The House matches at Locksley were played on the knocking out system. And this year a great stroke of luck befell Merevale's. The only other house with any pretentions to the cup, Dacre's, drew the School House for their first match. The School House won, Scott making 102 in an hour. And it was now evident that the cup lay between Merevale's and the School House. These two easily disposed of their opponents and qualified for the final.

There was much discussion in the school on the merits of the two teams. The general impression was that Merevale's would fail for want of bowling. Scott, it was thought, ought to have a day out against the inferior bowling of Merevale's. If he got out early, anything might happen, for Merevale's had the strongest batting side in the school.

Then it was that Charteris went to Venables, the captain of Merevale's, on the evening before the match.

"Look here, Venables," he said. 'I'll start by saying I'm not ragging, or you might have your doubts. I want you to put me on to-morrow when Scott comes in. Whoever's bowling, take him off, and give me an over. I shall only want one. If I can't get him in that, I shan't get him at all."

"Have you developed a new ball?" inquired Venables. It was Charteris's habit to announce every other day that he had developed a new ball. He was always burlesquing his bowling.

"Don't rag," said Charteris earnestly. "I'm quite serious. I mean it. I happen to know that Scott's in a funk for his first over, and that my rotten stuff worries him till he gets set. You might give me a shot. It can't do any harm."

"You really aren't pulling my leg?"

"I swear I'm not. Of course, it's a million to one that I shan't get him out, but it's quite true that he doesn't like my bowling."

"I don't wonder," said Venables. "It's uncanny stuff. All right."

"Thanks," said Charteris.

*   *   *   *

We now come to that portion of the story which more particularly illustrates the truth of the profound remarks, with which it began, on the serpentine snakiness of woman. Coming down to breakfast on the day of the match, Charteris saw a letter by the side of his plate. It was from Molly.

Their correspondence had become, since her first letter, quite voluminous. Writing to Molly was like talking to a sympathetic listener. No detail of a match or of school gossip was too small to interest her; and when, as he had been doing frequently that term, he made a fifty or even a century; there was no need for him to slur modestly over the feat; he was expected to describe it vividly from beginning to end.

The bulk of the letter was not unusual. It was in the postscript that, like most feminine letter-writers, she had embodied her most important words. Charteris re-read them several times before the colossal awfulness of them dawned upon him.

This was the postscript:

"Now I want you to do me a favour. I wish you would. Poor old Billy is quite cut up about his luck this season. You know how badly he has done in matches. That century against Dacre's is the only really good thing he's done at all. *Can't* you give him an easy ball when the School House play you? I don't mean to hit, but just so that he doesn't get out. He told me that he hated your bowling, and he *is* so nervous in his first over. Do! It *is* such hard lines on him making ducks, and I'm awfully

74

fond of him. So you will, won't you? P.P.S.—If you do, you shall have that photograph you wanted. The proofs have just come back, and they are *very* good. I like the one best where I've got my hair sort of done up."

Charteris did not join the usual after-breakfast gathering of house-prefects in Venables study that morning. He sat in his own den, and pondered. At a quarter to nine he might have been overheard to murmur a remark.

"And that," he murmured, "is the girl I thought really understood the finer points of cricket!"

⋆   ⋆   ⋆   ⋆

It is a pity that the Problem Story has ceased to be fashionable. I should have preferred this narrative to have ended at the above point. As it is, I must add two quotations—one from the school magazine, the other from a letter from Miss Molly Scott to Charteris. *Place aux dames.* Here is the extract from the letter:

"I am sending the photograph. I hope you will like it."

And here is the quotation from the magazine:

"W. L. Scott b Charteris 0; c Welch b Charteris 2."

An assistant editor at Punch *when P. G. Wodehouse began his contributions was another cricket lover named Edward Verrall Lucas (1868–1938) who had deliberately chosen his first job as a bookseller's assistant in his home town of Eltham in Kent in order to get mid-week days off and watch county cricket in the East of England! As a boy he dreamed of playing for Kent, but was never, he says, anything other than "a slow bowler and an even slower batsman". His real talent proved to be in writing, and after a period as a reporter he joined the staff of* Punch. *He had a particular gift for gentle satire and parody, and he found a ready market for his work in numerous magazines. He ultimately produced over 30 volumes of essays – in which may be found numerous items relating to cricket – as well as writing* Cricket All His Life *(1935) and editing that admirable anthology* The Hambledon Men *(1907) which includes the text of John Nyren's classic work, 'The Young Cricketer's Tutor' written in 1833. With this in mind it seemed most appropriate to include in this book Lucas's own amusing 'review' of another very different cricket manual published in 1891 . . .*

An Indian Cricket Tutor

by E. V. Lucas

Mohummud Abdullah Khan's Cricket Guide was published in Lucknow in 1891, the full title being *Cricket Guide intended for the use of Young Players, containing a Short but Comprehensive Account of the Game, embracing all the important Rules and Directions nicely arranged in due Succession.* The reason given by the Indian Nyren for putting forth this work was the wish to allay the fever which cricket seems then to have been provoking in his compatriots. Those who remember the *sang-froid*, the composed mastery, of Prince Ranjitsinhji may be surprised to learn that, at any rate in 1891, cricket had a way of rushing to young India's head. "Even those," wrote Mohummud Abdullah Khan, "who are very good and noble (say, next-door to angels) turn so rash and inconsiderate at certain moments that their brains lose the balance and begin to take fallacious fancies." More, they "boil over with rage, pick up quarrels with one another, and even look daggers at their own dearest friends and darlings," the cause being not only the

79

game itself, but an ignorance of the laws that should govern it and them, and without obedience to which "a human body is nothing but a solid piece of rocky hill, that is to say 'cleverness.' " Very well, then. Feeling as he did about it, Mohummud Abdullah Khan had no alternative but to write his book.

Practical as the instructions of this Oriental teacher can be, it is deportment that really lies nearest his heart. He is as severe on a want of seriousness as upon loss of temper. Thus, he says: "The fielders must take especial care not to exchange jokes with one another or try funny tricks that do secretly divide their attention and produce a horrible defect in their fielding." Again, "Behave like gentlemen after the game is over; avoid clapping and laughing in faces of the persons you have defeated." But there is no harm in a match being momentarily interrupted by a touch of courtesy. Thus: "If you are the Captain of your team and the fielders of the opposite party clap your welcome, you are required simply to turn or raise your night cap a little, and this is sufficient to prove your easy turn of disposition as well as to furnish the return of their compliments."

For the most part the directions are sound, even if they may be a little obscure in statement; but now and then one is puzzled. The game in India must have been animated indeed if no error has crept into the following note on the bowler: "During one and the same over the bowler is allowed to change his ends as often as he may desire, but cannot possibly bowl two overs in succession." And this reads oddly: "The bowler is allowed to make the batsman stand in any direction he may choose from the wicket he is bowling from." But no fault can be found here: "The bowler must always try to pitch his ball in such a style and position that its spring may always rest on the wickets to be aimed at. He must know the proper rules of *no balls* and *wides* and"—here we are again!—"must never be wishing to pick up any quarrel with the umpire of the opposite party."

And so we reach the umpires, upon whom the author becomes very earnest. Under the frenetic conditions to which cricket could reduce his countrymen, to act as umpire was no joke. Indeed he goes so far as to advise the reader never to fill that position except when the match is between teams personally unknown to him. For to umpire among friends is to turn those friends to foes. "Take special care, my dear umpires, not to call *over* unless the ball has finally settled in the wicket-keeper's hand, as well as avoid ordering a batsman *out* unless you are appealed to by the opposite party . . . Each and every one of the umpires must avoid using insulting terms, or playing on bets with any one of the fielders or persons in general, in his capacity of being an umpire."

The requirements of a perfect wicket-keeper are well set forth. After describing his somewhat "stooping condition" the mentor says, "I would like this man to be of a grave demeanour and humble mind, say the Captain of the Club, whose duties are to guide the fielders, order the change of their places if necessary," and "guard himself well against the furious attacks of the sweeping balls." Here Mohummud Abdullah Khan is among some of the best critics, who have always held that for the captain to be wicket-keeper (as, for example, in the case of Gregor MacGregor) is an ideal arrangement.

Point also needs some special qualities: "He must be a very smart and very clever man, of a quick sight and slender form." (Slender form? And yet one has seen "W. G." doing not so badly there!) "His place is in front of the popping-crease, about seven yards from the striker. He must take special care to protect his own person in case when fast bowling is raging through the field. Pay great attention to the game, my dear pointer, or suppose yourself already hurt."

I have no idea whether my next contributor, the novelist Eden Phillpotts (1862–1960), who was born in India, ever read Mohummud Abdullah Khan's extraordinary 'Guide', but he was certainly a keen student of the game and there was no more enthusiastic supporter in the South West of England where he ultimately settled. Phillpotts was certainly introduced to the game by his soldier father in India, and when he came to London as a young man to study for the stage, he several times played in Actors XI's with such distinguished thespians as C. Aubrey Smith and Henry Ainley. The lure of the stage waned on Phillpotts, however, and he abandoned this career to take up writing – although he did later acknowledge his early endeavours by writing several successful dramas for the London stage. He proved an incredibly prolific author, in fact, publishing over 250 books during his lifetime, making one wonder how he ever found time to watch an afternoon game in Exeter where he lived, let alone a county game or five day test! He was also a man who enjoyed travelling, and it is believed that on a trip to the West Indies he gathered the raw materials which he shaped into the next highly amusing story. If Phillpotts' English visitors extract a certain amount of fun at the expense of the cricket of those unsophisticated islanders back at the beginning of this century, their prowess today is such that the laugh is now very much on us!

A West Indian Cricket Match

by Eden Phillpotts

After the Royal Mail Steamship *Rhine* had been anchored in the harbour of a certain little island in the West Indies, for the space of two days, our First Officer, more generally known as the Model Man, received a rather remarkable communication. It was a letter from a black sportsman, who issued a challenge to our ship on behalf of a local club. This note reminded the Model Man of a most successful cricket match in the past, when an eleven from the shore was victorious; and it suggested that, during the present visit of our vessel, a return match might be played. We talked the matter over, and I said:

"Of course you will accept."

But our Purser, known to all men as the Treasure, answered:

"You see, there is always one great difficulty with black cricketers. They have a theory you cannot play the game properly in clothes, and they get themselves up for a match much the same as we should if we were going swimming."

I said: 'If they prefer to play undraped, I don't see that it much matters to us."

"Not personally, but a mixed audience cannot be expected to stand it," replied the Treasure. "Of course, to see an eleven taking the field in a state of nature makes dead against civilisation and human progress."

Finally, the Model Man wrote to say that it would give him great pleasure to bring a team to the ground upon the following morning if the local talent promised to wear clothes.

An hour later, a negro in a boat paddled out to us with an answer. He hailed us, and we asked him if his people would accept our terms.

"Yes, massa, we all put fings on."

"Right!" shouted back the Model Man. "We will be on the ground at ten o'clock."

The messenger rowed off, and a great discussion began as to the constitution of our team. Everybody wanted to go to the match, and sit in the shade and look on and criticise, but no one much cared about playing. The Captain of the *Rhine* absolutely refused, to begin with. He said:

"I would do anything for my officers—anything in reason; but cricket is out of the question. I shall, however, be on the ground with some ladies. A good appreciative audience is everything in these cases. Moreover, I will umpire if the tide turns against us."

The Treasure only consented to play after much pressure. He said:

"You know what the wicket is like; it's simply mountainous, and black men have no control over their bowling. For you medium-sized chaps it may be comparatively safe, but bowling at me is like bowling at a haystack—you cannot miss. When I go in, the blacks never bother about the stumps, but just let fly at random on the chance of winging me. Last match here, I hit their crack fast bowler all over the island, and he got mad at last, and gave up attempting to bowl me, but just tried to kill me."

"You scored off him, though," said our Fourth Officer, who remembered the incident.

"I did," admitted the Treasure. "I slapped one straight back, as hard as ever I could lay in to it, and he funked it, and tried to get out of the way and failed. I nearly knocked a limb off him, and then he abandoned the ball, and went and sulked and chattered to himself in the deep field."

Our Doctor said it would give him great pleasure to play, but he added that he should feel very averse from bowling against anybody with nothing on. Then the Model Man answered:

"You need not fear. The negroes are very particular about pads and such things. They don't wear shoes, for nothing could hurt their feet, but they never dream of batting without leg-guards, because a negro's shins are his weak spot. These fellows are not much good at cricket after you have once hit them hard. Either they get cross and throw up the whole thing, and leave the ground and go home to their families, or else they become frightened and servile. I have known them almost beg for mercy before each ball."

"You'll play, of course," said the Fourth Officer to me.

"Certainly, if you will," I answered. Then he replied:

"I shall undoubtedly play. I'm not a man who does much with the bat, but my bowling is rather out of the common. I have a natural leg-break which baffles fellows frightfully. Why, there was a question raised once about playing me for my county."

I did not ask him which county, because one should never goad a willing horse. The Fourth Officer had been in a thoroughly mendacious vein ever since we left St Kitts; the fault grew upon him, and now he began to utter transparent inaccuracies at all hours, from sheer love of them.

After much argument and conversation, our team was finally selected, the last man chosen being a black stoker of great size and strength.

"I regard him as a speculation," explained the Captain of our side; "either he will get out first ball or make a hundred. There are no half-measures with him."

As we approached the ground on the following morning, our Model Man confided to me a great source of anxiety. This was the fielding. He said:

"You see, men don't mind batting, but they get very unsportsman-like when it comes to going out into the field. Some actually hide, or

87

pretend they have engagements; others feign illness and retire; others, again, salve their miserable consciences by paying a negro a shilling to go and field for them. I only mention this. I know you're not the man to do such things; but, between ourselves, I fear the Doctor is just a sort of chap to escape fielding. There are others also I must keep an eye upon. Being captain of a scratch cricket team in the Tropics is no light task, I can tell you."

A considerable crowd had gathered to see the conflict. The negroes sat and lolled round the ground, while, behind them, buggies and horsemen were drawn up. Conspicuous in that gay throng appeared the Captain of the *Rhine*, seated on a brown horse, amid female equestrians. Beyond the audience rose a belt of tamarind and flamboyant trees, the latter with gigantic green and brown seed-pods hanging from their branches; and above these woods, sloping upwards to the blue sky, extended the hills, with winding roads visible here and there through the foliage that covered them, and with many a flagstaff and white cottage scattered upon their sides.

The ground itself suggested golf rather than cricket. Here and there a little dried-up grass occurred, but it collected in lonely tufts, between which extended great ravines and hillocks and boulders and patches of desolation. Upon a barren spot in the middle, the wickets had been pitched. When we arrived, they appeared to be an object of no little interest to sundry goats. These beasts, evidently regarding the stumps as some strange new form of vegetation sprung up in a single night from the arid soil, sauntered round them enquiringly, and a shabby he-goat, braver than his companions, nibbled the bails.

Our opponents had arrived. They constituted a motley, good-humoured gathering in all shades. One, John Smith, a genial hybrid, commanded them, and presently a great shout arose, when it transpired that he had secured choice of innings. The Doctor said, in a tone of reproof:

"Hang it, John, you've only won the toss. You couldn't make a bigger row if you'd won the match."

"Great fing to go in fus, sar," explained John; "we go in fus now, when we's fresh."

Then the Model Man led out his warriors.

I sauntered across the pitch with the Treasure and examined its peculiarities. We were discussing a curious geological formation, midway between the wickets, when our Fourth Officer approached in some glee at a great discovery. He had found a little hill, rather wide of the stumps, on one side, and he explained that whenever he dropped a ball on this elevation, he must bowl an Ethiop.

"You see, my natural leg-break will take the ball dead into the wicket every time," he said.

We hoped it might be so; and he begged us to keep the thing a profound secret, because, as he said, if it got about that we were going to utilise this hill to such an extent, the enemy would probably send out and have it removed, or alter the pitch.

After the goats were cleared away, and the juvenile spectators driven back a trifle, our Model Man arranged his field. More correctly speaking, the field arranged itself. Indeed, our team hardly proved as amenable as might have been wished. The Doctor insisted on taking long-leg and long-off.

"Why?" asked his Captain, looking rather distrustfully at a buggy with some red parasols in it, which would be extremely close to the Doctor at long-leg.

"It isn't that, old chap," replied our physician, cheerfully, following the Model Man's eye. "In fact, I'm not sure if I even know those girls. I only suggested a place in the long field because I'm a safe catch. That's important."

So he had his way.

Meantime, the Treasure found some other parasols—white ones—and placed himself within easy chatting distance. The Model Man said that he might just as well be on the ship as there. So he ordered his man up to take the wicket. The Treasure came reluctantly, and absolutely declined to keep wicket. He declared that it was simple murder to make a person of his size attempt such a thing on such a ground.

He led me aside privately, and said:

"Look here, you know that walking-stick of mine, manufactured from a shark's backbone—the one you are always worrying me to give you? Well, I will, when we go back to the ship, if you'll take the wicket. If you fall at your post, then your heirs shall have it."

I closed on this bargain promptly, and while I dressed up in all sorts of life-saving inventions used at cricket, the Treasure took an unobtrusive, circuitous route back to the white parasols.

John Smith himself and another negro, who was said to be related to him by marriage, came in first. They were padded up to the eyes, and evidently felt the importance of their position. Then a black umpire said: "Play, gem'men," and our Fourth Officer started with his world-famed, natural leg-break. He bowled three wides in succession as a preliminary. It is not easy to bowl wides underhand, but that Fourth Officer managed it; and I began to understand why, after all, his county had determined to struggle along without him.

"What's the matter, old man?" asked our Captain, who was fielding at short-slip.

"It's all right, old chap; you wait," answered the Fourth Officer, full of confidence.

"Yes, quite so, but they count one against us every time. I didn't know whether you knew it," explained the Model Man.

Meantime the bowler made further futile attempts to drop the ball upon the mound he had discovered. At last he actually did do so, but instead of breaking in and taking a wicket, as we, who were in the secret, hoped, the batsman got hold of it, and hit it high and hard to long-leg. All eyes turned to see if the Doctor's estimate of his own powers at a catch was justified. But he had disappeared entirely. He had not even left a substitute. Everybody shouted with dismay, and then the Doctor suddenly bounded on to the field. He distinctly came out of the buggy, from between the red parasols. If he had not actually known those girls, he must have introduced himself, or prevailed upon somebody else to do so. He tore into the scene of action, looking for the ball.

"It's in the air, you fool," yelled a dozen voices. Then it fell within a yard of the Doctor. A child could have caught it. We were all quite unsettled. The Model Man said:

"I'm not a bit surprised—it's just what I expected."

And the Fourth Officer said: "I don't really see what good it is my bowling for catches at long-leg if there's no long-leg."

And the Doctor said: "Wouldn't have done it for money. Hadn't the faintest idea you'd started. I saw you sending down balls all over the place, miles away from the wicket, and I thought you were merely practising." Which was rather an unpleasant thing for the Fourth Officer to hear.

Then the game steadied down and proceeded. Our Captain took the ball, after the underhand expert had got a few within sight of the wicket, and so finished his over. The Model Man was much more successful, for he clean-bowled a negro with this third delivery. It pitched in a sort of mountain-pass, about ten feet from the wicket; then it branched off to the right and hit a stone, and came back again, and finally took the off stump. I don't see how anybody alive could have played it. The batsman retired utterly bewildered, and the Model Man assured me he had never delivered a better ball.

A slogger came in next, and made runs rather rapidly, but nothing much happened until the Fourth Officer's third over. Then the bowler fell foul of me, and took exception to my method of keeping the wicket. He was being hit about pretty generally, and had become very hot, so, at another time, I should not have retorted upon him; but when he spoke I was hot too, and being hit about also, so I answered without deliberation. He said: "Can't you even try to stump them?"

And I replied: "I might, if my arms were ten feet long."

Then he said: "You've had dozens of chances. I always want a wicket-keeper for my bowling."

Whereupon I answered: "You want twenty—in a row. One's no good."

He said: "You don't like standing up to my fast ones, that's the truth."

And I responded: "Oh, bless you, I'd stand up to them all right, if I knew *where* to stand. A wicket-keeper's supposed to keep the wicket, not run all over the ground after wides."

During this unseemly argument, the Model Man, the Treasure, and the Doctor were all having an unpleasantness on their own account. The Doctor was imploring our Captain to take himself off and let somebody else bowl. He said: "Can't you see they've collared you? They've scored twenty runs. Don't think that *I* want to go on. Far from it. I'm only speaking for the good of the side."

But the Model Man refused to leave off bowling for anybody. He emphatically denied that they had collared him. Then he changed the subject, and turned upon the Treasure, and asked him where he supposed he was fielding.

The Treasure answered: "This is mid-on. I'm all right."

"You may think it's mid-on, but it isn't," shouted back the worried Model Man. "I've no doubt you're all right," he continued, bitterly, "but you're no sportsman."

After twenty more runs had been scored, the Fourth Officer unexpectedly and frankly admitted that he was not in form. He relinquished the ball, and said he had the makings of a sunstroke about his head, and went off to field among a few friends in a patch of shade under a tree, where all kinds of refreshments were being sold. Then our Captain held a consultation, and determined to try a complete change in the attack. He called upon the Doctor and the Treasure, and told them just to bowl quietly and carefully, and as straight as possible.

The Treasure started with yorkers; which was about the most effective thing he could have done, for, whenever he got one on the wicket, it bowled a black man. Two negroes, including the slogger, fell to him in his first over. Then the Doctor tried his hand, and began by being absurdly particular about the field. He put five men in the slips, and then started with terrifically fast full pitches to leg. A good player would have hit one and all of these right out of the island into the sea, but the people who were now at the wickets merely got out of the way, and let the Doctor's deliveries proceed to the boundary for three byes each.

Upon this he insulted me, as the Fourth Officer had done before him. He said: "Do stand up to them, old man."

I said: "Why should I? I'm out to enjoy myself. I'm a human being, not a target. Besides, long-stop will lose interest in the game if he has nothing to do."

"They don't have long-stops in first-class cricket," grumbled the Doctor. "You've got no proper pride."

Then I said: "Of course, if you are mistaking this display for first-class cricket, it's no good arguing with you."

In his second over the Doctor bowled a shade straighter, and began knocking the batsmen about, and hurting them and frightening them. If they had only kept in front of the wicket, and put their bats between their legs out of the way, they might have been safe enough, but they dashed nervously about and tried to escape; and the ball would shoot and hit their toes, or rise and threaten their heads, or break back into their stomachs. Then the bowler got a man "retired hurt," and a regular panic set in.

"I'm keeping down the run-getting, anyhow," said the elated Doctor.

"Yes, and you'll have to mend all these local celebrities for nothing after the match," replied our Treasure.

The latter had taken several more wickets, and now the score stood at sixty, with three further blacks to bat. About this time I made an appeal to the umpire upon a question of stumping a man, but he had his back turned and was buying a piece of sugar-cane. He apologised profusely. He said:

"I'se too sorry Massa, jus' too sorry, but I'se dam hungry, Sar."

Hungry! Whoever heard of an umpire being hungry? Thirsty they may be, and generally are, but hunger is a paltry plea to raise.

Soon afterwards, our black stoker made two brilliant catches, one after the other, the Treasure quickly bowled their last man, and the innings closed for seventy-three runs.

Then the rival teams scattered through St Thomas for luncheon, the spectators dispersed, and the goats had the cricket ground all to themselves until the afternoon.

Some lively betting took place during our meal. The Model Man was gloomy, and doubted the ability of his eleven to make the necessary score on such a wicket; but the Doctor appeared extremely sanguine, and the Fourth Officer actually guaranteed half the runs himself. He said:

"Though not a finished bat, yet it often happens that I come off with the willow when I fail with the leather."

It struck me that if his success with one was proportionate to his failure with the other, there seemed just reason for hoping he would get into three figures that afternoon.

Our Captain grew very anxious about the order of going in. Finally, he determined to start with the black stoker and myself. He said:

"You play steadily and cautiously and let him hit. If it chances to be his day, we may, after all, win with ten wickets in hand. Stranger things have happened at cricket.

"Not many," I replied; "but we will do our best."

Our best, unfortunately, did not amount to much. The match was resumed at half-past three, before an increased gathering of onlookers; and three distinct rounds of applause greeted the gigantic stoker and me as we marched to the wickets. It proved a fortunate thing that we got the applause then, because we might have missed it later. My own innings, for instance, did not afford the smallest loophole for enthusiasm at any time.

The black certainly began well. He hit the first ball he received clean out of the ground for six runs, but the second ball retaliated and smote him direfully somewhere in the small ribs. Thereupon, he fell down and rolled twenty yards to allay the agony, after which he rose up and withdrew, declaring that he had met his death, and that no power on earth would induce him to bat again. These negroes never forget an injury of this kind. If our black stoker lives over tomorrow, he will probably collect his colleagues from the ship, and row ashore by night and seek out the local bowler, and make it very unrestful and exciting for him.

The Model Man now came in, but he had the misfortune to lose my assistance almost immediately. I was caught at short leg after a patient innings of ten, slightly marred, however, by about the same number of chances. The Fourth Officer took my place. He began by nearly running out his Captain. If point had not stopped to dance and rub his leg, the wicket must have fallen. Then the new-comer settled down and played with great care, and irritated the bowlers extremely by giving them advice and criticising their efforts. Once they sent him so slow a ball that it never reached the wicket at all. Then our Fourth Officer rushed out and hit it after it had stopped, and so, rather ingeniously, scored two. It was a revolutionary sort of stroke, and the umpire said it must not be counted, but the batsman insisted upon having the runs put down. Of course, to argue with any umpire is madness. This black one simply waited for the next over, and then gave our Fourth Officer out "leg before." There was a great argument, but the umpire's ruling had to be upheld, and the batsman retired, declaring that he would never play cricket with savages again as long as he lived. He said:

"In the first place the ball was a wide, and in the second, after breaking a yard and a half, it hit my elbow. Then that black ass gives me out 'leg before.' It's sickening. Emancipation is the biggest error of the century. I'm going back to the ship."

But he did not. He found something under a yellow parasol that comforted him.

The Doctor came in next, and hit the first ball he received over the bowler's head for three. Encouraged by this success, he ran half across the ground to the next one, missed it, and would have been stumped under ordinary circumstances, but the ball, instead of going to the wicket-keeper, shunted off at a sort of junction, and proceeded to short-slip. He, desiring the honour of defeating the Doctor, would not give the ball up, and tried to put the wicket down himself. This the outraged custodian of the stumps refused to permit, and while they were wrangling about it, and the rest of the team were screaming directions, our batsman galloped safely back amidst loud applause.

We made fifty-eight for four wickets, the Model Man being the next to succumb. He had performed well, in something approaching style, for thirty runs. After him came the Treasure. He played forward very tamely at everything, until a ball suddenly got up and skinned two of his knuckles. The he grew excited, and began hitting very hard, and making runs at a tremendous pace.

Meanwhile the Doctor, finding his wicket still intact, suddenly became enthusiastic and took extraordinary interest in his innings. Between each ball he marched about the pitch and grubbed up tufts of grass and threw away stones, and patted the different elevations and acclivities with his bat. But he might just as well have patted the Alps, or any other mountain range. He hit a fast ball straight up into the air, when only five or six runs were wanted to win the match. It was one of those awkward, lofty hits that half the field can get to, if they only look alive. In this case, four negroes were all waiting to secure him, so the Doctor escaped again. Then, evidently under the impression that he bore a charmed life, he began taking great liberties, and pulling straight balls and strolling about out of his ground, and so forth. Finally, amid some intricate manœuvres, he jumped on to his own wicket, and retired well pleased with his performance. The Treasure went on hitting and being hit for a few minutes longer; then he made the winning stroke, and the contest came to a happy conclusion.

With one or two exceptions, everybody had much enjoyed the match; and that night, I recollect, we sat and smoked late on the deck of the *Rhine*, fought our battle once more, explained our theories of cricket to one another, and agreed that it was a great and grand amusement.

This next story brings us back to the more tranquil scenes of village cricket in England in the company of that master humorist and creator of Winnie the Pooh, A. A. Milne (1882–1956). Milne, who was educated at Westminster and Trinity College, Cambridge, was a better cricketer than he would admit, hiding his prowess behind the gentle banter which was such a feature of his character and his writing style. This style he first developed through the pages of the undergraduate magazine, Granta, *and then as a staff member of* Punch. *For both he wrote poems and essays about cricket, and not a few of these items were later collected in books such as* For The Luncheon Interval, Cricket & Other Verse *and* The Day's Play. *The story here, 'A Scratch Lot', written in 1910, bears all the hall-marks of personal experience – if not of author A. A. Milne himself, then probably of someone he knew well. Whichever is the case, there are elements that any amateur cricketer who has ever tried to field a team will recognise and doubtless chuckle over . . .*

A Scratch Lot

by A. A. Milne

I The Choosing of the Day

As soon as I had promised to take an eleven down to Chartleigh I knew that I was in for trouble; but I did not realise how great it would be until I consulted Henry Barton. Henry is a first-class cricketer, and it was my idea that he should do all the batting for us, and such of the bowling as the laws allowed. I had also another idea, and this I explained to Henry.

"As you are aware," I said, "the ideal side contains five good bats, four good bowlers, a wicket-keeper, and Henry Barton."

"Quite so," agreed Henry.

"That is the principle on which one selects an eleven. Now, I intend to strike out a line of my own. My team shall consist of three authors or journalists, two solicitors, four barristers, a couple from the Stock Exchange, some civil servants and an artist or two. How many is that?"

"Nineteen."

"Well, that's the idea, anyhow."

"It's a rotten idea."

99

"No, it's a splendid idea. I wonder nobody has thought of it before. I send a solicitor and a journalist in first. The journalist uses the long handle, while the solicitor plays for keeps."

"And where does the artist come in?"

"The artist comes in last, and plays for a draw. You are very slow to-day, Henry."

Henry, the man of leisure, thought a moment.

"Yes, that's all very well for you working men," he said at last, "but what do I go as? Or am I one of the barristers?"

"You go as 'with Barton.' Yes. If you're very good you shall have an 'H' in brackets after you. 'With Barton (H)' "

The method of choosing my team being settled, the next thing was the day. "Any day in the first week in July," the Chartleigh captain had said. Now at first sight there appear to be seven days in the week, but it is not really so. For instance, Saturday. Now there's a good day! What could one object to in a Saturday?

But do you imagine Henry Barton would let it pass?

"I don't think you'll get eleven people for the Saturday," he said. "People are always playing cricket on Saturday."

"Precisely," I said. "Healthy exercise for the London toiler. That's why I'm asking 'em."

"But I mean they'll have arranged to play already with their own teams. Or else they'll be going away for week-ends."

"One can spend a very pretty week-end at Chartleigh."

"H'm, let me think. Any day in the week, isn't it?"

"Except, apparently, Saturday," I said huffily.

"Let's see now, what days are there?"

I mentioned two or three of the better-known ones.

"Yes. Of course, some of those are impossible, though. We'd better go through the week and see which is best."

I don't know who Barton is that he should take it upon himself to make invidious distinctions between the days of the week.

"Very well, then," I said. "Sunday."

"Ass."

That seemed to settle Sunday, so we passed on to Monday.

"You won't get your stockbroker on Monday," said Henry. "It's Contanger day or something with them every Monday."

"Stocktaking, don't you mean?"

"I dare say. Anyhow, no one in the House can get away on a Monday."

"I must have my stockbrokers. Tuesday."

Tuesday, it seemed, was hopeless. I was a fool to have thought of Tuesday. Why, everybody knew that Tuesday was an impossible day for——

I forget what spoilt Tuesday's chance. I fancy it was a busy day for Civil Servants. No one in the Home Civil can get away on a Tuesday. I know that sounds absurd, but Henry was being absurd just then. Or was it barristers? Briefs get given out on a Tuesday, I was made to understand. That brought us to Wednesday. I hoped much from Wednesday.

"Yes," said Henry. "Wednesday might do. Of course most of the weeklies go to press on Wednesday. Rather an awkward day for journalists. What about Thursday?"

I began to get annoyed.

"Thursday my flannel trousers go to the press," I said—"that is to say, they come back from the wash then."

"Look here, why try to be funny?"

"Hang it, who started it? Talking about Contanger-days. Contanger—it sounds like a new kind of guano."

"Well, if you don't believe me——"

"Henry, I do. Thursday be it, then."

"Yes, I suppose that's all right," said Henry doubtfully.

"Why not? Don't say it's sending-in day with artists," I implored. "Not *every* Thursday?"

"No. Only there's Friday, and——"

"Friday is *my* busy day," I pleaded—"my one ewe lamb. Do not rob me of it."

"It's a very good day, Friday. I think you'd find that most people could get off then."

"But why throw over Thursday like this? A good, honest day, Henry. Many people get born on a Thursday, Henry. And it's a marrying day, Henry. A nice, clean, sober day, and you——"

"The fact is," said Henry, "I've suddenly remembered I'm engaged myself on Thursday."

This was too much.

"Henry," I said coldly, "you forget yourself—you forget yourself strangely, my lad. Just because I was weak enough to promise you an

'H' after your name. You seem to have forgotten that the 'H' was to be in brackets."

"Yes, but I'm afraid I really am engaged."

"Are you really? Look here—I'll leave out the 'with' and you shall be one of us. There! Baby, see the pretty gentlemen!"

Henry smiled and shook his head.

"Oh, well," I said, "we must have you. So if you say Friday, Friday it is. You're quite sure Friday is all right for solicitors? Very well, then."

So the day was settled for Friday. It was rather a pity, because, as I said, in the ordinary way Friday is the day I put aside for work.

II The Selection Committee

The committee consisted of Henry and myself. Originally it was myself alone, but as soon as I had selected Henry I proceeded to co-opt him, reserving to myself, however, the right of a casting vote in case of any difference of opinion. One arose, almost immediately, over Higgins. Henry said:

(*a*)   That Higgins had once made ninety-seven.
(*b*)   That he had been asked to play for his county.
(*c*)   That he was an artist, and we had arranged to have an artist in the team.

In reply I pointed out:

(*a*)   That ninety-seven was an extremely unlikely number for anyone to have made.
(*b*)   That if he had been asked he evidently hadn't accepted, which showed the sort of man he was: besides which, what was his county?
(*c*)   That, assuming for the moment he had made ninety-seven, was it likely he would consent to go in last and play for a draw, which was why we wanted the artist? And that, anyhow, he was a jolly bad artist.
(*d*)   That hadn't we better put it to the vote?

102

This was accordingly done, and an exciting division ended in a tie.

Those in favour of Higgins 1
Those against Higgins 1

The Speaker gave his casting vote against Higgins.

Prior to this, however, I had laid before the House the letter of invitation. It was as follows (and, I flatter myself, combined tact with a certain dignity):—

"Dear ———, I am taking a team into the country on Friday week to play against the village eleven. The ground and the lunch are good. Do you think you could manage to come down? I know you are very busy just now with

Contangers,
Briefs,
Clients,
Your Christmas Number,
Varnishing Day,
(*Strike out all but one of these*)

but a day in the country would do you good. I hear from all sides that you are in great form this season. I will give you all particulars about trains later on. Good-bye. Remember me to ———. How is ———? Ever yours.

"*P.S.*—Old Henry is playing for us. He has strained himself a little and probably won't bowl much, so I expect we shall all have a turn with the ball."

Or, "I don't think you have ever met Henry Barton, the cricketer. He is very keen on meeting you. Apparently he has seen you play somewhere. He will be turning out for us on Friday.

"*P.P.S.*—We might manage to have some bridge in the train."

"That," I said to Henry, "is what I call a clever letter."

"What makes you think that?"

"It is all clever," I said modestly. "But the cleverest part is a sentence at the end. 'I will give you all particulars about trains later on.' You see, I have been looking them up, and we leave Victoria at seven-thirty a.m. and get back to London Bridge at eleven-forty-five p.m."

The answers began to come in the next day. One of the first was from

103

Bolton, the solicitor, and it upset us altogether. For, after accepting the invitation, he went on: "I'm afraid I don't play bridge. As you may remember, I used to play chess at Cambridge, and I still keep it up."

"Chess," said Henry. "That's where White plays and mates in two moves. And there's a Black too. He does something."

"We shall have to get a Black. This is awful."

"Perhaps Bolton would like to do problems by himself all the time."

"That would be rather bad luck on him. No, look here. Here's Carey. Glad to come, but doesn't bridge. He's the man."

Accordingly we wired to Carey: "Do you play chess? Reply at once." He answered, "No. Why?"

"Carey will have to play that game with glass balls. Solitaire. Yes. We must remember to bring a board with us."

"But what about the chess gentleman?" asked Henry.

"I must go and find one. We've had one refusal."

There is an editor I know slightly, so I called upon him at his office. I found him writing verses.

"Be brief," he said, "I'm frightfully busy."

"I have just three questions to ask you," I replied.

"What rhymes with 'yorker'?"

"That wasn't one of them."

"Yorker—corker—por——"

"Better make it a full pitch," I suggested. "Step out and make it a full pitch. Then there are such lots of rhymes."

"Thanks, I will. Well?"

"One. Do you play bridge?"

"No."

"Two. Do you play chess?"

"I can."

"Three. Do you play cricket? Not that it matters."

"Yes, I do sometimes. Good-bye. Send me a proof, will you? By the way, what paper is this for?"

"*The Sportsman*, if you'll play. On Friday week. Do."

"Anything, if you'll go."

"May I have that in writing?"

He handed me a rejection form.

"There you are. And I'll do anything you like on Friday."

I went back to Henry and told him the good news.

"I wonder if he'll mind being black," said Henry. "That's the chap that always gets mated so quickly."

"I expect they'll arrange it among themselves. Anyhow, we've done our best for them."

"It's an awful business, getting up a team," said Henry thoughtfully. "Well, we shall have two decent sets of bridge, anyway. But you ought to have arranged for twelve aside, and then we could have left out the chess professors and had three sets."

"It's all the fault of the rules. Some day somebody will realise that four doesn't go into eleven, and then we shall have a new rule."

"No, I don't think so," said Henry. "I don't fancy 'Wanderer' would allow it."

III   In the Train

If there is one thing I cannot stand, it is ingratitude. Take the case of Carey. Carey, you may remember, professed himself unable to play either bridge or chess; and as we had a three-hour journey before us it did not look as though he were going to have much of a time. However, Henry and I, thinking entirely of Carey's personal comfort, went to the trouble of buying him a solitaire board, with glass balls complete. The balls were all in different colours.

I laid this before Carey as soon as we settled in the train.

"Whatever's that?"

"The new game," I said. "It's all the rage now, the man tells me. The Smart Set play it every Sunday. Young girls are inveigled into lonely country houses and robbed of incredible sums."

Carey laughed scornfully.

"So it is alleged," I added. "The inventor claims for it that in some respects it has advantages which even cricket cannot claim. As, for instance, it can be played in any weather: nay, even upon the sick bed."

"And how exactly is it played?"

"Thus. You take one away and all the rest jump over each other. At each jump you remove the jumpee, and the object is to clear the board. Hence the name—solitaire."

"I see. It seems a pretty rotten game."

That made me angry.

"All right. Then don't play. Have a game of marbles on the rack instead."

Meanwhile Henry was introducing Bolton and the editor to each other.

"Two such famous people," he began.

"Everyone," said Bolton, with a bow, "knows the editor of——"

"Oh yes, there's that. But I meant two such famous chess players. Bolton," he explained to the editor, "was twelfth man against Oxford some years ago. Something went wrong with his heart, or he'd have got in. On his day, and if the board was at all sticky, he used to turn a good deal from QB4."

"Do you really play?" asked Bolton eagerly. "I have a board here."

"Does he play! Do you mean to say you have never heard of the Trocadero Defence?"

"The Sicilian Defence——"

"The Trocadero Defence. It's where you palm the other man's queen when he's not looking. Most effective opening."

They both seemed keen on beginning, so Henry got out the cards for the rest of us.

I drew the younger journalist, against Henry and the senior stock-broker. Out of compliment to the journalist we arranged to play half-a-crown a hundred, that being about the price they pay him. I dealt, and a problem arose immediately. Here it is.

"A deals and leaves it to his partner B, who goes No Trumps. Y leads a small heart. B's hand consists of king and three small diamonds, king and one other heart, king and three small clubs and three small spades. A plays the king from Dummy, and Z puts on the ace. What should A do?"

Answer. Ring communication-cord and ask guard to remove B.

"Very well," I said to Dummy. "One thing's pretty clear. You don't bowl to-day. Long-leg both ends is about your mark. Somewhere where there's plenty of throwing to do."

Later on, when I was Dummy, I strolled over to the chess players.

"What's the ground like?" said the editor, as he finessed a knight.

"Sporting. Distinctly sporting."

"Long grass all round, I suppose?"

"Oh, lord, no. The cows eat up all that."

"Do you mean to say the cows are allowed on the pitch?"

"Well, they don't put it that way, quite. The pitch is allowed on the cows' pasture land."

"I suppose if we make a hundred we shall do well?" asked somebody.

"If we make fifty we shall declare," I said. "By Jove, Bolton, that's a pretty smart move."

I may not know all the technical terms, but I do understand the idea of chess. The editor was a pawn up and three to play, and had just advanced his queen against Bolton's king, putting on a lot of check side as it seemed to me. Of course, I expected Bolton would have to retire his king; but not he! He laid a stymie with his bishop, and it was the editor's queen that had to withdraw. Yet Bolton was only spare man at Cambridge!

"I am not at all sure," I said, "that chess is not a finer game even than solitaire."

"It's a finer game than cricket," said Bolton, putting his bishop back in the slips again.

"No," said the editor. "Cricket is the finest game in the world. For why? I will tell you."

"Thanks to the glorious uncertainty of our national pastime," began the journalist, from his next Monday's article.

"No, thanks to the fact that it is a game in which one can produce the maximum of effect with the minimum of skill. Take my own case. I am not a batsman, I shall never make ten runs in an innings, yet how few people realise that! I go in first wicket down, wearing my M.C.C. cap. Having taken guard with the help of a bail, I adopt Palairet's stance at the wicket. Then the bowler delivers: either to the off, to leg, or straight. If it is to the off, I shoulder my bat and sneer at it. If it is to leg, I swing at it. I have a beautiful swing, which is alone worth the money. Probably I miss, but the bowler fully understands that it is because I have not yet got the pace of the wicket. Sooner or later he sends down a straight one, whereupon I proceed to glide it to leg. You will see the stroke in Beldam's book. Of course, I miss the ball, and am given out l.b.w. Then the look of astonishment that passes over my face, the bewildered inquiry of the wicket-keeper, and finally the shrug of good-humoured resignation as I walk from the crease! Nine times out of ten square-leg asks the umpire what county I play for. That is cricket."

"Quite so," I said, when he had finished. "There's only one flaw in it. That is that quite possibly you may have to go in last to-day. You'll have to think of some other plan. Also on this wicket the ball always goes well over your head. You couldn't be l.b.w. if you tried."

"Oh, but I do try."

"Yes. Well, you'll find it difficult."

The editor sighed.

"Then I shall have to retire hurt," he said.

Bolton chuckled to himself.

"One never retires hurt at chess," he said, as he huffed the editor's king. "Though once," he added proudly, "I sprained my hand, and had to make all my moves with the left one. Check."

The editor yawned, and looked out of the window.

"Are we nearly there?" he asked.

IV   In the Field

It is, I consider, the duty of a captain to consult the wishes of his team now and then, particularly when he is in command of such a hetero-geneous collection of the professions as I was. I was watching a match at the Oval once, and at the end of an over Lees went up to Dalmeny, and had a few words with him. Probably, I thought, he is telling him a good story that he heard at lunch; or, maybe, he is asking for the latest gossip from the Lobby. My neighbour, however, held other views.

"There," he said, "there's ole Walter Lees asking to be took off."

"Surely not," I answered. "Dalmeny had a telegram just now, and Lees is asking if it's the three-thirty winner."

Lees then began to bowl again.

"There you are," I said triumphantly, but my neighbour wouldn't hear of it.

"Ole Lees asked to be took off, and ole Dalmeny" (I forget how he pronounced it, but I know it was one of the wrong ways)—"ole Dalmeny told him he'd have to stick on a bit."

Now that made a great impression on me, and I agreed with my friend that Dalmeny was in the wrong.

"When I am captaining a team," I said, "and one of the bowlers wants to come off, I am always ready to meet him half-way, more than half-way. Better than that, if I have resolved upon any course of action, I always let my team know beforehand; and I listen to their objections in a fair-minded spirit."

It was in accordance with this rule of mine that I said casually, as we were changing, "if we win the toss I shall put them in."

There was a chorus of protest.

"That's right, go it," I said. "Henry objects because, as a first-class cricketer, he is afraid of what *The Sportsman* will say if we lose. The editor naturally objects—it ruins his chance of being mistaken for a county player if he has to field first. Bolton objects because heavy exercise on a hot day spoils his lunch. Thompson objects because that's the way he earns his living at the Bar. His objection is merely technical, and is reserved as a point of law for the Court of Crown Cases Reserved. Markham is a socialist and objects to authority. Also he knows he's got to field long-leg both ends. Gerald——"

"But why?" said Henry.

"Because I want you all to see the wicket first. Then you can't say you weren't warned." Whereupon I went out and lost the toss.

As we walked into the field the editor told me a very funny story. I cannot repeat it here for various reasons. First, it has nothing to do with cricket; and, secondly, it is, I understand, coming out in his next number, and I should probably get into trouble. Also it is highly technical, and depends largely for its success upon adequate facial expression. But it amused me a good deal. Just as he got to the exciting part, Thompson came up.

"Do you mind if I go cover?" he asked.

"Do," I said abstractedly. "And what did the vicar say?"

The editor chuckled. "Well, you see, the vicar, knowing, of course, that——"

"Cover, I suppose," said Gerald, as he caught us up.

"What? Oh yes, please. The vicar did know, did he?"

"Oh, the vicar *knew*. That's really the whole point."

I shouted with laughter.

"Good, isn't it?" said the editor. "Well, then——"

"Have you got a cover?" came Markham's voice from behind us.

I turned round.

"Oh, Markham," I said, "I shall want you cover, if you don't mind. Sorry—I must tell these men where to go—well, then, you were saying——"

The editor continued the story. We were interrupted once or twice, but he finished it just as their first two men came out. I particularly liked that bit about the——

"Jove," I said suddenly, "we haven't got a wicket-keeper. That's always the way. Can you keep?" I asked the editor.

"Isn't there anyone else?"

"I'm afraid they're all fielding cover," I said, remembering suddenly. "But, look here, it's the chance of a lifetime for you. You can tell 'em all that——"

But he was trotting off to the pavilion.

"Can anybody lend me some gloves?" he asked. "They want me to keep wicket. Thing I've never done in my life. Of course I always field cover in the ordinary way. Thanks awfully. Sure you don't mind? Don't suppose I shall stop a ball though."

"Henry," I called, "you're starting that end. Arrange the field, will you? I'll go cover. You're sure to want one."

Their first batsman was an old weather-beaten villager called George. We knew his name was George because the second ball struck him in the stomach and his partner said, "Stay there, George," which seemed to be George's idea too. We learnt at lunch that once, in the eighties or so, he had gone in first with Lord Hawke (which put him on a level with that player), and that he had taken first ball (which put him just above the Yorkshireman).

There the story ended, so far as George was concerned; and indeed it was enough. Why seek to inquire if George took any other balls besides the first?

In our match, however, he took the second in the place that I mentioned, the third on the back of the neck, the fourth on the elbow, and the fifth in the original place; while the sixth, being off the wicket, was left there. Nearly every batsman had some pet stroke, and we soon saw that George's stroke was the leg-bye. His bat was the second line of defence, and was kept well in the block. If the ball escaped the earth-work in front, there was always a chance that it would be brought up by the bat. Once, indeed, a splendid ball of Henry's which came with his arm and missed George's legs, snicked the bat, and went straight into the wicket-keeper's hands. The editor, however, presented his compliments, and regretted that he was unable to accept the enclosed, which he accordingly returned with many thanks.

There was an unwritten law that George could not be l.b.w. I cannot say how it arose—possibly from a natural coyness on George's part about the exact significance of the "l." Henry, after appealing for the best part of three overs, gave it up, and bowled what he called "googlies" at him. This looked more hopeful, because a googly seems in no way to be restricted as to the number of its bounces, and at each bounce it had a chance of doing something. Unfortunately it never did George. Lunch came and the score was thirty-seven—George having compiled in two hours a masterly nineteen; eighteen off the person, but none the less directly due to him.

"We must think of a plan of campaign at lunch," said Henry. "It's hopeless to go on like this."

"Does George drink?" I asked anxiously. It seemed the only chance.

But George didn't. And the score was thirty-seven for five, which is a good score for the wicket.

V   At the Wickets

At lunch I said: "I have just had a wire from the Surrey committee to say that I may put myself on to bowl."

"That is good hearing," said Henry.

"Did they hear?" asked Gerald anxiously, looking over at the Chartleigh team.

"You may think you're very funny, but I'll bet you a—a—anything you like that I get George out."

"All right," said Gerald. "I'll play you for second wicket down, the loser to go in last."

"Done," I said, "and what about passing the salad now?"

After lunch the editor took me on one side and said: "I don't like it. I don't like it at all."

"Then why did you have so much?" I asked.

"I mean the wicket. It's dangerous. I am not thinking of myself so much as of——"

"As of the reading public?"

"Quite so."

"You think you—you would be missed in Fleet Street—just at first?"

"You are not putting the facts too strongly. I was about to suggest that I should be a 'did not bat.' "

111

"Oh! I see. Perhaps I ought to tell you that I was talking just now to the sister of their captain."

The editor looked interested.

"About the pad of the gardener?" he said.

"About you. She said—I give you her own words—'Who is the tall, handsome man keeping wicket in a M.C.C. cap?' So I said you were a well-known county player, as she would see when you went in to bat."

The editor shook my hand impressively.

"Thank you very much," he said. "I shall not fail her. What county did you say?"

"Part of Flint. You know the little bit that's got into the wrong county by mistake? That part. She had never heard of it; but I assured her it had a little bit of yellow all to itself on the map. Have you a pretty good eleven?"

The editor swore twice—once for me and once for Flint. Then we went out into the field.

My first ball did for George. I followed the tactics of William the First at the Battle of Hastings, 1066. You remember how he ordered his archers to shoot into the air, and how one arrow fell and pierced the eye of Harold, whereupon confusion and disaster arose. So with George. I hurled one perpendicularly into the sky, and it dropped (after a long time) straight upon the batsman. George followed it with a slightly contemptuous eye . . . all the way. . . .

All the way. Of course, I was sorry. We were all much distressed. They told us afterwards he had never been hit in the eye before. . . . One gets new experiences.

George retired hurt. Not so much hurt as piqued, I fancy. He told the umpire it wasn't bowling. Possibly. Neither was it batting. It was just superior tactics.

The innings soon closed, and we had sixty-one to win, and, what seemed more likely, fifty-nine and various other numbers to lose. Sixty-one is a very unlucky number with me—oddly enough I have never yet made sixty-one; like W. G. Grace, who had never made ninety-three. My average this season is five, which is a respectable number. As Bolton pointed out—if we each got five to-day, and there were six extras, we should win. I suppose if one plays chess a good deal one thinks of these things.

Harold, I mean Geroge, refused to field, so I nobly put myself in last and substituted for him. This was owing to an argument as to the exact wording of my bet with Gerald.

"You said you'd get him out," said Gerald.

"I mean 'out of the way,' 'out of the field,' 'out of——"

"I meant 'out' according to the laws of cricket. There are nine ways. Which was yours, I should like to know?"

"Obstructing the ball."

"There you are."

I shifted my ground.

"I didn't say I'd get him out," I explained. "I said I'd get him. Those were my very words. 'I will get George.' Can you deny that I got him?"

"Even if you said that, which you didn't, the common construction that one puts upon the phrase is——"

"If you are going to use long words like that," I said, "I must refer you to my solicitor Bolton."

Whereupon Bolton took counsel's opinion, and reported that he could not advise me to proceed in the matter. So Gerald took second wicket, and I fielded.

However, one advantage of fielding was that I saw the editor's innings from start to finish at the closest quarters. He came in at the end of the first over, and took guard for "left hand round the wicket."

"Would you give it me?" he said to Bolton. "These country umpires. . . . Thanks. And what's that over the wicket? Thanks."

He marked two places with the bail.

"How about having it from here?" I suggested at mid-on. "It's quite a good place and we're in a straight line with the church."

The editor returned the bail, and held up his bat again.

"That 'one-leg' all right? Thanks."

He was proceeding to look round the field when a gentle voice from behind him said: "If you wouldn't mind moving a bit, sir, I could bowl."

"Oh, is it over?" said the editor airily, trying to hid his confusion. "I beg your pardon, I beg your pardon."

Still he had certainly impressed the sister of their captain, and it was dreadful to think of the disillusionment that might follow at any moment. However, as it happened, he had yet another trick up his sleeve. Bolton hit a ball to cover, and the editor in the words of the local paper, "most sportingly sacrificed his wicket when he saw that his partner had not time to get back. It was a question, however, whether there was ever a run possible."

Which shows that the reporter did not know of the existence of their captain's sister.

When I came in, the score was fifty-one for nine, and Henry was still in. I had only one ball to play, so I feel that I should describe it in full. I have four good scoring strokes—the cut, the drive, the hook and the glance. As the bowler ran up to the crease I decided to cut the ball to the ropes. Directly, however, it left his hand, I saw that it was a ball to hook, and accordingly I changed my attitude to the one usually adopted for that stroke. But the ball came up farther than I expected, so at the last moment I drove it hard past the bowler. That at least was the idea. Actually, it turned out to be a beautiful glance shot to the leg boundary. Seldom, if ever, has Beldam had such an opportunity for four action photographs on one plate.

Henry took a sixer next ball, and so we won. And the rest of the story of my team, is it not written in the journals of *The Sportsman* and *The Chartleigh Watchman*, and in the hearts of all who were privileged to compose it? But how the editor took two jokes I told him in the train, and put them in his paper (as his own), and how Carey challenged the engine-driver to an eighteen-hole solitaire match, and how . . . these things indeed shall never be divulged.

When assembling this book I was very conscious of an earlier anthology, The Light Side of Cricket, *a collection of 'Stories, Sketches and Verse' assembled by a cricket-loving solicitor named E. B. V. Christian and issued by a long-defunct publisher named James Bowden in 1898. Indeed, I have a copy of the book with its decorated cover showing two young boys playing cricket under the amused eyes of their watching parents, on the shelf beside me as I write. Although much of the humour is now dated, it is still a model of its kind. Edmund Brown Viney Christian (1864–1938) had been an almost county standard cricketer in his youth, but chose the law as his profession. He was rarely to be found in his chambers in Holborn, however, when a major game was being played in London, and liked to write about the game from an amusing legal viewpoint. His essays such as 'Cricket in the Law Courts', 'Serious Charge Against a Well-known Cricketer' and 'The Great LBW Lawsuit' still make delightful reading today, as does his now hard-to-find book,* At the Sign of the Wicket *(1894). There is also something of the judicial about Mr Christian's short story, 'The Umpire's Remorse' and for that reason – if for no other beyond its wry humour – it seems a most suitable selection for these pages.*

The Umpire's Remorse

by E. B. V. Christian

I found Parker behind the refreshment-tent, grovelling upon the ground in agony.

This was at eleven o'clock on the morning of our match against Shalford. It is always the duffer's thankless task to see that the arrangements for a match are complete, the crease properly marked, the tents securely pegged, the bails not forgotten. So it happened that I was alone on the Heath an hour before stumps were to be pitched, and I alone was witness of Parker's distress. Even the refreshments had not arrived, or I might have jumped to erroneous conclusions.

"What's the matter, Parker?" I asked; "a touch of colic——"

"No, no, don't ask me!" cried Parker. "I am a miserable man! I am a miserable man!"

"Whereabouts?" I said, sympathetically. "Shall I hail the doctor for you?"

Parker rose, or rather adopted a sitting posture, and threw his cloth cap on to a furze bush; he looked at me, ran his fingers through his hair, and exhibited every sign of mental disturbance.

"It's no bodily trouble that ails me," he said, "it's my conscience that hurts. Oh, I am a sinner, a miserable sinner!"

"We are all sinners, Parker," I said, "especially umpires; but I don't recollect that we have ever had more than usual cause of complaint against you. What is it that is on your mind?"

"I will tell you, sir," he said, standing up; "it will ease my mind, mayhap, to tell you. I was to umpire for you to-day, but I couldn't ever put that white coat on again"—and he pointed to his garb of office, lying where he had hurled it in his despair—"till I had made confession. You have always thought me a fair man, a man who wouldn't favour his own side more than was decent, haven't you, sir? Well, sir, it's that that troubles me most. Here have I been going about, as I might say, wearing the white coat of an unpartial umpire, and all the while I have been gaining my own ends, giving decisions to suit my own purpose, giving gentlemen out, maybe, or not out, just as it seemed to suit my hand, if I may use such an expression. And it has all come home to me now, sir! I feel the burden on my own back now."

He turned away, groaning, and went through the process by which bus drivers endeavour to restore the circulation to their hands in cold weather. "Oh," he said, "I am a sinful man, a sinful man."

I suppose none of us ordinary mortals can express unusual emotion naturally. "All but very great actors," as George Henry Lewes said, "are redundant in gesticulation." Parker, no doubt, thought he was beating his breast with the most repentant sinner on the whole penitent form, but to me he seemed to be merely 'beating the booby." But he was so clearly in earnest that I could not laugh in his face.

"This is a serious matter, Parker," I said, to restrain my tendency to laugh; "would you like to see a clergyman? Mr Jones is coming up to play for us." (It is strange how we fly to the despised professions in any difficulty. I had already suggested medical help, and now spiritual consolation seemed necessary.) But Parker preferred to make me his confessor; he thought he would be able to speak more freely to me. I believe Parker fancied that the curate might have something to say on the irregularity of his church attendance. So I assured Parker he could rely on my giving careful consideration to all he said, and urged him to speak frankly.

"Well, sir," he said, "there was one case you may remember, about two years ago. It was at Dorking. I wanted to get home to Chilworth by the 7.3, and Mr Robinson was making a lot of runs. I knowed once he was out nobody would stay long, and I could get away in good time for the train. So I give him out caught at the wicket. I don't say I didn't hear a snick or something. But I shouldn't have given him out for that early in the day. But I did then, and caught the train easily. I remember that when I was in the carriage I chuckled to myself at my cleverness in getting the game over before seven, and saving myself a long walk. But I am sorry for it now deeply sorry."

"Did you ever treat any one else like that?"

"Oh, yes, many a one! I can say this for myself, sir, I never made no distinctions, unless, of course, it might be the captain or secretary of a side. Do you remember Mr Harvey who used to play for Albury?"

"Yes, Parker, very well; he used to play when I was a youngster. What of him?"

"Well, sir,—would you believe it?—three times in a fortnight I had to get him out. Once he was keeping me out on the wet ground that was giving me rheumatics to a certainty, and the other times he kept making runs when I was very tired and hungry and wanted to get home. But he was quite huffy about it, the third time; leg-before it was then. I didn't often give a gentleman out that way, however much I wanted to go. It was more often a catch. Quite huffy he was."

"I don't wonder, Parker."

"Nor I, sir. I see the error of my ways now. Ho, I am a miserable man!"

"Did you bet on the matches you umpired in, Parker?"

"No, sir; anyhow, not as a rule. At least, I don't think that affected my decisions. Of course, I didn't care to lose half a crown to some men, and then——. But no, I think I can say No. But for catches and stumpings and run-outs, whenever it was a near thing, if I wanted to go, why, the batsman had to go first."

So Parker continued the tale of his wrongdoing. The conversation struck me as humorous. To see an umpire so moved was strange; the umpire is generally the only man on the field who seems to have no emotion. And, when one thinks of it, any conversation with an umpire is unusual. One's remarks to him are commonly short, and either an interrogation or an objurgation. When Parker paused in his direful catalogue I asked what had brought him to a repentant mood.

"Well, sir," he said, "I am giving up this sort of thing, and I should like to leave off with a clean sheet, so to speak. I have taken a nice little business in the ham and beef line over at Guildford, but I couldn't go into business with my conscience so heavy. The scales wouldn't hang true, sir, and I should spoil the beef in the boiling and cut the ham thick. I know I should. I want to get clear of old associations——" and so forth. I tried to reassure Parker, and told him he was exaggerating his offences. Old Mr Harvey had suffered most: perhaps if Parker wrote to Mr Harvey confessing his offence, it might relieve his mind, and Harvey would be pleased. Such a letter might soothe his declining years. "But, Parker," I asked, as a painful recollection of last season recurred to my mind, "surely you haven't treated *me* like this?"

Parker, to his lasting disgrace, admitted that he had. "Do you remember being run out at Peaslake last year, sir? Well, sir, you were no more out than—than anything! Half a yard past your crease, you were. And when old Clarke stumped you at Abinger your right toe didn't move. And at Chilworth, caught at slip you were, but the ball touched the ground first, and at—"

"Parker!" I shouted, "this is abominable, this is wicked," and I expressed my indignation forcibly for some time. It really *was* too bad, for my stay at the wicket was rarely long enough to call for any extra-ordinary method of abbreviating it. And the undeserved tips I had given the man, and the cigars! For the first time I felt really angry at the miscreant's confessions.

When we were calmer, the umpire said, "what can I do, sir? Can't anything be done to ease my mind? Can't I put it right anyhow?"

"Parker," I said, with decision, "there is only one thing to be done. *You must make restitution.* Mr Jones would tell you that repentance is useless without restitution. You have been giving batsmen out all this time without cause; now you must lean a little in their favour. Give them more than the usual benefit of the doubt. Remember how often you have wronged them, and on this, your last opportunity, try to make it up to us, a little."

Parker promised, and no more was said. How well the fool kept his promise I shall never forget, nor will any single member of our eleven. The Shalford men won the toss, went in, and stayed there. There was no way of getting them out. The most palpable catches were useless, they stuck their legs in front of straight balls, they ran a yard out of their ground and walked back after the wicket-keeper had put the bails off. It made no difference. To every appeal Parker answered "Not out." The only way of getting rid of the batsmen was by clean bowling them, and even that was no use sometimes. The captain's leg stump was sent out of the ground before he had scored a dozen. Parker appeared distressed, hesitated, said slowly "No ball," and then the idiot looked round to me for approbation! He made restitution with a vengeance that day, and at our cost.

So I paid dearly for usurping clerical functions. I shall never do it again. Or, at least, I shall refuse in future to offer advice to penitent umpires until I know who has won the toss.

During the First World War, there must have been many an officer and private far away from England who dreamed of home and cricket matches on sunlit summer days. Certainly, there is the expression of such yearnings to be found in a number of novels and poems from the period, but nowhere else is it expressed with quite such wistfulness and good humour than in this next story written in 1916 by Stacy Aumonier (1887–1928). Aumonier had himself been a useful cricketer during his education at Cranleigh, but it was a career as a landscape painter which he first chose, and indeed a number of his paintings were exhibited at the Royal Academy. In 1908, however, he abandoned his art to become a society entertainer, giving recitals of his own original sketches as well as performing at the Comedy and Criterion theatres in London. His natural talent for humour also inspired him to produce essays and stories for the leading magazines of the day, and for some years he was regarded as one of the funniest writers of his generation. Aumonier never lost his enthusiasm for cricket, however, and later bought a house in St John's Wood almost next door to Lord's, and it was said of him that 'if he was not to be found entertaining on the stage he would certainly be watching cricket at Lord's!'

The Match

by Stacy Aumonier

It is all so incredibly long ago that you must not ask me to remember the scores. In fact, even of the result I am a little dubious. I only know that it was just on such a day as this that we were all mooning around Bunty Cartwright's garden after breakfast, smoking, and watching the great bumble-bees hanging heavily on the flowers. Along the flagged pathway to the house were standard rose-trees, the blossoms and perfume of which excited one pleasantly. It was jolly to be in flannels and to feel the sun on one's skin, for the day promised to be hot.

For years it had been a tradition for dear old Bunty to ask us all down for the week. There were usually eight or nine of us, and we made up our team with the doctor and his son and one or two other odds and ends of chaps in the neighbourhood. I know that on this day he had secured the services of Dawkin, a very fast bowler from a town near by, for Celminster, the team we were to play, were reputed to be a very hot lot.

As we stood there laughing and talking. Bunty and Tony Peebles were sitting within the stone porch, I remember, trying to finish a game of chess started the previous evening; there was the crunch of wheels on the road, and the brake arrived, accompanied by the doctor's son, a thin slip of a boy on a bicycle.

Then there was the usual bustle of putting up cricket-bags and going back for things one had forgotten, and the inevitable "chipping" of "Togs," a boy whose real name I have forgotten, but who was always last in everything, even in the order of going in. It must have been fully half an hour before we made a start, and then the doctor hadn't arrived. However, he came up at the last minute, his jolly red face beaming and perspiring. Some of the chaps cycled, and soon left us behind, but I think we were seven on the brake. It was good to be high up and to feel the wind blowing gently on our faces from the sea. We passed villages of amazing beauty nestling in the hollows of the downs, and rumbled on our way to the accompaniment of lowing sheep and the doctor's rich, burring voice talking of cricket, and the song of the lark overhead that sang in praise of this day of festival.

It was good to laugh and talk and watch the white road stretching far ahead, then dipping behind a stretch of woodland. It was good to feel the thrill of excited anticipation as we approached the outskirts of Celminster. What sort of ground would it be? What were their bowlers like? Who would come off for us?

It was good to see the grinning, friendly faces of the villagers and then to descend from the brake, to nod to our opponents in that curiously self-conscious way we have as a race, and then eagerly to survey the field. And is there in the whole of England a more beautiful place than the Celminster cricket ground?

On one side is a clump of buildings dominated by the straggling yards and outhouses belonging to the "Bull" inn. On the farther side is a fence, and just beyond a stream bordered by young willows. At right angles to the inn is a thick cluster of elms—a small wood, in fact—while on the fourth side a low, grey stone wall separates the field from the road. Across the road may be seen the spire of a church, the fabric hidden by the trees, and away beyond sweeping contours of the downs.

In the corner of the field is a rough pavilion faced with half-timber, and a white flagstaff with the colours of the Celminster Cricket Club fluttering at its summit.

Members of the Celminster Club were practising in little knots about the field, and a crowd of small boys were sitting on a long wooden bench, shouting indescribably, and some were playing mock games with sticks and rubber balls. A few aged inhabitants looked at us with lazy interest and touched their hats.

A little man with a square chin and an auburn moustache came out and grinned at us and asked for Mr. Cartwright. We discovered that he was the local wheelwright and the Celminster captain. He showed us our room in the pavilion and called Bunty "sir." Of course, Bunty lost the toss. He always did during that week, and this led to considerably more "chipping," and we turned out to field.

No one who has never experienced it can ever appreciate the tense joy of a cricketer when he comes out to begin a match. The gaiety of the morning, when the light is at its best and all one's senses are alert; the sense of being among splendid deeds that are yet unborn; and then the jolly red ball! How we love to clutch it with a sort of romantic exultation and toss it to one another! For it is upon *it* that the story of the day will turn. It is the scarlet symbol of our well-ordered adventure, as yet untouched and virginal, and yet strangely pregnant of unaccomplished actions. What story will it have to tell when the day is done? Who will drop catches with it? Who destroy its virgin loveliness with a fearful drive against the stone wall?

As I have stated, it happened all so long ago that I cannot clearly remember many of the details of that match, but curiously enough I remember the first over that Dawkin sent down very vividly.

A very tall man came in to bat. The first ball he played straight back to the bowler; the second was a "yorker" and just missed his wicket; the third he drove hard to mid-off and Bunty stopped it; the fourth he stopped with his pads; the fifth he played back to the bowler again; and the sixth knocked his leg stump clean out of the ground.

One wicket for no runs! We flung the scarlet symbol backward and forward in a great state of excitement, with visions of a freak match, the whole side of our opponents being out for ten runs, and so on. I remember the glum face of their umpire, a genial corn merchant, dressed in a white coat and a bowler hat, with a bewildering number of sweaters tied round his neck, glancing apprehensively at the pavilion. I remember that the next man in was the little wheelwright, and he looked very solemn and tense. The first three balls missed his wicket by inches, then he stopped them. My recollection of the rest of that morning was a vision of the little wheelwright, with his chin thrust forward, frowning at the bowlers. He had a peculiarly uncomfortable stance at the wicket, but he played very straight. He kept Dawkin out for about five overs, then he started pulling him round to leg. The wicket was rather fiery, and Dawkin was very fast. The wheelwright was hit three times on the thigh, twice on the chest, and numberless times on the arms, and one ball got up and glanced off his scalp, but he did not waver. He plodded on, lying in wait for the short ball to hook to leg. I do not remember how many he made, but it was a great innings. He took the heart out of Dawkin, and encouraged one or two of the others to hit with courage. He was caught at last by a brilliant catch by Arthur Booth running in from long leg.

One advantage of a village team like Celminster is that they have no "tail," or, rather, that you never know what the tail will do. You know by the costume that they have a tail, for the first four or five batsmen appear in complete outfits of white flannels and sweaters, and then the costumes start varying in a wonderful degree. Number six appears in a black waistcoat with white flannel trousers, number seven with brown pads and black boots, number eight with a blue shirt and brown trousers, and so on to the last man, who is dressed uncommonly like a verger. But this rallentando of sartorial equipment does not in any way represent the run-getting ability of the team, for suddenly some gentleman inappropriately garbed, who gives the impression of never having had a bat in his hand before, will lash out and score twenty-five runs off one over.

On this particular occasion I remember one man who came in about ninth, and who wore one brown pad and sand-shoes, and had on a blue shirt with a dicky and a collar, but no tie, and who stood right in front of his wicket, looked grimly at Dawkin, and then hit him for two sixes, a four, and a five, to the roaring accompaniment of "Good old Jar-r-ge!" from a row of small boys near the pavilion. The fifth ball hit his pad and he was given out l.b.w. He gave no expression of surprise, disappointment or disgust, but just walked grimly back to the pavilion. Celminster were all out before lunch, but I cannot let the last man—the verger— retire (he was bowled first ball off his foot) before speaking of our wicket-keeper, Jimmy Guilsworth.

Jimmy Guilsworth was, in my opinion, an idea wicket-keeper. He was a little chap and wore glasses, but his figure was solid and homely. He was by profession something of a poet, and wrote lyrics in the celtic-twilight manner. He played cricket rarely, but when he did, he was instinctively made wicket-keeper. He had that curious, sympathetic mothering quality which every good wicket-keeper should have. The first business of a wicket-keeper is to make the opposing batsman feel at home. When the man comes in trembling and nervous, the wicket-keeper should make some reassuring remark, something that at once establishes a bond of understanding between honourable opponents. When the batsman is struck on the elbow it is the wicket-keeper who should rush up and administer first-aid or spiritual comfort. And when the batsman is bowled or caught, he should say: "Hard luck, sir!"

At the same time it his business to mother the bowlers on his own side. He must be continually encouraging them and sympathizing with them, but in a subdued voice, so that the batsman does not hear. And, moreover, he must be prepared to act as chief of staff to the captain. He must advise him on the change of bowlers and on the disposition of the field. All of this requires great tact, understanding and perspicacity.

All these qualities Jimmy Guilsworth had in a marked degree. If he sometimes dropped catches and never stood near enough to stump anyone, what was that to the sympathetic way he said "Oh, hard luck, sir!" to an opposing batsman when he was bowled by a long hop, or the convincing way he would call out, "Oh, well hit, sir!" when another opponent pulled a half-volley for four. What could have been more encouraging than the way he would rest his hand on young Booth's shoulder after he had bowled a disappointing over, and say: "I say, old chap, you're in great form. Could you pitch 'em up just a wee bit?" When things were going badly for the side, Jimmy would grin and whisper into Cartwright's ear. Then there would be a consultation and a change of bowlers, or some one would come closer up to third-man, and, lo! in no time something would happen.

But it is lunch-time. In the pavilion a long table is set, with a clean cloth and napkins and with gay bowls of salad. On a side-table is a wonderful array of cold joints, hams, cold lamb, and pies. We sit down, talking of the game, curiously enough, we do not mix with our opponents. We sit at one end, and they occupy the other, but we grin at one another, and the men sitting at the point of contact of the two parties occasionally proffer a remark.

Girls wait on us, and a fat man in shirt-sleeves, who produces ale and ginger-beer from some mysterious corner. And what a lunch it is! Does ever veal-and-ham pie taste so good as it does in the pavilion after the morning chasing a ball? And then tarts and fruit and custard and a large yellow cheese, how splendid it all seems, with the buzz of conversation and the bright sun through the open door! Does anything lend a fuller flavour to the inevitable pipe than such a lunch, mellowed by the rough flavour of a pint of shandy-gaff?

We stroll out again into the sun and puff tranquilly, and some of us gather round old Bob Parsons, the corn merchant, and listen to his panegyric of cricket as played "in the old days." He's seen a lot of cricket in his time, old Bob. His bony, weather-beaten face wrinkles, and his clear, ingenuous eyes blink at the heavens as he recalls famous men: "Johnny Strutt, he was a good 'un. Aye, and ye should ha' seen old Tom Kennett bowl in his time. Nine wicket' he took against Kailhurst, hittin' the wood every toime. Fast he were, faster'n they bowl now. Fower bahls he bahl fast, then put up a slow."

He shakes his head meditatively, as though the contemplation of the diabolical cunning of bowling a slow ball after four fast ones was almost too much to believe as though it was a demonstration of intellectual callisthenics that this generation could not appreciate.

It is now the turn of the opponents to take the field, while we eagerly scan the score-sheet to see the order of going in, and restlessly move about the pavilion, trying on pads, and making efforts not to appear nervous.

And with what a tense emotion we watch our first two men open the innings! It is with a gasp of relief we see Jimmy Guilsworth cut a fast ball for two, and know, at any rate, we have made a more fortunate start than our opponents did.

I do not remember how many runs we made that afternoon, though as we were out about tea time, I believe we just passed the Celminster total, but I remember that to our joy Bunty Cartwright came off. He had been unlucky all the week, but this was his joy-day. He seemed cheerful and confident when he went in, and he was let off on the boundary off the first ball! After that he did not make a mistake.

It was a joy to watch Bunty bat. He was tall and graceful, and he sprang to meet the ball like a wave scudding against a rock. He seemed to epitomize the dancing sunlight, a thing of joy expressing the fullness of the crowded hour. His hair blew over his face, and one could catch the gleam of satisfaction that radiated from him as he panted on his bat after running out a five.

He was not a great cricketer, none of us were, but he had a good eye, the heart of a lion, and he loved the game.

I believe I made eight or nine. I know I made a cut for four. The recollection of it is very keen to this day, and the satisfying joy of seeing the ball scudding along the ground a yard out of the reach of point. It made me very happy. And then one of those balls came along that one knows nothing about. How remarkable it is that a bowler who appears so harmless from the pavilion seems terrifying and demoniacal when he comes tearing down the crease towards you!

Yes, I'm sure we passed the Celminster total now, for I remember at tea time discussing the possibilities of winning by a single innings if we got Celminster out for forty.

After tea, for some reason or other, one smokes cigarettes. We strolled into a yard at the back of the "Bull" inn, and there was a wicket gate leading to a lawn where some wonderful old men, whose language was almost incomprehensible, were drinking ale and playing bowls. At the side were some tall sunflowers growing amid piles of manure.

Some one in the pavilion rang a bell, and we languidly returned to take the field once more.

I remember that it was late in the afternoon that a strange thing happened to me. I was fielding out in the long field not thirty yards from the stream. Tony Peebles was bowling from the end where I was fielding. I noted his ambling run up to the wicket and the graceful action of his arm as he swung the ball across. A little incident happened, a thing trivial at the time, but which one afterwards remembers. The batsman hit a ball rather low on the off side, which the doctor's son caught or stopped on the ground. There was an appeal for a catch, given in the batsman's favour, but for some reason or other he thought the umpire had said "out," and he started walking to the pavilion. He was at least two yards out of his crease when the doctor's son threw the ball to Jimmy Guilsworth at the wicket. Jimmy had the wicket at his mercy, but instead of putting it down he threw it back to the bowler. It was perhaps a trivial thing, but it epitomized the game we played. One does not take advantage of a mistake. It isn't done.

The sun was already beginning to flood the valley with the excess of amber light which usually betokens his parting embrace. The stretch of level grass became alive and vibrant, tremblingly golden against the long, crisp shadows cast from the elms. The elms themselves nodded

131

contentedly, and down by the stream flickered little white patches of children's frocks. Everything suddenly seemed to become more vivid and transcendent. As if aware of the splendour of that moment, all the little things struggled to express themselves more actively. The birds and little insects in solemn unison praised God, or, rather, to my mind, at that moment they praised England, the land that gave them such a glorious setting. The white-clad figures on the sunlit field, the smoke from the old buildings by the inn trailing lazily skyward, the comfortable buzz of the voices of some villagers lying on their stomachs on the grass. Ah! My dear land!

I don't know how it was, but at that moment I felt a curious contraction of the heart, like one who looks into the face of a lover who is going on a journey. Perhaps a townsman gets a little tired at the end of a day in the field, or the feeling may have been due to the Cassandra-like dirge of a flock of rooks that swung across the sky and settled in the elms.

The bat, cut from a willow down by the stream, the stumps, the leather ball, the symbol of the wicket, the level lawn, cut and rolled and true—all these things were redolent of the land we moved on. They spoke of the love of trees and wind and sun and the equipoise of man in Nature's setting. They symbolized our race, slow-moving and serene, with a certain sensuous joy in movement, a love of straightness, and an indestructible faith in custom. Ah, that the beauty of that hour should fade, that the splendour and serenity of it all should pass away! Strange waves of misgiving flooded me.

If it should be all *too* slow-moving, *too* serene! If at that moment the wheels of the Juggernaut of evolution were already on their way to crush the splendour of it beneath their weight!

Ah! my dear land, if you should be in danger! If one day another match should come in which you would measure yourself against— some unknown terrors! I was aware at that moment of a poignant sense of prayer that when your trial should come it would find you worthy of the clean sanity of that sunlit field; and if in the end you should go down, as everything in nature *does* go down before the scythe of Time, the rooks up there in the elm should cry aloud your epitaph. They are very old and wise, these rooks: they watched the last of the Ptolemys pass from Egypt, they moaned above Carthage and Troy, and warned the Roman prætors of the coming of Attila. And the epitaph they shall make for you—for *they* saw the little incident of Jimmy Guilsworth and the doctor's son—shall be: "Whatever you may say of these people, they played the game."

I think those small boys down by the pavilion made too much fuss about the catch I muffed. Of course, I did get both hands to it, and as a matter of fact the sun was *not* in my eyes; but I think I started a bit late, and it seemed to be screwing horribly. Ironical jeers are not comforting. Bunty, like the dear good sportsman he is, merely called out:

"Dreaming there?"

But it was a wretched moment. I remember slinking across at the over, feeling like an animal that has contracted a disease and is ashamed to be seen, and my mental condition was by no means improved by the cheap sarcasms of young Booth or Eric Ganton. We did not get Celminster out for the second time, and the certainty that the result would not be affected by the second innings led to introduction of strange and unlikely bowlers being put on and given their chance.

I remember that just at the end of the day even young "Togs" was tried. He sent down three most extraordinary balls that went nowhere within reach of the batsman, the fourth was a full pitch, and a young rustic giant who was then batting, promptly hit it right over the pavilion. The next ball was very short and came on the leg side. I was fielding at short leg and I saw the batsman hunching his shoulders for a fearful swipe. I felt in a horrible funk. I heard the loud crack of the ball on the willow, and I was aware of it coming straight at my head. I fell back in an ineffectual sort of manner, and despairingly threw up my hands in a sort of self defence. And then an amazing thing happened: the ball went bang into my left hand and stopped there. I slipped and fell, but somehow I managed to hang on to the ball. I remember hearing a loud shout, and suddenly the pain of impact vanished in the realization that I had brought off a hot catch.

It was a golden moment. The match was over. I remember all our chaps shouting and laughing, and young "Togs" rushing up and throwing his arms round me in a mock embrace. We ambled back to the pavilion and it suddenly struck me how good looking most of our men were, even Tony Peebles, whom I had always looked upon as the plainest of the plain. My heart warmed towards Bunty with a passionate zeal when he struck me on the back and said: "Good man! You've more than retrieved your muff in the long field."

I know they ragged me frightfully in the pavilion when we were changing, but it was no effort to take it good-humouredly. I felt ridiculously proud.

We took a long time getting away, there was so much rubbing down and talking to be done, and then there was the difficulty of getting Len Booth out of the "Bull" inn. He had a romantic passion for drinking ale with yokels, and a boy had stuck a pin into one of Ganton's tyres, and he had to find a bicycle shop and get it mended. It was getting dark when we all got established once more in the brake.

I remember vividly turning the corner in the High Street and looking back on the solemn profile of the inn. The sky was almost colourless, just a glow of warmth, and already in some of the windows lamps were appearing. We huddled together contentedly in the brake, and I saw the firm lines of Bunty's face as he leaned over a match lighting his pipe.

The grass is long to-day in the field where we played Celminster, and down by the stream are two square, unattractive buildings, covered with zinc roofing, where is heard the dull roar of machinery. The ravages of time cannot eradicate from my memory the vision of Bunty's face leaning over his pipe, or the pleasant buzz of the village voices as we clattered among them in the High Street, or the sight of the old corn merchant's face as he came up and spoke to Bunty (Bunty had stopped the brake to get more tobacco) and touched his hat and said:

"Good noight, sir. Good luck to 'ee!"

Decades have passed, and I have to press the spring of my memory to bring these things back; but when they come they are very dear to me.

I know that in the wind that blows above Gallipoli you will find the whispers of the great faith that Bunty died for. Eric Ganton, young Booth, and Jimmy Guilsworth, where are they? In vain the soil of Flanders strives to clog the free spirit of my friends.

"Good noight, sir. Good luck to 'ee!"

Again I see the old man's face as I gaze across the field where the long grass grows, and I see the red ball tossed hither and thither, with its story still unfinished, and I hear the sound of Jimmy's voice:

"Oh, well hit, sir!" as he encourages an opponent.

The times have changed since then, but you cannot destroy these things. Manners have changed, customs have changed, even the faces of men have changed; and yet this calendar on my knee is trying to tell me that it all happened *two years ago to-day!*

And overhead the garrulous rooks seem strangely flustered.

Cricket, the theatre and my next contributor are also inseparable – for didn't Ben Travers (1886–1980) write some of the most uproarious farces ever seen on the London stage as well as describing his life-long fascination with the game in one of the funniest of all cricketing memoirs, 94 Declared, *published shortly after his death? And if the book itself with its delightful catalogue of incidents and characters both on and off the field isn't remarkable enough, then the fact he wrote and typed the entire script single-handed at the age of 94 surely is! He was educated at the Abbey School, Beckenham and Charterhouse, and not only delighted in playing cricket, but reading about it, too. "From my early boyhood I have read books on cricket and have revelled in them," he once wrote. "Volumes and volumes of elderly* Wisdens *bear still my fingerprints in chocolate upon their pages. There were also anthologies on cricket, novels on cricket, even tracts on cricket – I well remember how I used to read all the descriptive passages of* Baxter's Second Innings *and to skip the religious application!" Despite his jovial nature, Ben Travers was a brave man and served with distinction in the RAF in both World Wars, winning an Air Force Cross in the first, and rising to the rank of Squadron Leader in the second. His work for the theatre as well as his hugely successful novels such as* Rookery Nook *(1923) earned him widespread praise, yet he particularly cherished his membership of the MCC and in* Who's Who *described his hobby as "watching cricket". He well deserved the CBE he was awarded in 1976. From all his study and reading about cricket, Ben Travers concluded what he called "the one genuine and original reason for cricket" which he explained in an essay in 1950. "There are many people," he said, "who, if you told them the real reason for cricket, would look at you with horror, almost as though you had said something profane. But the fact remains that the only real reason for cricket is FUN." And in the story which follows, written in 1923, and published with sketches by H. M. Bateman which are also reproduced, he demonstrates this belief to comic perfection . . .*

135

A Buffer's Wicket

by Ben Travers

There are people who like to watch children at play and there are people who like to play with children and there are people (not the nicest sort) who wish children at the devil. Likewise there are children who hate being watched when they are playing, who hate still more being played with, and who would rather (these have had bitter experiences) that grown-ups minded their own business and kept themselves to themselves.

Major Wodell, C.B., was of the variety that likes to play with children, and it never entered his head that the children with whom he disported himself might possibly enjoy themselves still more if he left them alone.

Major Wodell was a buffer. So he frequently described himself. A good-natured, easy-going, hearty sort of buffer. Rubicund, grizzled of moustache, convex at the zone, full of friendly breeziness—a harmless old buffer.

And he had a genuine taste for young people. The younger they were, the better they pleased him. It was a weakness of his to stop perambulators and make inexpert inquiries of the attendant nursemaids. When a little girl in the park asked him if please he would tell her the time he became so delightfully facetious, watch in hand, that the child usually gazed at him with open-eyed solemnity and returned somewhat hurriedly to her guardian.

One May morning, accompanying a small niece in Kensington Gardens, he bowled a wooden hoop, unaided, for a hundred yards along the Broad Walk; bragged of it afterwards to his friends, without ever realising how absurd he must have appeared. He was that sort of man. It did not occur to him that his niece might prefer to bowl the hoop herself; that his antics were offensive in her eyes.

I have said enough, I think, to indicate that to Major Wodell the spectacle of a number of small boys playing cricket on Shrubwood Common would be particularly attractive. He had strolled out this summer Saturday afternoon when he might have been more profitably dozing in his host's garden, and he came upon Billy Chaffinch, Teddie and Ernie Spattow, Artie Lettuce, and a few more of the younger generation of Shrubwood athletes, playing cricket. Major Wodell fixed his monocle and beamed. The odour of the gorse pleased him and the song of the larks and the shrill voice of the peacock in his host's garden, but none of these things pleased him so much as the sight of Billy and his friends playing cricket.

The sight was the more pleasant because the Major himself had been a bit of cricketer in his time. No event had caused him such poignant distress as the reluctant but final abandonment, ten years before, of the scarlet, orange and violet blazer of the Leather-hunters. This he had put aside after the last of the buttons had flown off and hit the umpire in the eye, as he was endeavouring to pull to the leg boundary an innocent-looking left-handed slow which seemed to turn a somersault under his bat before leaping, with a laugh, at the wicket. Of course he ought not to have been wearing his blazer, but the Leather-hunters invariably flaunted their colours when batting, on the theory that they might distract the bowlers.

Though he played no longer, the Major still followed the game; dozed happily at Lords, and felt capable of making a century yet, given the right sort of wicket and "on his day." As he beamed at Billy and his friends, it seemed to him that here possibly was the right sort of wicket, and that this perhaps might be his day. That is how he really felt, but if you had challenged him, he would not have admitted it. What he believed himself to feel was the innocent desire to add to the pleasure of these youngsters. Billy and his friends were obviously happy. It was the Major's privilege to make them yet happier.

Scarcely aware that he was moving, Major Wodell gradually approached the pitch. When he was about six yards away a furious dispute broke out. Long Willie was declared Out, to a catch. Billy said decisively that he was Out. Long Willie, with equal decision, insisted that Fatty Spottle had fallen on the ball in the furze bush and had risen with it in his hands in order to deceive. Billy Chaffinch advanced up the pitch to wrest the bat from Long Willie by main force.

"Take your blinkin' bat," said Long Willie. "I'm sick of it."

Long Willie edged towards Fatty Spottle with a heart full of bitterness and revenge.

"What you boys want is an umpire," said Major Wodell.

Billy looked at him amiably, politely trying to conceal the absence of enthusiasm. He handed the bat to Ernie Spattow, picked up the ball, and spat in his palms.

"What you boys want is an umpire," said Major Wodell.

139

"I'll take a turn for you," said Major Wodell, and gave Ernie "centre."

Off the very first ball Ernie was caught. A storm of voices ascended. Ernie was in the minority, but he clung to the bat and stuck his chin out.

"Garn! Never touched it!" he shouted. Billy advanced along the pitch towards him; calm, deliberate, full of purpose.

"Out! said the Major.

"Take your blinkin' bat," said Ernie and threw the offensive weapon on the ground.

Circumstances favoured Billy's bowling, and two more wickets fell during the next four balls.

"I rather think that must be Over," said the Major.

"None of the others can't bowl—not for nuts," Billy objected.

"Umpire's decision is final," replied the Major, smiling.

"Gimme the bat, young Sid," cried Billy, suddenly submitting to judgment. "You 'ave a bowl."

The umpire no-balled young Sid twice running, and then gave Billy Out for obstructing the wicket. There was a death-like silence. Billy flushed, keeping his eyes on the bat. The other boys looked from Billy to the Major, from the Major to Billy, and hoped for the worst. They were surprised and disappointed, for Billy walked up to the Major and offered him the bat.

"You take a knock, sir," he said quietly.

"Well now, that's very sporting of you," said the Major. "Mind you I haven't handled a bat for a considerable time. Not since our celebrated match with the Shulamites. You never heard of that match, I dare say. No, of course not. You weren't born." The Major sighed. He patted the bat on the turf and found it a trifle small. Then he looked smilingly about him.

"Sure you don't mind a buffer like me butting in?"

He posed himself at the wicket.

Billy placed his field with elaborate care. He spat on his hands with vigour. He began to bowl viciously at the Major's legs. The third ball hit the Major severely on the shin.

"Ow's that?" Billy shouted.

"Nonsense, boy. Nonsense," said the Major. He spoke crossly, for the blow had been painful. "Still it's not for the batsman to arbitrate," he continued more calmly, as the pain diminished. "We must have another umpire."

It happened that at this moment Mr. Festlock, gardener at the house where the Major was staying, happened to be crossing the common from the "Cat and Fiddle." The Major called to him. This was a disastrous thing to do, for Festlock had a "down" on the village boys. Against most of them he could produce nothing stronger than suspicion; but Billy and the elder Spattow he had actually caught astride the orchard wall, their pockets full of apples which he would have been willing—aye, anxious—to identify in a court of law if the squire could have been persuaded to prosecute.

Knowing his employer's weakness of character, Festlock on that occasion had taken the law into his own hands, and there had been a feud between him and the boys ever since. He scowled on them now, touched his hat to the Major, and took up his stand at the wicket. That he knew next to nothing about the game he did not disclose.

Each time that Billy ran up to the wicket to bowl he had to listen to a growling admonition from the umpire.

"Good fer nothing' young varmint!" said the umpire.

"Come ter the gallus yet, see if yer don't," he said.

"Wait till I catch yer among my fruit again, that's all."

Three times Billy managed to hit the Major on the leg, and three times he shouted " 'Ow's that?"

"Not out!" growled the umpire, enjoying himself.

Then Billy tucked up his sleeves still higher, gritted his teeth, and determined to hit the Major's middle stump. The Major began to swipe, and to almost every swipe the umpire awarded a boundary. The umpire, moreover, constituted himself the keeper of the score, and was soon able to inform the Major that he was nearing his half-century.

Left to himself, his better self, the Major might have had the decency to retire, but the umpire's encouraging cries stirred his blood—the blood of an old Leather-hunter. He passed the fifty, for the first time in his career. The vision of a century flashed before his eyes. Evidently it was the right wicket. Likewise it was his day. He had "got his eye in." The gorse-tufted expanse of Shrubwood Common vanished. It seemed to him that he stood in the middle of the arena at Lord's, that applauding thousands were behind him on the Mound Stand and that more discriminating, but not less appreciative, spectators were watching his strokes through field-glasses from the aristocratic white seats before the pavilion.

Making one of his rare runs between the wickets . . . brought his score to
ninety-seven

"Eighty-five!" shouted the umpire. Then, in an aside to the
perspiring Billy, "Call yerself a bowler? Good fer nothin' yew ain't,
'cept stealin' apples. An' not much good fer that neither."

But Billy kept pegging away. Thanks to the peculiar uniformity of
the batsman's strokes, always in the nature of a pull to leg, Billy did not
suffer so severely as he might have done from the attenuation of the
field. For the field had strangely thinned since the arrival of Festlock.
One by one the boys had crept away; had slunk behind furze, or gorse,
and vanished. There remained only Artie Lettuce, admirably energetic
at long leg, hurling the ball back to Billy like an automaton and
projecting murderous, but ineffective, glares at the back of the Major's
head and into the small of his back.

The clock of the village church chimed five as the Major, making one
of his rare runs between the wickets, with the breathing noise of a
walrus, brought his score to ninety-seven. The next ball he hit to what
the umpire declared to be the boundary. A century! Festlock applauded
vigorously.

"Thank you, Festlock," said the Major, wiping his forehead. "Quite
irregular, of course. Umpire should be unbiassed, un—er—
unemotional. Still it is an occasion. I am bound to admit that this is
something of an occasion."

The next ball scattered the Major's wickets.

"Not out!" cried the umpire.

"'E sent you a no-ball," the umpire explained.

Billy picked up a stump. Nobody knows what he proposed to do with it. He did not know himself. It is true that Festlock had removed his hat, thereby bringing his aggravating bald head, damp and steaming, temptingly into range. It is true that Billy had been known to hit a rabbit at twelve yards by flinging a stump at it, and the Major was less than twelve feet away. But at the very moment that Billy picked up a stump a child's voice was heard at the edge of the common.

"Bill-ee! Bill-ee!" cried the voice. "Come to tee-ee! Muvver ses she'll warm yer if yer don't come ter tee-ee."

"Well, it's been a good game," said the Major returning the bat to Billy. He glanced round the common. "God bless my soul! Where have all the boys gone?"

"Sneaked away an hour ago," the umpire volunteered.

The Major asked Billy why he had remained firm at his post when the rest of the team had deserted.

The next ball scattered the Major's wickets.

143

"Them's my stumps an' bat," Billy answered modestly.

"An' it's my ball," added Artie Lettuce. The Major did not appear to be listening.

"Well, you cut along and get your tea," he said. "We'll look after your traps. Call at the Lodge for them. And here's——" The Major slipped a coin into Billy's palm. "Share it with the rest of the eleven; that is"—he poked Artie Lettuce in the midst with the bat—"with this young Strudwick here."

"Muvver ses she'll warm yer," the shrill call continued.

"Comin'!" bellowed Billy.

"You take the ball for a bit, Festlock," said the Major.

Lovers of humorous writing will also need little introduction to Harry Graham (1874–1936) creator of those immortal Ruthless Rhymes *and of Reginal Drake Biffin, a gentleman reknowned to know 'something about everything and everything about something'. Less well-known, though, was Graham's passion for cricket: his ever-present attendance at test matches and occasional appearances for a village team in Surrey, the identity of which he carefully concealed, though there are tantalising hints to be found in his hilarious essay, 'Village Cricket' written in 1919. There is evidently something of Graham in Reginald Drake Biffin, though I doubt that he would have claimed for himself what he does for Biffin. 'Of all matters connected with sport,' he wrote introducing a selection of the stories, 'Biffin proved himself over and over again to be an authority whose opinions were unquestioned, whose experience was unrivalled; and it is no exaggeration to say that he himself could not be described more truthfully than in the three words, "the complete sportsman".' My favourite Biffin story is the one which follows, set against the background of a test match against Australia. Have those who gather for such games ever been described with such penetrating wit and humour as in the pages which follow?*

Biffin on Acquaintances

by Harry Graham

We were sitting in the pavilion at Lord's cricket ground, Reginald Biffin and I, eagerly watching a Test Match, in company with a host of other middle-aged enthusiasts. It was a typical English summer's day. A cold north wind swept across the ground, blowing up our legs and down our necks, making the draughty wooden benches seem better ventilated than ever. But though we might perhaps have been pardoned for feeling a trifle chilled and miserable, the excitement of the occasion kept us warm, and we huddled happily together, determined to miss no single incident of a momentous match upon the issue of which so much of our national honour depended.

The game that had just begun promised to be of a more than usually thrilling character. The two Australian batsmen who had opened the innings were playing with the confidence and caution that one has learnt to expect from first-class cricketers. In an hour and twenty-seven minutes one of them had succeeded in making eighteen runs, and although his partner had not yet scored, it was evident to such experts as Biffin and myself that within the next half-hour or so he would be tempted to open his shoulders and punish the bowling severely by snicking a ball past silly-point for at least one run.

147

In the pavilion the excitement was intense. Many of the older members, unable to stand the strain, had hurried away to the ground-floor bar, leaving umbrellas and match-cards on their seats to reserve their places and act as dumb witnesses of their passionate interest in the game. On a single row of benches I counted no less than fourteen of these tokens, and the distant clink of glass upon glass showed that their owners had not forsaken them, however temporarily, without a cause.

Biffin was as usual deriving a considerable amount of innocent pleasure from pointing out to me many of the celebrities by whom we were surrounded whom I already knew quite well by sight. There in a far corner, with his back to us, was a deservedly popular figure, which, if only it could have been induced to turn round, we felt sure we should recognize as that of a well-known playwright and novelist. Next to him sat a man, who but for his clerical collar and episcopal gaiters, presented all the appearance of a famous pugilist. His eyes were half-closed, and his mouth half-open, and it was fairly evident that the worthy prelate was engaged in praying against rain.

All round us sat the great men of the day (or of past days)—politicians, soldiers, civil servants, statesmen—an ex-Prime Minister refilling his pipe, an ex-Lord Chancellor returning flushed from the tea-room, a well-known Sea Lord talking to a better-known Landlord, a distinguished Law Lord talking to himself: all the lovers of sport who have helped to make England what she is to-day but upon whom so brave a responsibility seemed at the moment to lie but lightly. Here and there among them, too, crouched the lesser fry, men like Reginald and myself, clergymen, schoolmasters, writers, rugged men with rugged faces (and occasionally rather rugged trousers), the best product of our public-school system, all united in the one desire to see the best side win, but fervently hoping that it would not do so unless it happened to be our own.

"You've heard of Sir George Tuff," said Biffin suddenly, rather unnecessarily rousing me from a few moments' well-earned slumber.

"No," I said, "never."

"Well, that's him over there." He pointed to a large man in a grey billycock hat, who was sitting in a centre seat behind the bowler's arm, secretly grappling with the crossword in a morning paper. "A great leader of men," he explained, "and a great follower of women."

"Oh, really," I said. "How extremely interesting."

I turned over on the other side and settled down again, but Reginald was feeling remorselessly conversational.

"You know Colonel Barbecue?" he asked a moment later.

"No," I said, "I'm afraid I don't. Who is he?"

"I don't know," said Biffin, "but that's him over there, scratching himself with a match-card."

"Indeed?"

I could not help wishing I had brought my opera-glasses so that I could have examined the irritable colonel more closely.

The conversation flagged for a few moments.

"Did you ever meet old Lord Gorbals?" I asked at length, for it was clearly my turn to speak and I was determined not to be put to shame by my friend's superior knowledge of the world.

"No," said Biffin. "Did you?"

"No," I said, "but I thought that old gentleman by the flagstaff might be he."

"Why did you think it might be him?" he asked.

"I didn't. I thought it might be he."

"Do you know him by sight?" said Reginald.

"No."

"Then why——"

"I don't know."

"By the way," I added, "how's the Duke?"

"Which Duke?" said Biffin, bridling modestly.

"Any Duke."

"Oh."

Another brief silence ensued, broken at last by Biffin leaning across and whispering something unintelligible in my ear.

"What's that?" I asked.

"Sh-sh!" he answered in a low voice. "Don't look round!"

"Why not?"

"There's a fellow sitting just behind us," he replied, "who was at school with me."

"Good Lord!" I said. "I quite understand."

One of the great disadvantages of attending a popular cricket match at Lord's is that one is in constant danger of meeting old acquaintances whom one had believed—nay, even hoped—to be long since dead. It is almost impossible to walk round the ground without being greeted as a long-lost brother by boyhood's friends, whose names one had mercifully forgotten, whom one had justifiably counted upon never setting eyes on again. Oddly enough, too, one's contemporaries have all become excessively old, if not actually in their dotage, and I know few things more disturbing than to find that the majority of men who were at school with one are suffering from senile decay. At Lord's this is a constant and bitter experience which it is very difficult to avoid. Biffin, however, has his own method of dealing with it.

As he and I were strolling across to examine the pitch, during one of those numerous intervals which help to make cricket so thrilling a game, we were suddenly accosted by a very old gentleman with a long grey beard and an Inverness cape, who looked as though the moth had been at him for some time.

"Well! Well! Well!" he exclaimed with every symptom of genuine delight as soon as he caught sight of my companion, "If it isn't Reginald Biffin!"

The remark itself was a singularly inane one, for of course if it wasn't Biffin it must have been somebody else, which it could not possibly be. In such circumstances, however, it seems to be a very favourite cliché.

"You don't remember me, eh?" the dotard continued, wagging his beard in a painfully roguish fashion.

"I'm afraid not," said Biffin rather coldly.

"We used to go caterpillar-hunting together at St. Domino's," the stranger explained, while a moth which at that moment flew out of his beard seemed to bear silent witness to the truth of his assertion.

"I was never at St. Domino's," said Biffin cruelly, "and I particularly dislike caterpillars." He brushed away the moth as he spoke, for it was obviously making advances to his hat.

"But——"

"My name is not Biffin," said Reginald. "I am Colonel Montmorency of the King's Own Loyal Buffs. Good afternoon!" With that, raising his hat (in which the moth had by this time succeeded in laying several eggs), he moved away, leaving the old gentleman a prey to the utmost perplexity and embarrassment.

"Aren't you being rather unkind, Reginald?" I said, as soon as we were out of earshot. (I belong to a society for the prevention of cruelty to beavers, and would willingly have subscribed to buy the old man a packet of moth-balls.)

"Nonsense," said Biffin. "Nonsense! Come away quickly!" he added, seizing me by the arm, for at that moment a tall familiar figure could be seen bearing rapidly down upon us, and we had both recognized another companion of our youth from whom it was essential to escape.

Sir Pugsley Grout—for it was no less distinguished a man than he—is perhaps the most popular as well as one of the most eminent of our modern English surgeons. In the days when operations for appendicitis were still fashionable there were but few members of the British aristocracy who had not allowed Sir Pugsley to relieve them of some if not all of those superfluous internal organs with which Nature had so unnecessarily provided them. Many of the wealthiest residents of Mayfair still carry about with them mementos of his skill in the shape of various surgical appliances which in the hurry of the moment he so often leaves behind him. No wonder, then, that if Sir Pugsley is deservedly popular in Society he should be even better beloved by the medical fraternity, for whom his continual discovery of new and possibly fatal diseases supplies scope for much interesting experimental work of an amusing and lucrative character.

Only last year, you may remember, he wrote to the public press, prognosticating the imminent arrival, long overdue, of a particularly virulent epidemic of Russian influenza which was to decimate society. When this prophecy was not actually fulfilled—the public mind having unfortunately been temporarily diverted to the more absorbing subject of our lapse from the Gold Standard—when, as I say, the ravages of the fell disease did not at all come up to expectations, he was clever enough to invent a hitherto unknown nervous disorder which he named "Sciuridosis" and attributed to an obscure infection spread among the community by squirrels. The commonest symptoms included matudinal lassitude, a sense of fullness after meals and a general disinclination to work, and the ailment was chiefly confined to the wealthier classes.

You will recall the panic that ensued among all parents whose offspring possessed tame squirrels; how a special Squirrel Week was instituted to deal with these otherwise charming little creatures, and how the Board of Trade finally forbade the importation of foreign squirrels and suggested elaborate means of exterminating what had hitherto been regarded as a fairly harmless type of vermin.

In Sussex alone, in less than a month, three hundred red squirrels were shot or wounded by zealous hygienists; the head master of Eton was forced to flog three members of Third Form for attempting to conceal squirrels in their ottomans, and the head master of Harrow issued an edict to the effect that any boy in Lower Shell found in possession of a squirrel, would be deprived of his straw hat and compelled to attend three military parades a week. Meanwhile Lord Porpentine wrote to *The Times* to boast that on his Berkshire estates not a single squirrel survived, and in the fur market the price of skunk fell to a ridiculously low figure.

It must be six months at least since Sir Pugsley has been able to infect the public mind with any fresh ailment of a serious nature, but his labours are unceasing and, given the wholehearted co-operation of his colleagues and a sufficiently hard winter, they will doubtless bear fruit before the year is out.

Sir Pugsley—Grout *minor* as we then knew him—had been at a private school with Biffin and myself. His intense love of Nature which there expressed itself in the habit of blowing addled birds' eggs and eviscerating the semi-decomposed carcasses of deceased mice in the dormitory, had caused him to be regarded with mixed feelings by his less scientifically-minded fellows. As far as I was concerned a long period of absence had in no way lessened my distaste for his society, and Reginald obviously shared my views.

"Come away quick!" he said, as the great surgeon hove in sight.

Alas! he had not spoken soon enough. As we looked round for a loophole of escape the chances of eluding our ancient playmate seemed excessively remote. All around us surged a crowd of bustling spectators obeying the summons of the first warning bell and hurrying back to the stands. They compassed us about on every side: they compassed us about, I say, on every side, while one obvious line of retreat was cut off by half a dozen brawny groundsmen who advanced towards us dragging the immense roller with which they had just been levelling the pitch. The situation was indeed a delicate and difficult one, but Biffin is a man of infinite resource and rose gallantly to the occasion.

Sir Pugsley Grout bore ruthlessly down upon us, as I have explained—and that "bore" is the *mot juste* (as M. Hugo would say) all his friends will readily admit. Scarcely, however, had he time to extend a welcoming hand and exclaim: "Well, well, well, if it isn't—"before Reginald had seized his fingers with a grip of iron and proceeded to push him gently but implacably backwards into the track of the oncoming roller. At the same time he accidentally allowed the handle of his umbrella to become entangled round the surgeon's left ankle.

As the result of this brilliant manœuvre Sir Pugsley was forced to step backwards and, in so doing, lost his balance, slipped up and fell heavily upon the turf at our feet. The efforts of six agonized groundsmen were alas! insufficient to bring the roller to a standstill before it had passed over his prostrate form. Amid the scenes of confusion that followed, while First Aid was being administered and ambulances summoned, Reginald and I managed to slink nonchalantly back to our seats in the pavilion, where we were soon engrossed once more in the details of the day's play.

Owing to recent heavy rains and the consequent softness of the ground, Sir Pugsley's accident inflicted a considerable amount of damage upon the outfield. He himself, on the other hand, was not nearly so seriously hurt as might have been expected. Unfortunately, however, he had been carrying in his tailcoat pocket a spare pair of forceps with which he proposed that very evening to extract the tonsils of a lady of title, and with the impact of the heavy roller these instruments became somewhat deeply embedded in his spine. He was consequently fated to experience much of the discomfort from which patients of his had often suffered, and spent nearly two months in a fashionable nursing-home which had just been opened in one of London's noisiest thoroughfares. Here, for the sum of twenty-five guineas a week, he was privileged to occupy a small attic bedroom on the sixth floor, and to enjoy a bill of fare consisting chiefly of underdone plaice and tepid tapioca pudding.

No account of the accident ever appeared in the press, though one of our more sensational Sunday papers published a paragraph cautiously headed:"Alleged Attempted Suicide of Alleged West End Club Man." Sinister rumours, however, were spread in certain Australian circles hinting that an attempt had been made to ruin the pitch and thus deprive the Commonwealth of a hard-won victory. The head groundsman was luckily in a position to be able to issue a *dementi*, and the amicable relations between the Motherland and her farflung outposts were never seriously endangered. The story that described the grey squirrels from Regent's Park as holding a nocturnal mass meeting and thanksgiving service at Lord's cannot be regarded as credible, though it is true that the spread and popularity of Sciuridosis waned considerably during Sir Pugsley's convalescence.

When I reproached Reginald for what I could not help regarding as the rather callous attitude that he adopted towards old acquaintances, he excused himself by evolving the following theory. Friends (he said) are all very well in their way, for to a certain extent one is able to pick and choose one's friends, though not so easily of course as one can choose one's enemies. Acquaintances, on the other hand, stand in a totally different category, and there is practically nothing to be urged in favour of encouraging their advances. To begin with, one has little or no say in their selection; they are more often than not wished upon one by circumstances or environment, and, as a rule, may be justly said to serve no useful purpose whatsoever. Furthermore, it is appalling to consider the waste of time involved in the revival of old acquaintanceships.

After a merciful interval of many years two acquaintances are re-united, much to their mutual embarrassment.

"Hullo, old man! This *is* a surprise!" says one of them with an imitation of heartiness that deceives nobody. "It's *ages* since we met, eh?"

"Ages!" agrees the other thankfully.

"What are you doing with yourself these days?" asks the first—a purely rhetorical question which it would be impossible to answer in less than half an hour.

"Oh, I don't know. What are you?" is the recognized reply.

Thereupon conversation reaches an impasse, each of the two protagonists vainly searching his mind for a suitable excuse to get away from the other as quickly as possible. At the very bottom of either's mind lies the profound conviction—the certainty, rather—that the perfectly good reason why two persons have not met for ages is that neither of them has ever felt the slightest inclination to meet the other, or he would undoubtedly have done so; in fact, that they had both sincerely hoped that they would never meet again.

"Come, come, Reginald," I said, when he had finished propounding these very cynical views. "That won't do at all!"

"Why not?"

"Should old acquaintance be forgot?" I asked, for I am a confirmed sentimentalist at heart.

"Undoubtedly," he replied with conviction, "and never brought to mind!"

"Perhaps you're right," I said, and as by this time it had begun to snow, we left our pavilion seats and hastened to join the more sensible of our fellow members in the bar.

For a number of years between the wars a character named 'The Man in the Pavilion' delighted readers of Passing Show *with stories about the funny side of the game – some of which seemed improbable and not a few highly unlikely! He was the creation of Herbert Farjeon (1887–1945) a cricket-loving theatre critic and playwright. Farjeon had idolised the players of his youth, and began to express his enthusiasm for the game around the turn of the century by compiling his own cricket annuals – playing county championships with dice and recording every score of the imaginary season! From back garden cricket with his brothers and friends (in which 'Bertie' insisted on being the Surrey fast bowler, Tom Richardson), Farjeon developed into 'a steady bat, able to make a century (though not, I believe, often doing it), a useful bowler, and a very safe fieldsman', according to his other writer brother, J. Jefferson Farjeon. He played for University College School and was for many years a member of the Old Broughtonians. 'Had he devoted himself seriously to cricket he might have got his name in Wisden's,' his brother wrote years later. As it was, the theatre absorbed Herbert Farjeon's energies, though he continued to watch first-class games and test matches, as well as taking the occasional break from his critiques and plays to write highly amusing pieces such as the one which follows. For many British readers, it was a sad day indeed when 'The Man in the Pavilion' was no longer around to regale them with eccentric yarns of bat on leather . . .*

Some Record Catches

by Herbert Farjeon

Talking of catches, said the Man in the Pavilion, one of the most remarkable catches *I* ever saw (*that* was a lucky snick!) happened when I was playing for charity some years ago against a team composed of variety artistes—comics and conjurers and jugglers and all sorts. I've seen some pretty startling things in my time, but I've only once seen a batsman caught out by three fielders simultaneously (why *don't* they run up!)—and I've only once seen a ball caught while it was still about eighteen feet up in the air. As a matter of fact (that's the *fourth* long hop this over!) I was the unfortunate victim.

It was a small ground (now *that's* what I call a life!) and I was having an A1 time, because, as you know, when I *do* get my eye in, I *can* make them go a bit, and before long practically every man was fielding on the boundary. That wasn't any use, because I was seeing them as big as footballs and lifting them high over the ropes for six pretty nearly every other ball (I *thought* they'd put Mudlark on soon!) and they simply couldn't catch me out owing, as editors say, to lack of space. They just stood and stared at the ball as it sailed over their heads time after time.

I've seldom felt more comfortable than I did that day, and I haven't a doubt I should have got my century if it hadn't been for the tactics of the opposing skipper, who really *was* rather a brainy cove for a music-hall chap. (Good lord, *what* a stroke!) Of course, I saw him alter his field, but I couldn't for the life of me think what he was doing, placing three men absolutely shoulder to shoulder on the square-leg boundary, and I hadn't a notion that those three men were the famous Pasquagli Brothers, though I'd often seen them in tights at the Palladium. So when I got a nice half-volley outside the leg-stump (what *is* that woman doing right in *front* of the bowling-screen?) I lammed it for all I was worth in their direction and stood and watched it go for what I felt quite sure would be another six.

But it wasn't another six. I could scarcely believe my eyes. You'll hardly believe it yourself when I tell you. Do you know, no sooner had I hit that ball than the second Pasquagli Brother leapt up on to the shoulders of the first Pasquagli Brother, and the third Pasquagli Brother clambered quick as lightning on to the shoulders of the second Pasquagli Brother, and bless my soul if he didn't stretch up his arm, catch the ball, jump to the ground, and shout out "Voilà!" The umpire answered "Out!" And they entered me in the score-book, "caught Pasquagli Brothers"—rather an unusual entry, wasn't it? (Fifty up, *and* about time, too!)

Of course, said the Man in the Pavilion, the umpire's decision was right enough, but I can't say the same for a decision given against me in another match, when I was caught out in a different way, but no less surprising. I was slogging away again, and having dispatched two balls to Kingdom Come, they had to get out a third ball, which was rather an ancient specimen. Well I banged it about a bit (these two fellows only need a *straight* one to get them out!) and then I got a full toss and absolutely let fly for all I was worth, and hang me if the bally ball didn't come in half. And one half of the ball sailed away to the boundary, and the other half was caught by point.

I never expected point would have the cheek to appeal, but he did (*beat* him again!) and there was a long discussion between the umpires, and in the end they told me that I could add four to my score but that I must also consider my innings over. I think that's the only case on record (my word, I *should* like to have a go at this bowling!) of a batsman hitting a boundary and getting caught off the same ball, but I once saw a bowler bowl two no-balls simultaneously. Oh, yes, it's possible enough. What the fellow did was to drag his foot over the crease *and* throw the ball at the same time, and the umpire gave us two runs for it. (If these two fellows sit on the splice much longer, I shall drop off to sleep!)

The most tragic catch I ever saw, said the Man in the Pavilion, was a catch at the wicket off a fast ball. I wasn't the victim this time. If I had been, I shouldn't be here to tell the tale. The pitch was very fiery—not like *this* easy wicket—the bowler was a real lightning merchant, and the ball got up nastily, hit the shoulder of the bat, struck the batsman a fearful whack on the temple, and was caught by the man behind the stumps. There was an immediate appeal, and the umpire said "Out!" and the batsman lay full length on the ground. And the terrible thing was that he was stone dead. We were all pretty gloomy—of course, it stopped the game—but it raised a very nice point.

You see, the doctor said that death had been absolutely instantaneous, which meant that the batsman had been caught *after* he had been killed, and the question arose: *Can* a batsman be caught out after he's dead? If not, should he be entered "Retired dead?" And if so, isn't it pretty rotten luck for a fellow's batting average to be lowered *after* he's kicked the bucket? Well, they say it's the unexpected always happens at cricket. (And if these two fellows last much longer, it's the unexpected'll happen in *this* match. I never saw such an exhibition of batting in all my life. Not even in the match when . . .)

The Australians feature again in this next story by Hugh de Selincourt (1878–1951) author of The Cricket Match *(1924) which has been described by J. M. Barrie as 'the best book ever written about cricket'. One would add that it also contains perhaps the finest description of a village cricket match. Selincourt was a wholehearted devotee of the village match, believing it to be the purest of all forms of English games, a view he expressed with some conviction in a famous essay entitled 'Ours Is The Real Cricket' written in 1931. He was also something of a cricketer, playing regularly in Authors XI's in the twenties and thirties, usually opening the bowling and quite capable of a good score when at the wicket. Selincourt's love of the game is reflected in his other books such as* Over! *(1932),* Move Over *(1934) and* The Saturday Match *(1937) which again returned to the topic of village cricket. For completists of Selincourt's work, there is also a fine chapter 'Cricket and the Something More' in his novel of childhood,* Young 'Un *(1927). My selection, though, is his tale with the intriguing title, 'How Our Village Beat the Australians' written in 1930. I like it not only for its style and humour, but also because it represents a dream shared, surely, by every small cricket club. The reader will also doubtless spot the strange manner of the dismissal of one of the Australians, and how it parallels a similar dismissal that took place at a crucial moment in the most recent test series against the Aussies. A case of life imitating art, once again?*

How Our Village Beat the Australians

by Hugh de Selincourt

Here they were – these great Australians with their unbeaten record –
to speak to any of whom by chance even or mistake, in a railway
carriage, would have been an unforgettable honour; here they actually
were in full strength dressed and ready to play us, stepping about on our
own ground – cracking jokes like ordinary men. No wonder our hearts
beat, our eyes bulged, our knees weakened, for after all it is one thing to
talk of having a go at the Australians and quite another to see them in
flesh and blood before you. The thing seemed barely credible. Sam
Bird, who always likes to be careful in his statements – never anxious,
you understand, to commit himself in any way – said to me as I stood
quailing:

'On the whole they're a pretty decent side, I should say; perhaps the
strongest side that has ever appeared on a village ground.'

'Ah, well, on paper!' – I answered, my natural optimism asserting

165

itself immediately. 'And there is always the luck of the game to be taken into account.'

'True for you,' Sam slowly laughed. 'You never know your luck!'

One kept blinking to make quite sure that one's eyes were not playing tricks: but they were not. They were recording plain facts as faithfully as human eyes ever can – which persist, however, in affirming the monotonous rigidity of the earth, against our certain knowledge that it is rushing round the sun in space.

There stood Mr. Armstrong, a little larger even than life, tossing with our Captain. Mr. Armstrong, as always, tossed with great skill, and showed no surprise at winning. He elected to bat without a moment's hesitation, not pausing for a moment to consider the old familiar argument that it is a good thing to know what you have to make before going in to make them. He showed no nervousness of any kind: indeed it was desolating for us to observe the complete confidence that marked the deportment of our visitors. Some of us were cowardly enough to wish that we had left the Australians unchallenged. There was a look too of amusement on the faces of the spectators, who were crowding upon the ground, as though they had left their homes not so much to watch a game of cricket as to see some fun.

Jovial remarks were flung out to us from the safety of the crowded ring – to keep our tails up – to show what we were made of – to remember that no game was lost till it was won. I regret to say they were on the facetious rather than on the encouraging side.

Mr. Collins and Mr. Gregory opened the batting to the bowling of Sid Smith and Mr. Gauvinier. Our side was fairly strong, the same indeed, with two exceptions, as that which defeated Raveley. On paper our side did not look much perhaps; on the field, however, there were great possibilities about it.

Sam Bird, asked to give centre to Mr. Collins, could hardly speak or move; but eventually Mr. Collins obtained as good a block as he has ever obtained in a Test Match.

The curious happenings, which I shall accurately relate as my eyes beheld them, began immediately. For Sid Smith, bewildered by the occasion, bowled as soon as Sam Bird stood back and a little too soon for Mr. Collins, who was not quite ready. Had this occurred in a Test Match, Mr. Collins would undoubtedly have stepped away declining to play the ball, but in this game, as the ball was a full toss, Mr. Collins perhaps opined that he was ready enough to place it out of the ground: for this he gallantly tried to do, but unfortunately he missed the ball altogether and it hit his middle stump.

He looked pardonably and intensely annoyed; Sid and Paul Gauvinier, both real sportsmen, instantly ran up, Sid apologizing and Mr. Gauvinier pointing out that the umpire had omitted to cry 'Play!' (which was true: Sam Bird's lips had indeed moved, but no audible sound had emerged from them). Mr. Gauvinier begged Mrs. Collins to remain where he was, not wishing to take an unfair advantage of any visiting team; in the interests of the game he begged him to stay, and Mr. Collins very obligingly consented to do so. The ball was considered as a no ball, as thought it had never been bowled; and the game was resumed, or perhaps it would be more accurate to say, properly begun.

Sam Bird found his voice and bravely shouted 'Play!' and we all got ready on our toes, taking heart at the mere sight of an Australian wicket broken, however the breaking may have been caused.

Now I am a trained observer and was in a position to see what happened next. Sid bowled his usual medium-to-slow-paced ball on the off stump, and it was a perfect length. Mr. Collins played well forward – to drive it, firmly but not hard, past mid-off: but the ball, instead of striking the bat, rose, as though bouncing on some invisible substance or lifted by some unseen spirit hand, and, describing a near half-circle over the shoulder of his bat, hit the centre of the off stump.

There was a hush of surprise, then a roar of applause. Mr. Collins looked at his bat and looked at the wicket and looked at the pitch. Mr. Collins looked scared. He stooped to pick up the ball; he pinched it, he smelt it, as though in doubt of its being a cricket ball at all; then he uttered a deep-felt ejaculation of regret and withdrew towards our pavilion. He will worry about that ball as long as he worries about anything, and how it came to bowl him. But it was all over, as these tragic and mysterious things always are, in a tiny fraction of a second and no one exists who can really enlighten us as to their exact nature. Even if we happen to be told the truth, we are not able to believe it. We are in fact the merest Horatios and there is far, far more in heaven and earth and also on the cricket field than is dreamed of in our philosophies.

0 – 1 – 0, the score-board read; a familiar, and I may add, under the circumstances, a refreshing sight. Our Secretary, Mr. John McLeod, walked up to Sid Smith, and told him that it was the finest ball he had

ever seen bowled. Sid blushed and believed him and hoped that a member of the English Selection Committee was on the ground, and making a note of his name.

Mr. Armstrong came in next, slow, massive and imperturbable, his enormous belief in his side and himself towering above the little wanton vagaries of Chance.

'Not a bad ball *that*, I should say!' he remarked cheerfully to Sid, twiddling his bat round in his hand, making it look a funny little instrument for such a great man to be using.

Still thrilled by what my eyes had beheld, I rather hoped that nothing unforeseen would happen to him. Moreover 0 – 2 – 0 on the score-board would really be past a joke, would indeed appear almost blasphemous treatment of our august visitors. The Australian Captain was the Australian Captain, and *lèse majesté* is not an empty formula to any but a Communist heart. Perhaps some such thoughts moved Sid, for much to my relief his next ball was a half-volley outside the leg stump which Mr. Armstrong swept gracefully clean out of the ground, narrowly missing a motor that was passing along in the road, its occupants oblivious of who were playing in our field: thus many golden opportunities are missed, as we rush along our modern way at an ever faster pace. Eager small boys found and returned the ball, hopeful of much similar work: but Mr. Armstrong, though his confidence towered above Chance, yet took no liberties with that fickle lady; and played the remaining four balls of the over as any decent first-wicket batsman would have played four good-length balls in his first over.

Tillingfold crossed over, and Mr. Gauvinier started to bowl to Mr. Gregory, and it was clear that Mr. Gregory had the length of the game well in mind, and was determined to waste no time, for the first ball he slashed confidently past cover with such force that it overcame the longish grass and reached the boundary. Two ones followed, confident hard drives which young Mr. Trine flung back from the deep. Mr. Armstrong was backing up with a little more exuberance perhaps than he would have done in a Test Match, suggesting a readiness to play the excellent game of tip-and-run; Mr. Gauvinier bowled a good-length ball on the off stump: Mr. Gregory stepped out and drove it straight back with tremendous force to the bowler, whose hand the ball viciously smacked and then struck the wicket. Unfortunately Mr. Armstrong was a good yard outside his crease and his own umpire was obliged to give him out in response to the yell of appeal that came simultaneously from point, slip, and Mr. Gauvinier, and was taken up immediately from sheer joyous excitement by most of our remaining fieldsmen.

Mr. Armstrong reluctantly withdrew, an illustrious victim of misfortune, and all of us within earshot condoled with him, sincerely, crying out, 'Oh, bad luck, sir, bad luck!'

He smiled and remarked without a quaver in his voice, like the great sportsman that he is: 'It's all in the game, boys; it's all in the game.'

Somehow, we most of us felt guilty, and longed to put him back again at the wicket; but it could not of course be done. Even a great Australian Captain must bow before his fate and the rules of the game.

Mr. Ryder strode in to join Mr. Gregory, and caused considerable amusement to the spectators by hastening to take centre before he realized that he was not to receive the bowling.

Sam Bird started to run from square-leg to the wicket, confident that he and not the famous batsman must be at fault.

He paused half-way and looked wildly round, before returning to his place with his accustomed composure.

Not in the least daunted by the bad start, Mr. Ryder and Mr. Gregory played good free cricket, and it seemed probable that they might make a stand, as the bowling neither of Sid Smith nor of Mr. Gauvinier appeared to trouble them greatly. Twenty was on the score-board; and though Mr. Armstrong and Mr. Collins were out – two useful men to see the back of in any match – signs of uneasiness began to be shown among the Tillingfold team.

Mr. Gregory was lashing good-length balls a little outside the off stump between point and cover; Teddy White was fielding cover and retreated to the boundary by the hedge. Our Secretary, Mr. John McLeod, fearless and short and stout (fearless, that is, of anything but the possible effect of a sudden stoop), was fielding point and came squarer, though the balls seemed generally to have passed him before he was quite aware that they had been hit. He was unaccustomed to the shot and to its pace. Once or twice he had fallen over in a frantic but tardy effort to reach the ball. This had called forth little shouts of laughter from the happy spectators who were not fielding point to Mr. Gregory, and old John McLeod felt that he was somehow being made game of, for a smile was noticeable even upon the courteous face of Mr. Gregory.

I watched this little side-show, as it were, with increasing interest, full of that strained ominous sensation, familiar to us all in dreams, that something startling was about to happen.

Mr. Gregory, with those steel-strong wrists of his, lashed at the ball and hit it a beautiful smack: and I saw Mr. McLeod bound yards to the right with his arm extended, and his arm seemed to stretch out like a piece of elastic; there was another smack, following the first quickly as two reports from a gun. Mr. McLeod spun completely round and sat quietly down with a dazed look upon his face, holding up the caught ball in his right hand, between his fingers and thumb.

Mr. Gregory had started running, thinking his hit was safely away to Teddy White – the howls and yells of joy at the catch stopped him. He stared at Mr. McLeod, bewildered.

'I caught it all right,' our Secretary faltered, and began slowly to rise from his sitting posture. 'It stuck, you know.'

Mr. Gregory continued to stare, first at Mr. McLeod, then out towards Teddie White, in the direction he was sure the ball had travelled, half suspecting, I believe, that Mr. McLeod had played a trick upon him and produced another ball, like a conjurer, from the slack of his breeches.

But Mr. Gregory, though a little dazed with astonishment, was clear-minded enough to perceive that there was no slack to Mr. McLeod's breeches, or, indeed, to any other part of his attire, which fitted him like a glove. The Australian umpire answered his questioning look with becoming promptness:

'Out!' he called, and added to Mr. Gauvinier: 'The most wonderful catch I have ever seen.'

Our Secretary quickly recovered from his momentary surprise as we crowded round him, asking him however he had managed to bring it off. He was so happy that he was on the brink of tears. 'The sort of catch I've often dreamed of making,' he stammered. 'And now I've done it, bless my soul! Now I've done it; and in this game too!'

'We are all inspired once in our lives,' said young Trine, who had come hurrying up from the deep.

'Inspired! Ah, that's the very word,' gasped old John, more breathless than usual. 'Do you know I was that mad to catch it, I felt lifted up and shoved towards it, and as though my arm had got stretched out three times it natural length at least.'

'That's exactly what it looked like, mate,' said Sid Smith in solemn tones. And to the world at large he added: 'This is what comes of playing cricket on a Sunday!' a remark which it baffled me to understand, though local people are often superstitious. Old John McLeod, I thought, looked hurt. But the happy cluster round our honest Secretary broke up as Mr. Andrews strode to the wicket, and the catch, like other great events in human existence, became a thing of the past; a thing to be recounted to grand-children by every person who had seen it; a thing of history; a thing, moreover, so rarely wonderful in itself that it could not possibly be embellished in the telling.

24 – 3 – 11. Tillingford were not doing so badly. It was clear that they were no longer content to make an exhibition of themselves for the country's sake; they were all out now to make a game of it; forgetting in their enthusiasm and excitement that any batsman on the other side might be considered good enough for at least a hundred. If fat old John McLeod could at a pinch hold a catch like that, hang it all! why shouldn't anyone? Thus ran the tenor of their thought.

'Does he often do that?' Mr. Andrews asked our stumper pleasantly, as he made his block, smiling.

'Oh, well! Not very often, now,' our stumper bashfully replied.

Sid Smith was now bowling with more than his usual unconcern, as though he were at length convinced that he could but do his best and that the outcome of his effort lay in other hands than his. There was something impersonal and aloof about his attitude, and his attitude was perhaps a wise one under the circumstances, though in an ordinary game it might have robbed his bowling of sting and intention. But this, it will be noted, was not an ordinary game.

Of course in cricket, the game being played with a moving ball (sometimes a very swiftly moving ball), things happen so quickly and are over so soon that no one can be quite sure precisely what did happen to any given ball. Thus it is we hear even from experts such divergent accounts of the same stroke. The game, indeed, is wrapped in a cloud of mystery which can never be pierced. Herein lies its fascination. The player feels himself in touch with some hidden power, when, for example, leaping out to his full length the bowler takes and holds a flying ball he can barely see. It is not done by taking thought. The man who has ever held a hot return from his own bowling feels that it has somehow been done for him, and feels grateful; the man who has unaccountably missed a sitter at mid-off, which ninety-nine times out of a hundred he would have held, feels that he has been the victim of a spiteful trick.

On the cricket field we are in touch with powers to which, though we may not be in a position to name and label them, as in this mechanical age we like to name and label everything, it is as well to be respectful. It was natural that in such a game as this these powers should be in special evidence, and it was natural that such a simple unsophisticated soul as Sid Smith should be specially open to their influence. There was something comic, no doubt, in the dogged perseverance of his bowling, but there was also something very touching in its faithfulness and simplicity.

Now some of us read with surprise that Jack Hobbs, after playing the Australian bowling for a whole day, was bowled on the opening of the second day by a full toss from Mr. Mailey. We had learned at our preparatory schools that a full toss was a good ball to smite. Jack Hobbs himself, however, in the interesting account of the tour which he contributed to a daily newspaper, described himself as being quite content to be out to such a ball, which, we were told, was deceptive in pace, swerved in its flight, hung in the air, and beat him all ends up before bowling him.

I must own to having been sceptical about this until with my own eyes I saw the ball with which Sid Smith disturbed the wicket of Mr. Ryder. It, too, was a full toss, a slow full toss, which I thought, and Mr. Ryder obviously thought, must reach him knee-high wide of the wicket on the leg side. But, halfway in its flight, just after Mr. Ryder had turned, his mind, in that fraction of a second during which a batsman unconsciously decides to act, made up, his strength summoned – half-way in its flight, I say, the ball miraculously seemed to pause and swerve inwards. Mr. Ryder, observing this, made a superb effort to change his mind, only possible to such a fine batsman as he is, but in spite of his almost superhuman quickness of eye and wrist, he was too late; he over-balanced as the ball swerved gently past him and on to the middle stump and neatly saved himself from a fall by the help of his bat. A clumsier man would certainly have fallen.

Mr. Macartney came in next, looking perceptibly worried at the way things were going. A village wicket might be accountable for a great deal, but no wicket could be blamed for disaster caused by a full toss.

There was a business-like look about him, the air of one who without being the least downhearted or inclined to sit upon the splice, was yet determined to take no foolish risks. It was evident that he considered the previous batsmen had been victims either of gross ill-luck, like Mr. Armstrong, or of their own folly.

Three runs were made without any untoward incident. Mr. Macartney and his partner seemed to be wondering how four good wickets could have fallen; their voices as they called, to run or not to run, had that settled confidence of men who are ready to go quietly on till their Captain sees fit to declare. But this was not to be.

Mr. Macartney drove Mr. Gauvinier past mid-off into the deep to young Mr. Trine. As the batsmen passed, Mr. Andrews said, 'There's another,' and there seemed no doubt whatever that there was ample time for a second run.

Mr. Trine was fielding alertly and well – he saw their intention to take a second run: at full speed he picked the ball up and flung it in with such force and accuracy that the middle stump was knocked clean out of the ground. It was fortunate the stump was not broken, as there might have been considerable difficulty in obtaining another: and we never like to ask any side to finish the game with incomplete kit. Mr. Andrews, noticing the amazing velocity of the throw, quickened his pace, but being a good yard outside the crease was forced to retire.

You could not call the piece of work that dismissed him with any justice a fluke. True, Mr. Trine did not usually throw with such pace and accuracy: indeed, he seemed spirited to the ball even as the ball was spirited to the wicket; but most men rise to an occasion once at least in their lives; and that was the occasion on which Mr. Trine rose; nor could he have chosen a better. It is unlikely that he will ever forget that piece of fielding; it is certain that he will never repeat it.

Tillingfold continued to do quite nicely; five wickets were now down for thirty-three. Of course, the Australian tail might wag, though tails rarely did on our own ground, for long.

Now our Captain, Mr. Gauvinier, is always mad to win; some people say that he is over-anxious, too keen. He may possibly be; but I think he was wise to remind the side that they had to face some pretty decent bowling. He did not overdo it, as he would have done had he gone on to remind us that on several well-authenticated occasions all ten wickets of a side had fallen without a run being scored. We had all read these lamentable records at the end of Mr. Somerset's score-book; and they had long been present somewhere at the back of most of our minds as a painful possibility, though no one, I am glad to say, had had the indecency to put the horrid thought into words.

Mr. Mailey came in quite unabashed by the figures on the score-board. By the way he took centre you felt he was going to make things hum. He did. He leaped out at Mr. Gauvinier's first ball and hit it full and tremendously hard. I thought it must have gone well into the next field. I was astonished accordingly to hear Mr. Gauvinier call out, in a loud commanding voice, 'Mine!' I looked up, and there the ball was soaring higher and higher; so high indeed that Mr. Mailey and Mr. Macartney easily ran two before the ball descended into Mr. Gauvinier's safe hands, about a yard and a half behind the umpire. The way in which Mr. Gauvinier avoided treading on the wicket was extremely clever.

Tillingfold have always been proud of their fielding. They had certainly never shown to better advantage. 'The feller deserves to be out,' growled Mr. Macartney, 'swiping at his first ball in that silly fashion.'

Mr. Mailey walked jauntily out, laughing to himself, pretending bravely, as many another good cricketer has pretended on that sad walk to the pavilion after failing to score, that after all it didn't so very much matter.

Small boys were pacing up and down before the pavilion, peering in to catch a glimpse of Mr. Armstrong's face; but the features of such a man are under perfect control, and they learned nothing of what was passing behind the cheerful mask within the great man's mind. All captains should strive to acquire this imperturbability of feature, as a rattled skipper is apt to mean a disjointed side. Mr. Armstrong's bearing was indeed a lesson to us all. His plan had no doubt been to make a couple of hundred or so for the loss of one or perhaps two wickets, to take tea and then skittle us twice out for twenty or perhaps thirty. But the gods who preside over cricket had decided otherwise; the unforeseen had happened; and six good wickets were down for thirty-three. Nothing can alter a fact of this kind: each fallen wicket helped to form, like boulders, a horrid little cairn of incontrovertible fact.

The remaining Australian batsmen gave us little trouble, and nobody expected that they would. As Sid Smith wisely remarked: 'We had 'em on the run,' and a side in that condition, as everyone knows, can do nothing right. Our men, on the other hand, did nothing whatever wrong. Every semblance of a catch was held, and some, indeed, that hardly bore any ordinary resemblance to a catch. That, for instance, with which young Mr. Trine dismissed Mr. McDonald was quite miraculous. The ball, travelling at the deadly breast-high level of a furious drive, seemed well out of reach; but Mr. Trine, speeding over the rough ground with the effortless ease of a man moving like a porpoise through water in his dreams, did reach it and he held it superbly in his outstretched hand. Wonderful as the catch was, he never looked like missing it.

The Australian innings closed at thirty-nine – a trebly unlucky number.

There was time for thirty-five minutes' batting before the tea interval at five. It created a very favourable impression that quite a number of the Australian team walked with a hand on the roller, while we rolled the wicket.

Some of us were wondering whether Mr. Armstrong, in view of important matches that were to be played during the week, would think it wiser to rest his fast bowlers, in spite of the fact that the wicket would certainly suit them; and distrustful eyes were turned on certain unobtrusive plaintains that, do what we would, continued to disfigure the square.

As the roller was shoved up by the hedge I noticed an Eastern gentleman who was staying in the village and was rumoured to be a Tibetan monk of very high grade, left standing alone. He approached each wicket and inspected the stumps, stroking each one gently between his finger and thumb, as though to find out the quality of the material of which they were made. Sam Bird told me that, before the game began, he had asked to be allowed to handle the ball, and Sam had allowed him to do so.

'Ah, how ingenious men are!' he had remarked, as he politely handed the ball back to Sam.

Sam Bird likes to do everything properly. He realized that our visitors were accustomed to play on county grounds where a bell is rung to warn spectators off the ground and to prepare the team for taking the field. There is no bell on our ground; the umpires stroll out and we follow at our leisure; so thoughtful Sam, afraid that the Australians might be put off their game by the absence of the tintinnabulation to which their ears were accustomed, had brought a small bell and this he produced from his trouser pocket and shook violently for some moments, standing discreetly, being a shy man, behind the small scoring-box. Then, with some difficulty replacing the bell in his trouser pocket, he joined his colleague and proceeded with a solemn shy smile upon his broad face to the wicket, followed by the Australian team in a laughing, compact body.

Our Secretary, dear old John McLeod, who was going in first and always took first ball, turned a little pale when he saw that Mr. Armstrong, suitably impressed by Tillingford's magnificent fielding, was setting his field for a fast bowler.

'Oh dear!' he said. 'Bless my soul, now. Oh, well. One ball. How I should dearly love to play a ball or two.'

'You just stop there till tea,' said Mr. Gauvinier pleasantly, patting him on the back. 'And we shall be all right.'

'It's no good waiting,' said Mr. Bois, a preparatory schoolmaster who lived in the village and had played much really good cricket. 'Come on. The sound old rules hold good, you know. Keep your eye on the ball and use a nice straight bat.'

They made their brave way to the wicket.

Dear old John McLeod must have felt not more than about three inches high, as all alone he faced Mr. McDonald and the ten Australian fieldsmen, placed by a master mind on the exact spot towards which, if he did happen to stroke the ball, the ball must certainly fly. Mr. McDonald came thundering along his terrific run to the wicket, a giant with a cannon ball which a man feeling like a midget was to receive with a bat that felt like half a wax match in the midget's grasp. The odds were disproportionate. But our Secretary, all honour to him, gripped the handle of his bat, glued his eye on something he took to be the ball and played the ball.

Its impact on the centre of his bat gave Mr. McLeod such confidence that he grew from a mere midget of a few inches to almost half his full stature as a man. True, he dwindled a little as Mr. McDonald walked leisurely into the outfield preparatory to delivering his next ball, but during the course of the five seconds' sprint to the wicket he had time to grow once more, and once more the ball met the bat though sooner than Mr. McLeod had expected. This second stroke drew a round of applause from the spectators, confident now that the batsman had taken the measure of the bowling. The next ball, however, missed the bat. Mr. Oldfield, confident that it must hit the wicket, missed it also and it sped to the boundary for four runs.

Thus Tillingfold's worst fears of dismissal without scoring were allayed. A jubilant smile spread slowly over many of the faces of the team in the pavilion.

'Oh Lord,' Horace Cairie muttered, 'if we could only beat them!' And he kept doing the sum six sixes are thirty-six and a bye or a leg-bye could sometimes score six.

The next ball also missed the bat, and missed the wicket. I was standing straight behind the stumps and I was as surprised as Mr. Oldfield and Mr. McDonald at Mr. McLeod's escape. I could have sworn that the top of the wicket faced for that fraction of a second when the ball should have struck it. But there stood the wicket, bails on, unbroken. Mr. Oldfield walked up to the stumps, put both his gloved hands on them, and pressed them, as wicket-keepers sometimes do, backwards and forwards, as though to assure himself that there was no deception.

Mr. McDonald may be pardoned for stamping with vexation when the same thing happened to all the remaining balls of his over except the last, which Mr. McLeod steered with a quick flick of his wrist through a small crowd of slips bang against the pavilion for four.

I did not know that Mr. McLeod kept such a shot in his locker. But it has been well said that good bowling evokes latent powers from a batsman. Mr. Bois was never tired of impressing this upon us when urging us, as he frequently did, to make a point of playing better sides. It was chiefly through his advocacy, as the son of a millionaire who had great influence in Melbourne attended his school, that the game had been arranged.

Mr. Bois played with his usual unruffled composure, though his wicket too was often missed by a miracle. Once the wicket was perceptibly hit and perceptibly trembled, but the bails remained stolidly in their place; and there was nothing wrong with the set of the wicket or with the bails, because Mr. Oldfield tapped the stumps lightly with his finger and the bails dropped lightly off. Their umpire, too, came forward and shook the wicket as Mr. Oldfield had done.

It must have been thankless work for their bowlers, for I suppose our first-wicket batsmen might perhaps be considered mere rabbits to bowlers of their class, and to keep shaving the stumps of a rabbit is distressing to any bowler. Then these men, it must be remembered, had the honour of a great Commonwealth to sustain; and to them therefore these elusive wickets must have been doubly, nay, trebly trying. They clutched their heads, they stamped their feet, they jerked their arms down as though punching imaginary heads: and ever the confidence of the two batsmen became more bland and smiling, as well it may have done. The way the Australian bowlers stuck to their thankless task commanded our admiration and roused our unstinted applause.

Runs, however, did not come so fast as in the first over. Mr. Oldfield was alert behind the stumps; the small crowd of slips were on their toes: the fielding, though not miraculous, was very good. Ten, however, crept up on the board, and our batsmen would certainly have remained together until the tea interval, had not Mr. Bois, in playing back to Mr. McDonald, unfortunately struck his wicket with his bat. The one blemish to his style is that he is apt to cramp his freedom of movement by making his block unnecessarily far back from the front crease.

11 – 1 – 5 the score-board read, and though Tillingfold as a team would have liked to have knocked off the thirty-nine runs without loss, the start could not be described as other than quite satisfactory. Mr. Bois, however, was extremely annoyed. He was quite at home, he said, and could have stayed there for hours, had it not been for his execrable luck.

Young Mr. Trine, who came in next, noticing that Mr. Oldfield was standing well back and that there was no fieldsman in the deep, determined to have a go. As Mr. McDonald was taking his sprint to the wicket he shambled along out of his ground to meet him and letting madly fly, drove him well out of the ground. A few small boys remained husky for the remainder of the day after the prolonged yell which the fine daring of this hit elicited.

He tried to repeat this manœuvre on the last ball of the over, but he started too soon and got too far out of his ground, so that Mr. McDonald and Mr. Oldfield foresaw his intention and acting like one man, Mr. McDonald bowled a slow high full toss over Mr. Trine's head into the hands of Mr. Oldfield who, still on the run, stumped him – a brilliant piece of concerted work between bowler and wicket-keeper.

'Ah!' said Sid Smith sagely, wagging his head. 'You dussn't take no liberties with such as they.'

178

During tea, as is usually the case, the strain of the contest was relaxed. The Tillingfold team, especially those who had not yet faced the fast bowlers, seemed to enjoy the honour of eating with their distinguished visitors even more than the honour of playing cricket with them.

Crowds paraded in front of the pavilion, glancing in, as to many it was quite as thrilling to know how the Australians drank their tea and ate their cake and bread and butter as to watch them bat and bowl. Our visitors showed no surprise at this interest, since the trait is common to the inhabitants of both continents, and were no more put off their food by spectators than they were put off their game by them.

Many of the Tillingfold team, however, unused to the glare of publicity, were painfully affected and, much to the distress of their thoughtful captain, ate and drank next to nothing – comparatively speaking – though the caterer had provided a special tea and had raised the price from ninepence to one shilling.

Punctual to the moment Sam Bird, a cake in his mouth, a pastry in his hand (sensible fellow, his bashfulness had limits), tore himself from the table and producing the little bell from his trouser pocket, rang it vigorously, faithful to duty and unheeding the rude remarks of small boys who gathered eagerly about him as he leaned against the small scoring-box.

The umpires went out together. Mr. Armstrong led his men once more into the field, with a look at the score-board which read $17 - 2 - 6$. The great game was resumed, Mr. Fanshawe joining our Secretary at the wicket.

Mr. Fanshawe takes his cricket very seriously. He is a religious bat, treating a half-volley or a long hop on the leg with reverence. He was in fact the ideal man to bat first in a Test Match where time is no consideration: during the first week he would have played himself steadily in, and towards the end of the second week he would have begun to make runs, and no one knows how freely he might not have scored as the innings proceeded. But in the Tillingfold games, having always felt hurried, he had never really done himself justice – a born Test Match player in village cricket: another square peg in a round hole. Alas! Life abounds with them.

No doubt Mr. McDonald and Mr. Gregory hoped that, after being refreshed with a cup of tea and bite of bread and butter, they would be able to hit the wickets; but though they bowled uncommonly well and frequently beat the batsmen the wickets remained intact, as they had done before tea.

In the first half-hour two leg-byes were scored off their bowling; and Mr. Armstrong, feeling that his fast bowlers were expensive and fatiguing themselves to no good purpose, made a double change, going on himself with Mr. Mailey.

Mr. McLeod, never a forcing bat, became infected with Mr. Fanshawe's religious caution, and the atmosphere was so charged with reverence that a run off the bat began to appear like a profanity.

The crowd, at first respectful at the steady resistance to the Australian attack, at last grew restive and disrespectful. Indeed they showed signs of barracking, thinking possibly that it was a mistake to be playing for a draw with twenty-one runs to make to win and more than an hour's time to make them in. They barracked to deaf ears: Mr. McLeod and Mr. Fanshawe, even had their tenacity of purpose allowed them to hear a sound were not light-natured enough to be distracted by popular opinion, much as each loved his fellow man off the cricket ground. Mr. Mailey tried every conceivable wile to tempt Mr. Fanshawe to hit; but Mr. Fanshawe was not to be tempted. Around both batsmen all the fieldsmen clustered in indescribable positions, sillier than silly. But both batsmen were well content to smother every ball that might under ordinary circumstances have hit the wicket, and let all others severely alone. In the second half-hour after tea, one more leg-bye had been scored. Twenty stood on the score-board – it looked with a quarter of an hour to go as though the match must end in a draw.

But cricket is a game of infinite uncertainty. At last, in desperation, Mr. Andrews, unable to bear it any longer, literally flung himself at Mr. Fanshawe's bat just as the ball struck it, and caught him well within the crease. It looked more like a tackle at Rugby football than a catch at cricket; and Mr. Fanshawe, rather bewildered, appealed against it, but he appealed in vain. The catch was unusual and unorthodox, but he was indubitably out.

Teddie White came in next. Australians or no Australians he came in, as he always came in, at a half-trot, shouldering his bat, to get to business with as little delay as possible. He disliked formalities, leaving them gladly to what he called 'the rank and stink.'

Mr. Armstrong, caught no doubt after this slow hour in the general

180

assumption that runs were a profanity, or perhaps thinking that the Tillingfold captain had given his men instructions to play for a draw neglected to replace his field: they were only a little less on the cluster round Teddie White than they had been round Mr. Fanshawe.

Teddie White did not go in for niceties; he didn't bother about the field; it didn't matter to him where they happened to be placed; his one aim in batting was to put the ball out of their reach, out of the ground, much the safest place. But he had a kind heart and noticing that the fieldsmen were crowded rather nearer to him than they usually were, as Mr. Armstrong bowled, he cried out: 'Look out for yourselves then,' as he might have done to careless boys at the village net, and lashed it for four.

There was a roar of applause. But Teddie White was not pleased. It was an ass of a shot – all along the ground – he had not properly got hold of it at all – you could never hit a six like that, the only really safe shot.

Mr. Armstrong much dislikes to be caught napping. He set his master mind to work, sized up his man exactly with one piercing look, and proceeded to dot his men carefully along the leg-side boundary, confident that the next ball would prove this reckless hitter's downfall.

Teddie chafed at the delay, muttering to himself: 'If I be dratted fool enough not to beat it over their Aussie 'eads!'

At length, Mr. Armstrong, satisfied with the exact position of his field, swung in his next delivery with a quiet smile of confidence. Teddie White burst at it in mad fury like an explosion; not a muscle, not a nerve in his body but he used for that frenzied blow – the vein on his forehead even bulged, as he smote the ball whizzing over the pavilion.

'That's one on 'em!' he muttered, crumpling off his little cap and rubbing his thick neck with it. 'Two more of 'em and we wins – with a few to spare.'

Just as some writers, charming gentle fellows to meet, can only become vocal when they are in a thoroughly bad temper with life, so Teddie White could only do himself full justice as a batsman in a mood of concentrated fury, as though it were an outrage that eleven men should band themselves together to do him out of a knock – especially when he never failed to pay his subscription to the club.

The delay in collecting the ball added to his exasperation. Like some sort of inspired fiend he crashed at Mr. Armstrong's next delivery and whanged it over the hedge, over the road and into the garden of a house opposite the ground.

The excitement became delirious. Everyone stood up and shouted and yelled and cheered: men waved their hats, and flung them towards the sky: women waved their scarves and handkerchiefs.

'That's another of 'em,' Teddie White muttered, giving his face and neck another vindictive rub with his little cap.

'Well hit, sir, well hit!' said Mr. Armstrong, the sportsman in him never wavering at the most critical moment of any game.

Teddie White glared. He was not to be conciliated by any honeyed words. He growled to himself, 'Well 'it!' I'll show the blokes well 'it.' But his fury was part of his batting rather than of his nature, and he looked very red and very shy and very happy.

There was a hush in the roaring, a stillness among the fluttering, waving apparel, one of those tense moments that last a lifetime as Mr. Armstrong delivered the last ball of his over. Spectators held their breath and stared: the only sound was the puff-puff of a belated traction engine as it slowly passed the ground. No one noticed anything funny in the way Teddie White's little crumped cap sat balanced upon his square head.

For once in his life Mr. Armstrong was rattled and did not bowl the ball he intended to bowl; the indended half-volley across which Teddie would certainly have hit became a full toss, at which Teddie viciously slashed with all his furious strength; the ball soared a terrific height, higher and higher; the outfielder hopefully watched it, retreating towards the hedge. Then as the clamour of joy rose, it began to fall and fell straight down the smoke-vomiting chimney of the belated traction engine.

But what is this that is happening? Mr. Oldfield excitedly appealing! The Australians flocking round the wicket! Could the game not be ours now after such a hit? We were all in consternation – having kept our eyes fixed on the ball. But Teddie in the fury of his last blow had managed to jolt off his little crumpled cap which had impishly floated on to the wicket and now sat perched there even more comfortably than it had before perched on his own square head.

It appears that Teddie, feeling an instant draught on his bald head, had started to snatch his cap from the stumps. To the eternal honour of the Australians they had persuaded him from this rash act, for had he dislodged the bail in removing his cap before the ball had safely landed down the traction engine's chimney he would of course have been out. As it was, he was still in . . .

The whole ground rose and flew at him, the air was thick with fluttering scarves, roaring men, yelling boys, waving arms; even the pavilion rose and streamed like a pennon through the air. The Downs themselves swelled to mountains – the houses capered like lambs, as we carried Teddie White, chanting songs of triumph, through the village High Street.

*   *   *   *

And I awoke, alone on the Tillingfold Cricket Ground, with a few toddlers playing about, that lovely Sunday afternoon; and walked smiling home to tea.

William Aubrey Darlington (1890–1979), the author, journalist and drama critic of the Daily Telegraph, *was a noted opening batsman and the record books indicate he made some enviable scores for two fine amateur sides, the 'Cryptics' and the 'Incogs' in the inter-war years. Darlington was a man of effervescent good humour, who began to write for* Punch *in 1916 and then became a household name with his book,* Alf's Button *(1919) about a Cockney Private, Alf Higgins, who suddenly finds himself the possessor of a terrifying djinn which appears every time he polishes a button on his uniform. This spirit is Alf's slave and able to carry out any command – sometimes with the most unexpected results!* Alf's Button *was an immediate best-seller and was soon afterwards filmed. During the Second World War, Darlington wrote a sequel,* Alf's New Button *(1940), which was also popular. In the light of this success, it is perhaps not surprising that he should have had the idea of getting a spirit to help a rather depressed cricketer to a little luck. The result was the following story, 'The Guardian Angel' which he wrote for* Pearson's Magazine *in June 1930. The spirit in question is, however, rather more pleasant than Alf Higgin's djinn – but, as you will discover, none the less unpredictable . . .*

The Guardian Angel

by W. A. Darlington

James Carter is always being referred to by journalists as "one of our best-known merchant princes," and everybody who reads the gossip columns of the papers knows that he has a passion for cricket; and so, even if you are not yourself specially interested in cricket, you may remember the excitement that was caused a couple of years back by his sensational hat-trick. The story has been told often, and often been garbled in the telling; but no garbled version is quite so surprising as the truth, now put on paper for the first time.

James is one of the most fortunate of men, not merely because he is rich, but because he is a man of simple and temperate desires, with an unspoilt capacity for enjoyment. He has good health, a delightful wife, and a satisfactory son who, having captained Cambridge at Lord's, is now settling down to do his share in the business.

The chief quality that has brought James his success is a patient persistence which in the end wears down opposition and gets him whatever he wants. But besides this there is an element of luck, which has held steady ever since he became head of the business at his father's death. James himself has never denied this luck, but accepts it in an attractive spirit of humility. He used to have a sentence which had become a formula, through constant use when people tried to flatter him.

"My guardian angel looks after me pretty well," he would say. "I have no complaints."

He does not use that sentence quite so often now.

As a cricketer, James is what is technically called a "keen rabbit." He has one of the finest private grounds in England, and when Barstead Village play their home matches on it James generally turns out for them, and is put on to bowl first—which is less a tribute to his skill than to his benefactions to the club and the fact that the captain is the local grocer and depends on James's custom for a large part of his income. All the same, James has a good natural action, and when he can manage to find a length, has been known to take wickets. And it is generally understood that in his youth he got his Second XI colours at Radford, and would have been in the First if the business had not called him away from school while he was still only seventeen.

Bowling for the Village gives James a thrill far keener than any business triumph could bring with it. But his proudest moment used to come when he took the field at the head of his team in his own big annual match. ("Used to come," I say advisedly; for though "Carter's Match" is still an annual event, James has not played in it himself since the year of his hat-trick.)

This match has become an institution in amateur cricket. To be asked to play in it is accounted an honour in the very highest circles. Even heroes who have appeared for the Gentlemen at Lord's have been known to angle shamelessly for invitations; for James is a discriminating host, and to be asked to stay in his house means that you are something more than a good cricketer.

The sides in the big match are known officially as "Mr. James Carter's XI" and "Mr. Kenneth Carter's XI." Kenneth's side has been nominally Kenneth's ever since, as a preparatory schoolboy whose pads seemed bigger than himself, he was allowed to go in last as an extra batsman, after his mother had stipulated that the bowlers should promise not to hurt him. Later, in all the glory of his Radford First colours, he was promoted to No. 1 in the batting order and made a perfect 32. On leaving school, he took to selecting for himself a team which consisted of Blues in a steadily increasing proportion, till somebody suggested that an appropriate title for the match would be "Gentlemen of England *v*. Combined Universities."

Everybody knew and sympathised with the pride which used to surge through James's breast as he walked on to the field at the head of his magnificent teams. He was never without at least one county captain in the side; and though he never failed to suggest that one or other of these heroes should take command on the field, it stands to their credit that not one of them had ever consented to do so.

But nobody except his wife Margaret, knew that behind James's pride was a deep-seated bitterness. He never forgot that for all the cheerful deference with which his team obeyed him, he was a "passenger" on his own side—so much dead weight which the others must drag along with them. Even in the village team, his place in the batting order was low; here it was uncompromisingly last. His fielding, keen and painstaking, had no dash, no power of anticipation. And he knew well enough that his bowling, even at its best, could present no difficulties to Kenneth's lusty undergraduates.

He knew all this, and he resented it. For far at the back of his mind James cherished a conviction that if fate and his father had not ruled otherwise, he had had it in him to be as good a cricketer as Kenneth.

Old Samuel Carter, James's father, had only consented with the greatest reluctance to his wife's wish that James should be sent to Radford. What was the use, he had asked, of a public school education to a lad in his position? Much better let him go into the business as errand-boy, and work up, instead of wasting his time learning Latin and playing games. Samuel was overruled, but had remained antagonistic. When he heard that James had got into his house cricket eleven, he grunted.

When, next year, James had come home with his Second XI cap, and revealed that one of the masters, an old Oxford Blue, had told him that he was certain of getting his First colours next year, and had hinted at greater things to follow, Samuel had become really alarmed. He removed James from Radford and started him in the business.

In view of his subsequent good fortune, you will see that it is not a sign of triviality in James's character to say that the loss of his school colours had been not merely the chief tragedy of his youth, but the one big disappointment of his life. It still rankled. How deeply it rankled he had realised when Kenneth had written home to say that he had been given his First, and James had felt as much jealousy as paternal pride at the news.

One night in July, 1927, James Carter retired to bed and lay thinking of his match, due in a few days' time.

It seemed likely to be a great success. The ground was in beautiful order, the weather was dry and warm and seemed likely to stay so— though you never could tell, of course. And never before had either he or Kenneth got together such strong sides.

The famous Harry Larborough, captain of England, was playing for James, and all the other nine had either been in that year's team against the Players at Lord's or had been well in the running for places. And Kenneth, having skimmed the cream of two very strong 'Varsity elevens, had a side which was remarkable, if only because it had no tail. Perhaps the least reliable batsman on the side was Pethick, and he had been Number 7 in the Oxford batting order, and had taken 53 of the best off the Cambridge bowling in the big match.

Reflecting sadly that this year he would be even more obviously out of his element than usual, James dropped off to sleep, and dreamed that the match had begun, and that he had put himself on to bowl, and was "running through" Kenneth's team as if they had been schoolgirls.

James had just bowled Thorp, the Cambridge captain, with a ball that broke at right-angles, when a young man with a bright and shining countenance came walking into his dream, pushing it aside as one pushes the two halves of a hanging *portière*, and seated himself easily in mid-air just above the foot of James's bed.

"Good evening," he said pleasantly.

James was less surprised than annoyed at the interruption.

"What can I do for you?" he asked.

The young man laughed.

"Nothing. In fact, that's just what I came to ask you. You see, I'm your guardian angel. I've dropped in to inquire if there's any little extra favour you'd care to ask for."

At the moment the only favour James could think of was that the visitor should leave him to go on with his extremely satisfactory dream, so he said nothing.

"You see," the angel went on, "I've been putting in some pretty hard work, looking after you; and I'm bound to say that you've always shown yourself properly grateful, and given me the credit. Now, that is unusual. Looking after a successful business man is generally about as thankless a job as a guardian angel can get. So I'd like to do you some little extra good turn; by way of what you'd call in the City a bonus. Nothing large, mind—just some little pet scheme you particularly want to bring off."

"Thank you very much," said James.

"Not at all. A pleasure. Think it over and I'll come back again to-morrow night and see what you've decided on."

Suddenly the angel was gone, and James found himself broad awake and staring at the ceiling. The light between the twin beds was still burning, and Margaret—who was in the habit of reading herself to sleep—looked up in surprise, for once James had dropped off he rarely woke again till morning.

"Hallo," she said. "Am I disturbing you?"

"No. It's not that. I say, have I been talking in my sleep or—or anything?"

She shook her head.

"You've been lying on your back, that's all. Turn over and you'll be all right."

She slipped out of bed and settled him comfortably, and he was asleep again almost before she had snuggled down once more to her book.

Next day James tried hard to convince himself that his experience was no more than an ordinary dream; but the memory of his conversation with the angel remained so clear in his mind that it refused to be lightly dismissed. Almost in spite of himself, James found himself making up his mind what favour he would ask, supposing his visitor did return that night.

When bedtime came he found himself in such a state of excitement that sleep seemed impossible to contemplate. He took an aspirin tablet to soothe his nerves, which was a proceeding so unusual with him that Margaret, in mild alarm, forwent her reading and turned out the light at once.

For five minutes or so James tossed uneasily, and had just resigned himself to a wakeful night, when sleep must have leapt upon him suddenly from behind; for there once again was the angel. James sighed with relief. It was true, then!

"Well?" said the angel. "Have you made up your mind?"

"I have."

"Something to do with the business, I suppose?"

"No," said James. "Much easier than that. Something to do with cricket."

The angel's face fell.

"Oh, I see—cricket," he said in a tone of disappointment.

"Why, what's the matter?"

"Well, I'm not very fond of cricket."

"Why not?" James asked in surprise.

"I find it a boring game to watch; and as your guardian angel, I have to watch such a lot of it."

He spoke in the tone of one who at last allows himself to air a long-standing grievance. To James this sounded like rank heresy. An angel, he felt, should have known better.

"It's the finest game in the world," he said warmly.

"Oh, I admit that there may be finer points in it that escape me. But that doesn't alter facts. I find it slow. Give me the excitement and bustle of business every time. . . . If only I were a little less angelic, I'd have put a stop to your cricket long ago. As it is, when you're playing that game, I remove my attention from you so far as my conscience permits."

He stopped, with a sigh for the restraints and obligations imposed upon him by his celestial nature.

"And is that the reason," James asked, "why I have always been successful in business and have never had any luck with my cricket?"

"That's it. In business you've had me behind you. Your cricket has depended on your own unaided efforts."

James thought this over.

"In that case," he said slowly at last, "I think you owe a good turn to my cricket. My annual match begins on Friday, you know."

"Don't I know it!" The angel's voice was weary.

"Well, since you've got to be there anyhow, won't it make it less boring for you to have a part to play in it?"

"Perhaps. What are you leading up to?"

"I want to do the hat-trick."

"What *is* a hat-trick?"

James stifled a sigh.

"A hat-trick," he explained patiently "is when a bowler gets three batsmen out with three consecutive balls. I want to put myself on to bowl in the big match; I shall begin bowling with my cap on, and when I take it off that will be the signal for you to arrange that each of my next three balls takes a wicket. That's all."

"And you mean to say that that will give you more pleasure than a successful plunge in the City?" the angel asked in contemptuous astonishment.

"Much more pleasure."

"Very well, then. There's no accounting for tastes. You bowl the ball and I'll do the rest."

The angel rose to depart.

"One moment," said James. "You know the rules of the game, I suppose? We don't want any mistakes."

"There shall be no mistakes," said the angel. "Good-bye. You won't see me again, but I'm always there." And he walked out of James's consciousness, leaving it full of wild and whirling dreams.

But next morning, with the sun pouring in, and Margaret in the next bed drinking her early cup of tea, James was more than a little inclined to believe that his guardian angel had been only a dream, after all.

All the same, he arrived on the field on the Friday morning with an air of expectancy. His intellect told him he had been dreaming, but something deeper inside him told him he had not. At the back of his mind he was convinced that this year he was going to vindicate himself as a cricketer. For once he would not be a passenger on his own side. At the most critical moment of the match he would put himself on to bowl and would dismiss three first-class batsmen. All he had to do was to deliver three reasonably good-length balls; the angel would do the rest, and thenceforward cricketers would speak of James with a new respect.

Harry Larborough, strolling down on to the field, composed in his mind a tactful formula with which to set aside the suggestion—which he was sure that James would make—that he, Larborough, should act as captain in the match. But he found that the formula would not be necessary, for as he reached the pavilion, James and Kenneth came out together in order to toss for choice of innings. Larborough was surprised, and even a little bit hurt. He did not allow this to appear, for Larborough was a good sportsman and a modest man; and besides, everybody knew how old Carter enjoyed his little hour. Still, his sense of propriety was a little upset that the offer should not have been made. It was due to his position as captain of England.

"Perhaps," he reflected, "the old boy is afraid I should feel bound to accept, and do him out of his fun."

The thought soothed his *amour propre*, and he grinned pleasantly as James came into the dressing-room.

"We bat," he said. "Will second wicket suit you, Larborough?"

"Anywhere you say, skipper," answered the great man in an amiable tone. "Last, if you like."

James laughed.

"Last," he answered, inscribing his own name as he spoke, "is booked."

Of the early part of James's match there is no need to write at any great length. James's glittering side made 200 for three wickets, Larborough getting 80 odd; and then the last batsmen, taking things too light-heartedly, collapsed, and were all out for 253.

Kenneth's side began badly, losing four wickets for 40. Then the solid strength of the side began to tell against tired bowling, and when Kenneth (exercising the unselfish captain's privilege of putting himself in last) had helped Fordyce, the Oxford wicket-keeper, to put on nearly 60 for the tenth wicket, the score was 336. So ended the first day's play.

Next day, James's side took things more seriously, and in spite of the fact that Larborough was caught in the slips before he had scored, and that Peter Graham, the Cambridge fast bowler and Kenneth's bosom friend, had an inspired spell of bowling in which he took four wickets, the innings closed at half-past three for 305, leaving Kenneth's youngsters 223 to get to win and plenty of time to do it.

By tea-time their opening pair, Thorp and Pearson, had made 60 without being parted, and the odds seemed heavily against a win for James and his stalwarts. Tea dissolved the partnership, as so often happens; but Thorp was still in, and the 100 went up for only two wickets. Then the fortunes of the game veered round sharply. P. J. Carruthers, the slow left-hander for whom everybody was prophesying a place in the next Test Match side, suddenly struck his best form. Six men were out for 150, only Thorp being able to play Carruthers with confidence.

"If P. J. keeps this up," said Larborough to James, as they crossed at the end of an over, "we may just win. But I wish young Thorp would get out."

James grunted in a preoccupied way. Now that there were only four wickets to fall, and his great moment was upon him, he began to feel qualms. Suppose the angel had been only a figure in a dream, after all! Suppose he, James, put himself on to bowl now and succeeded only in making a fool of himself—and perhaps lost the game for his side as well!

It was true that if the angel's visit had indeed happened, one over from James at this point would practically settle the match. But supposing there was no angel—and James's intellect told him more clearly every moment that there could be none—it would be madness for James to put himself on now. James had bowled once or twice at the nets to young Thorp, who had hit him all over the place with cheerful indifference; and as for Peter Graham, who had just come in at the fall of the sixth wicket, he was a regular visitor to the house, and James had been bowling to him for years without ever causing him a moment's uneasiness. A single over from James, unaided by celestial power, to either of these two boys might give away 20 runs; and 20 runs at such a moment might make all the difference between victory and defeat.

He dared not take the risk. Dismissing his dream of glory with a sigh, he put on Benson, the steadiest amateur bowler in the country, to keep the runs down at the other end while Carruthers got the wickets.

The cricket became slow and tense. There was still a long time to go before stumps were drawn, for the light would hold till half-past seven if necessary. The score mounted run by run, Thorp batting like the genius he was; Graham grimly keeping up his wicket at first, but batting with increasing confidence as time went on.

A burst of clapping went round the ground as the 200 appeared on the score-board, and five minutes later a tremendous cheer greeted Thorp's century.

"Best knock I've seen this year," said Larborough. "Eh, P. J.?"

And Carruthers, who knew that he had seldom bowled so well to so little purpose, agreed heartily.

As the field crossed over, 210 went up.

"All over now, I'm afraid," Larborough commented to James. "Even if we get one of these out, there's Fordyce, Pethick and Kenneth to come, and only 13 wanted."

James had been so intent upon the immediate problem of the game that he had almost forgotten his own private problem. But Larborough's words brought it home to him that now—now that the game was virtually over—was his real chance.

"I've half a mind to have a bowl myself," said he.

Larborough gave his pleasant grin.

"I should, skipper. Jolly good tactics, as a matter of fact."

With the last ball of his next over Carruthers at last got through Peter Graham's defence. While they were waiting for Fordyce to arrive, James went over to the English captain.

"D'you think I'd better bowl this over after all?" he asked anxiously. "I mean, now Graham's out, there just a chance. . . ."

Larborough shook his head.

"Not a real chance in this world," he said. "What we want now is a miracle, not bowling. And when it comes to miracles you're as likely to work 'em as the next man."

After which prophetic utterance, he moved to his place at cover, while James, feeling more frightened than he had ever felt in his life, settled his famous old Radford Second XI cap on his head, measured his run, and prepared to deliver the ball to Thorp.

A trickle of clapping, led by James's colleagues in the village team, went round the field as it was realised that the owner of Barstead Hall was about to bowl, but it was accompanied by an almost visible slackening of tension. So long as Carruthers and Benson were bowling, there was always a hope that something sensational might happen; but if Mr. Carter had put himself on, then obviously all was over. People began, unobtrusively, to gather their belongings together.

James began his run. If only, he thought, he could get Thorp out without the angel's help, his cup of joy would be full. He would not remove his cap until he must.

He delivered the ball. In the class of cricket in which James generally played it was not a bad ball. It pitched on the leg stump a little—but only a little—short of a good length. An orthodox batsman in village cricket would have treated it with respect. Thorp shifted his right foot across the wicket and cracked the ball to the leg boundary with delightful ease. Nine runs were now wanted to give Kenneth's side the match.

Obviously, it was no good giving Thorp anything on the leg side. James bowled again. This time it was to the off, but the length was no better than before. Thorp's left leg came across with the precision of a machine; and Larborough retrieved the ball, after a hunt, from under a car which was parked beside a remote wall.

Five runs wanted.

James waited for the ball to be returned to him. Then, wondering whether the angel would recognise the signal agreed upon—or, indeed, if there were any angel to recognise it—he took off his cap, and handed it to the umpire.

"Means business, this time!" Kenneth remarked to Peter Graham in the pavilion.

James trotted up to the wicket. But this time, partly from nerves, partly from the fact that his mind was occupied with wondering whether or not anything out of the way was about to happen, he lost all control of the ball, which slipped from his hand and ballooned up into the air—the simplest full-pitch to leg that any batsman could pray for.

"Hit it!" called Kenneth involuntarily.

Thorp did hit it. The ball, cleanly struck in the middle of the bat, soared up and up, flew clean over the pavilion and fell into the middle of a clump of trees.

There was that curious sound that happens when everybody in a gathering of people says "Oo!" at the same moment. And then a roar of cheering went up for the biggest hit that had ever been made on the Barstead ground—and the winning hit of the match, at that.

But suddenly the cheering died away, as it was seen that Thorp was walking out—walking out, not in company with his partner as having won the match, but alone, and with a rueful grin on his face; while the fielders had gathered round James and were obviously "ragging" him for having taken a good wicket with one of the worst balls ever seen on a cricket field.

In their astonishment people forgot to applaud Thorp's gallant century. He reached the pavilion in an almost unbroken silence.

"What happened, John?" said Kenneth, rummaging in his bag for the pads he had not expected to need.

"Trod on my wicket. Most extraordinary thing. I've never lost my balance like that before."

"Rotten luck to get out for a hit like that," said Pethick on his way to the pitch.

"My own silly fault, I suppose," answered Thorp, and disappeared into the dressing-room while Kenneth called out in stentorian but mocking tones, "Well bowled, father!"

James waved his hand, and tried to look as if he were enjoying the joke as much as anybody; but he was not amused. He had no doubt, now, of his guardian angel's existence; and he had to admit that the angel had shown a good deal of ingenuity in making so brilliant a batsman as Thorp get out to such a ball. But there was an unsportsman-like flavour about getting a batsman out by pushing him on to his stumps which offended James. He realised now, too late, that he ought to have instructed the angel to make him bowl three balls of superlative merit and so take his three wickets worthily. But the angel (who knew, as he had confessed, nothing about the finer points of the game) would naturally see no greater merit in any one way of getting a man out than in any other. James saw that unless he could manage, by his own unaided skill, to bowl two reasonably good balls to the two remaining batsmen, his heaven-sent hat-trick might easily make him a laughing-stock instead of a hero.

Pethick was now taking guard, and James prepared to bowl. Thoroughly demoralised, he ran up to the wicket, and in his eagerness to avoid another full pitch, hung on to the ball far too long. The ball, with about as much life in it as an insufficiently poached egg, flopped on to the pitch a little beyond half-way, gave a couple of feeble hops, and trickled slowly towards the batsman's wicket. Pethick eyed it contemptuously. Then he lifted his bat to smite it. Then he decided that it wasn't worth smiting and brought his bat down again to stop it.

But just before it reached the ball, Pethick's bat seemed to hesitate just long enough for the ball to trickle under it and bump gently into the middle stump. For a second or so it seemed that its force had not been enough to break the wicket; then one of the bails flew off with surprising velocity as though it had been flicked off by an unseen hand.

"Good God!" said Larborough in the purest astonishment. The trickling grub is a ball which not seldom proves deadly when small girls

198

of tender years play one another on the seashore, but it is not often bowled in first-class cricket, and still less often does it take a wicket.

Pethick gazed in stupefaction at his stumps and then at his bat, and bowed his head in shame and departed, blushing hotly. James blushed even more hotly, but nobody was tactless enough to look at him. And nobody laughed.

Kenneth came in, with determination written all over him. The very set of his shoulders as he took guard said that there was to be no more of this nonsense. There were two balls of James's over to go, and five runs wanted to win. Kenneth knew exactly what his father's bowling was like, and he was confident of his ability to get the necessary runs off the two balls, and so prevent any possibility of Carruthers having another over and defeating Fordyce.

But Kenneth knew nothing about the angel.

James delivered the ball; and Kenneth seeing that it was the simplest of half-volleys, stepped out and let drive. Humanly speaking, it was a certain four; but as he made the stroke the blade of the bat cracked clean across, and the ball rose gently in the air and fell into the hands of Carruthers at mid-off.

The match was over. James and his side had won a sensational victory; but nobody felt moved to cheer, and there was a general sense that anybody who dared to congratulate James on his achievement would be asked to leave Barstead by the next train. The players moved quietly off the field, talking in hushed tones as though somebody had met with a serious accident.

There was still no laughter; but James knew that that would come later, and it did. And when it came, it continued, and spread, and went on spreading. In a thousand country houses and clubs and cricket pavilions the story was told, with any embroideries that happened to occur to the teller as he went along. The gossip-writers of the Press had each his version, and the nation at large became aware of James as the bowler who, by performing the worst hat-trick ever known on the cricket-field, had turned a fine sporting finish into a complete anti-climax.

There was no hope, after this, that James could ever be taken seriously as a cricketer. Men smiled reminiscently at the very sight of him, and he had to learn to look as if he too enjoyed his notoriety; and only Margaret knew how far from enjoyment his real feelings were.

Next year, when his big match came round, James did not play. He handed over the management of his team to Harry Larborough.

He himself put on a white coat and acted as umpire. It gave him a grim satisfaction to feel that his guardian angel was thus still compelled to look on at the game whose finer points he had failed so signally to understand.

Lord Dunsany – or Edward John Moreton Drax Plunkett, 18th Baron Dunsany (1878–1957) to give him his full title – was one of those larger-than-life Irish figures about whom legends abound. He was an explorer and big-game hunter in Africa, a chess champion and once dubbed 'the worst dressed man in Ireland'. He fought in the Boer War and the First World War, was wounded in the Irish Easter Rebellion in 1916, and narrowly escaped imprisonment in Greece in the Second World War. He was also a prolific poet, dramatist and writer, particularly in the areas of humour and fantasy fiction, and he is widely credited as being the 'father of the invented fantasy world in short story form'. In all he wrote over 60 volumes, each and every one composed in typically eccentric manner with a quill pen!

Yet another of Dunsany's obsessions was cricket, at which he excelled. According to W. P. Hone, author of Cricket in Ireland (1955), Dunsany stood 6ft 2ins tall and was a good bowler who 'favoured fast full pitches aimed at the top of the stumps and calculated to upset the morale of rural batsmen'. He batted left-handed, had a good eye, and his favourite shot was a wide sweep to leg. From 1898 onwards, Dunsany organised regular games in the grounds of his castle in County Meath, cutting the wicket from a green pasture field! His love of practical jokes also extended to cricket, as W. P. Hone has told us: 'In the tent which was pitched at the edge of the pasture, he kept a clockwork duck which he used to send waddling out to meet any incoming batsman who had failed to score!' Alec Waugh relates a similar story about the eccentric nobleman: 'I never saw him play,' he wrote a few years back, 'but in 1938 when J. B. Priestley organised for charity a rag match played with a soft ball between Actresses and Actors, Dunsany arrived in an impressive blazer, carrying a heavy and well-worn bag, to treat the proceedings with an unsmiling solemnity, as though he was taking part in a real match. He was the one person on the ground who not only behaved like a cricketer, but looked like one!' Dunsany endowed this sense of humour to his most amusing character, Jorkens, a sardonic raconteur who tells the most outrageous

201

and often hilarious stories to a group of cronies in the Billiards Club. Several of these stories feature cricket – including 'The Devil in the Willows' and 'The Unrecorded Test Match' – but I have plumped for 'How Jembu Played For Cambridge' (1931) both for its amusement and because in it Dunsany mixes cricket with the foreign climes with which he was also, of course, familiar . . .

How Jembu Played for Cambridge

by Lord Dunsany

The next time that Murcote brought me again to his Club we arrived a little late. Lunch was over, and nine or ten of them were gathered before that fireplace they have; and that talk of theirs had commenced, the charm of which was that there was no way of predicting upon what topics it would touch. It all depended upon who was there, and who was leading the talk, and what his mood was; and of course on all manner of irrelevant things besides, such as whiskey, and the day's news or rumour.

But to-day they had evidently all been talking of cricket, and the reason of that was clearer than men usually seem to think such reasons

203

are. I seemed to see it almost the moment that I sat down; and nobody told it me, but the air seemed heavy with it. The reason that they talked about cricket was that there was a group there that day that were out of sympathy with Mr. Jorkens; bored perhaps by his long reminiscences, irritated by his lies, or disgusted by the untidy mess that intemperance made of his tie. Whatever it was it was clear enough that they were talking vigorously of cricket because they felt sure that that topic if well adhered to must keep the old fellow away from the trackless lands and the jungles, and that, if he must talk of Africa, it could only be to some tidy trim well-ordered civilised part of it that he could get from the subject of cricket. They felt so sure of this.

They had evidently been talking of cricket for some time, and were resolute to keep on it, when shortly after I sat down amongst them one turned to Jorkens himself and said, "Are you going to watch the match at Lord's?"

"No, no," said Jorkens sadly. "I never watch cricket now."

"But you used to a good deal, didn't you?" said another, determined not to let Jorkens get away from cricket.

"Oh yes," said Jorkens, "once; right up to that time when Cambridge beat Surrey by one run." He sighed heavily and continued: "You remember that?"

"Yes," said someone. "But tell us about it."

They thought they were on safe ground there. And so they started Jorkens upon a story, thinking they had him far from the cactus jungles. But that old wanderer was not kept so easily in English fields, his imagination to-day or his memory or whatever you call it, any more than his body had been in the old days, of which he so often told.

"It's a long story," said Jorkens. "You remember Jembu?"

"Of course," said the cricketers.

"You remember his winning hit," said Jorkens.

"Yes, a two wasn't it?" said someone.

"Yes," said Jorkens, "it was. And you remember how he got it?"

That was too much for the cricketers. None quite remembered. And then Murcote spoke. "Didn't he put it through the slips with his knee?" he said.

"Exactly," said Jorkens. "Exactly. That's what he did. Put it through the slips with his knee. And only a leg-bye. He never hit it. Only a leg-bye." And his voice dropped into mumbles.

"What did you say?" said one of the ruthless cricketers, determined to keep him to cricket.

"Only a leg-bye," said Jorkens. "He never hit it."

"Well he won the match all right," said one, "with that couple of runs. It didn't matter how he got them."

"Didn't it!" said Jorkens. "Didn't it!"

And in the silence that followed the solemnity of his emphasis he looked from face to face. Nobody had any answer. Jorkens had got them.

"I'll tell you whether it mattered or not, that couple of leg-byes," said Jorkens then. And in the silence he told this story:

"I knew Jembu at Cambridge. He was younger than me of course, but I used to go back to Cambridge often to see those towers and the flat fen country, and so I came to know Jembu. He was no cricketer. No no, Jembu was no cricketer. He dressed as white men dress and spoke perfect English, but they could not teach him cricket. He used to play golf and things like that. And sometimes in the evening he would go right away by himself and sit down on the grass and sing. He was like that all his first year. And then one day they seem to have got him to play a bit, and then he got interested, probably because he saw the admiration they had for his marvellous fielding. But as for batting, as for making a run, well, his average was less than one in something like ten innings.

"And then he came by the ambition to play for Cambridge. You never know with these natives what on earth they will set their hearts on. And I suppose that if he had not fulfilled his ambition he would have died, or committed murder or something. But, as you know, he played for Cambridge at the end of his second year."

"Yes," said someone.

"Yes, but do you know how?" said Jorkens.

"Why by being the best bat of his time I suppose," said Murcote.

"He never made more than fifty," said Jorkens, with a certain sly look in his eye as it seemed to me.

"No," said Murcote, "but within one or two of it whenever he went to the wickets for something like two years."

"One doesn't want more than that," said another.

"No," said Jorkens. "But he did the day that they played Surrey. Well, I'll tell you how he came to play for Cambridge."

"Yes, do," they said.

205

"When Jembu decided that he must play for Cambridge he practised at the nets for a fortnight, then broke his bat over his knee and disappeared."

"Where did he go to?" said someone a little incredulously.

"He went home," said Jorkens.

"Home?" they said.

"I was on the same boat with him," said Jorkens drawing himself up at the sound of doubt in their voices.

"You were going to tell us how Jembu played for Cambridge," said one called Terbut, a lawyer, who seemed as much out of sympathy with Jorkens and his ways as any of them.

"Wait a moment," said Jorkens. "I told you he could not bat. Now, when one of these African natives wants to do something that he can't, you know what he always does? He goes to a witch doctor. And when Jembu made up his mind to play for Cambridge he put the whole force of his personality into that one object, every atom of will he had inherited from all his ferocious ancestors. He gave up reading divinity, and everything, and just practised at the nets as I told you, all day long for a fortnight."

"Not an easy thing to break a bat over his knee," said Terbut.

"His strength was enormous," said Jorkens. "I was more interested in cricket in those days than in anything else. I visited Jembu in his rooms just at that time. Into the room where we sat he had put the last touches of tidiness: I never saw anything so neat, all his divinity books put away trim in their shelves, he must have had over a hundred of them, and everything in the room with that air about it that a dog would recognise as foreboding a going away.

" 'I am going home,' he said.

" 'What, giving up cricket?' I asked.

" 'No,' he answered and his gaze looked beyond me as though concerned with some far-off contentment. 'No, but I must make runs.'

" 'You want practice,' I said.

" 'I want prayer,' he answered.

" 'But you can pray here,' I said.

He shook his head.

" 'No, no,' he answered with that far-away look again.

"Well, I only cared for cricket. Nothing else interested me then. And I wanted to see how he would do it. I suppose I shouldn't trouble about it nowadays. But the memory of his perfect fielding, and his keenness for the one thing I cared about, and his tremendous ambition, as it seemed to me then, to play cricket for Cambridge, made the whole thing a quest that I must see the end of.

" 'Where will you pray?' I said.

" 'There's a man that is very good at all that sort of thing,' he answered.

" 'Where does he live?' I said.

" 'Home.'

"Well it turned out he had taken a cabin on one of the Union Castle line. And I decided to go with him. I booked my passage on the same boat; and, when we got into the Mediterranean, deck cricket began, and Jembu was always bowled in the first few balls even at that. I am no cricketer, I worshipped the great players all the more for that; I don't pretend to have been a cricketer; but I stayed at the wickets longer than Jembu every time, all through the Mediterranean till we got to the Red Sea, and it became too hot to play cricket, or even to think of it for more than a minute or two on end. The equator felt cool and refreshing after that. And then one day we came into Killindini. Jembu had two ponies to meet us there and twenty or thirty men."

"Wired to them I suppose," said Terbut.

"No," said Jorkens. "He had wired to some sort of a missionary who was in touch with Jembu's people. Jembu you know was a pretty important chieftain, and when anyone got word to his people that Jembu wanted them, they had to come. They had tents for us, and mattresses, and they put them on their heads and carried them away through Africa, while we rode. It was before the days of the railway, and it was a long trek, and uphill all the way. We rose eight thousand feet in two hundred miles. We went on day after day into the interior of Africa: you know the country?"

"We have heard you tell of it," said someone.

"Yes, yes," said Jorkens, cutting out, as I thought, a good deal of local colour that he had intended to give us. "And one day Kenya came in sight like a head between two great shoulders; and then Jembu turned northwards. Yes, he turned northwards as far as I could make out; and travelled much more quickly; and we came to nine thousand feet, and forests of cedar. And every evening Jembu and I used to play stump cricket, and I always bowled him out in an over or two; and then the sun would set and we lit our fires."

"Was it cold?" said Terbut.

"To keep off lions," said Jorkens.

"You bowled out Jembu?" said another incredulously, urged to speech by an honest doubt, or else to turn Jorkens away from one of his interminable lion-stories.

"A hundred times," said Jorkens, "if I have done it once."

"Jembu," some of us muttered almost involuntarily, for the fame of his batting lived on, as indeed it does still.

"Wait till I tell you," said Jorkens. "In a day or two we began to leave the high ground: bamboos took the place of cedars; trees I knew nothing of took the place of bamboos; and we came in sight of hideous forests of cactus; when we burned their trunks in our camp-fires, mobs of great insects rushed out of the shrivelling bark. And one day we came in sight of hills that Jembu knew, with a forest lying dark in the valleys and folds of them, and Jembu's own honey-pots tied to the upper branches.

"These honey-pots were the principal source, I fancy, of Jembu's wealth, narrow wooden pots about three feet long, in which the wild bees lived, and guarded by men that you never see, waiting with bows and arrows. It was the harvest of these in a hundred square miles of forest that sent Jembu to Cambridge to study divinity, and learn our ways and our language. Of course he had cattle too, and plenty of ivory came his way, and raw gold now and then; and, in a quiet way, I should fancy, a good many slaves.

"Jembu's face lighted up when he saw his honey-pots, and the forest that was his home, dark under those hills that were all flashing in sunlight. But no thought of his home or his honey-pots made him forget for a single instant his ambition to play for Cambridge, and that night at the edge of the forest he was handling a bat still, and I was still bowling him out.

"Next day we came to the huts of Jembu's people. Queer people. I should have liked to have shown you a photograph of them. I had a small camera with me. But whenever I put it up they all ran away.

"We came to their odd reed huts.

"Undergrowth had been cleared and the earth stamped hard by bare feet, but they did not ever seem to have thinned the trees, and their huts were in and out among the great trunks. My tent was set up a little way from the huts, while Jembu went to his people. Men came and offered me milk and fruit and chickens, and went away. And in the evening Jembu came to me.

" 'I am going to pray now,' he said.

"I thought he meant there and then, and rose to leave the tent to him.

" 'No,' he said, 'one can't pray by oneself.'

"Then I gathered that by 'pray' he meant some kind of worship, and that the man he had told me of in his rooms at Cambridge would be somewhere near now. I was so keen on cricket in those days that anything affecting it always seemed to me of paramount importance, and I said 'May I come too?'

"Jembu merely beckoned with his hand and walked on.

"We went through the dark of the forest for some few minutes, and saw in the shade a great building standing alone. A sort of cathedral of thatch. Inside, a great space seemed bare. The walls near to the ground were of reed and ivory: above, it was all a darkness of rafters and thatch. The long thin reeds were vertical, and every foot or so a great tusk of an elephant stood upright in the wall. Nuggets of gold here and there were fastened against the tusks by thin strands of copper. Presently I could make out that a thin line of brushwood was laid in a wide circle on the floor. Inside it Jembu sat down on the hard mud. And I went far away from it and sat in a corner, though not too near to the reeds, because, if anything would make a good home for a cobra, they would. And Jembu said never a word; and I waited.

"Then a man stepped through the reeds in the wall that Jembu was facing, dressed in a girdle of feathers hanging down from his loins, wing feathers they seemed to be, out of a crane. He went to some sort of iron pot that stood on the floor, that I had not noticed before, and lifted the lid and took fire from it, and lit the thin line of brushwood that ran round Jembu. Then he began to dance. He must have been twelve or fifteen feet from Jembu when he began to dance, and he danced round him in circles, or leapt is a better word, for it was too fierce for a dance. He took no notice of me. After he had been dancing some time I saw that his circles were narrowing; and presently he came to the line of brushwood at a point that the fire had not reached, and leapt through it and danced on round Jembu. Jembu sat perfectly still, with his eyes fixed. The weirdest shadows were galloping now round the walls from the waving flames of the brushwood; and any man such as us must have been sick and giddy from the frightful pace of those now narrow circles that he was making round Jembu, but he leapt nimbly on. He was within a few feet of my friend now. What would he do, I was wondering, when he reached him? Still Jembu never stirred, either hand or eyelid. Stray leaves drifting up from the dancing savage's feet were already settling on Jembu. And all of a sudden the black dancer fainted.

"He lay on the ground before Jembu, his feet a yard from him, and one arm flung out away from him, so that that hand lay in the brushwood. The flames were near to the hand, but Jembu never stirred. They reached it and scorched it: Jembu never lifted a finger, and the heathen dancer neither moved nor flinched. I knew then that this swoon that he had gone into was a real swoon, whatever was happening. The flames died down round the hand, died down round the whole circle; till only a glow remained, and the shadow of Jembu was as still on the wall as a black bronze image of Buddha.

"I began to get up then, with the idea of doing something for the unconscious man, but Jembu caught the movement, slight as it was, although he was not looking at me; and, still without giving me a glance of his eye, waved me sharply away with a jerk of his left hand. So I left the man lying there, as silent as Jembu. And there I sat, while Jembu seemed not to be breathing, and the embers went out and the place seemed dimmer than ever for the light of the fire that was gone. And then the dancing man came to, and got up and bent over Jembu, and spoke to him, and turned; and all at once he was gone through the slit in the reeds by which he had entered the temple. Then Jembu turned his head, and I looked at him.

" 'He has promised,' he said.

" 'Who?' I asked.

" 'Mungo,' said Jembu.

" 'Was that Mungo?' I asked.

" 'He? No! Only his servant.'

" 'Who is Mungo?' I asked.

" 'We don't know,' said Jembu, with so much finality that I said no more of that.

"But I asked what he had promised.

" 'Fifty runs,' replied Jembu.

" 'In one innings?' I asked.

" 'Whenever I bat,' said Jembu.

" 'Whenever you bat!' I said. 'Why! That will get you into any eleven. Once or twice would attract notice, but a steady average of fifty, and always to be relied on, it mayn't be spectacular, but you'd be the prop of any eleven.'

"He seemed so sure of it that I was quite excited; I could not imagine a more valuable man to have in a team than one who could always do that, day after day, against any kind of bowling, on a good wicket or bad.

" 'But I must never make more,' said Jembu.

" 'You'll hardly want to,' I said.

" 'Not a run more,' said Jembu, gazing straight at the wall.

" 'What will happen if you do?' I asked.

" 'You never know with Mungo,' Jembu replied.

" 'Don't you?' I said.

" 'No man knows that,' said Jembu.

" 'You'll be able to play for Cambridge now,' I said.

"Jembu got up from the floor and we came away.

"He spoke to his people that evening in the firelight. Told them he was going back to Cambridge again, told them what he was going to do there, I suppose; though what they made of it, or what they thought Cambridge was, Mungo only knows. But I saw from his face, and from theirs, that he made that higher civilisation, to which he was going back, very beautiful to them, a sort of landmark far far on ahead of them, to which I suppose they thought that they would one day come themselves. Fancy them playing cricket!

"Well, next day we turned round and started back again, hundreds of miles to the sea. The lions. . ."

"We've heard about them," said Terbut.

"Oh well," said Jorkens.

But if they wouldn't hear his lion-stories they wanted to hear how Jembu played for Cambridge: it was the glamour of Jembu's name after all these years that was holding them. And soon he was back with his story of the long trek to the sea from somewhere North of a line between Kenya and the great lake.

He told us of birds that to me seemed quite incredible, birds with horny faces, and voices like organ-notes; and he told us of the cactus-forests again, speaking of cactus as though it could grow to the size of trees; and he told us of the falls of the Guaso Nyero, going down past a forest trailing grey beards of moss; there may be such falls as he told of above some such forest, but we thought more likely he had picked up tales of some queer foreign paradise, and was giving us them as geography, or else that he had smoked opium or some such drug, and had dreamed of them. One never knew with Jorkens.

He told us how they came to the coast again; and apparently there are trees in Mombasa with enormous scarlet flowers, that I have often seen made out of linen in windows of drapers' shops, but according to him they are real.

Well, I will let him tell his own story.

"We had to wait in that oven" (he meant Mombasa) "for several days before we could get a ship, and when we got home the cricket season was over. It was an odd thing, but Jembu went to the nets at once, and began hitting about, as he had been doing in the Red Sea; and there was no doubt about it that he was an unmistakable batsman. And he always stopped before there was any possibility that he could by any means be supposed to have made fifty.

"I talked to him about Mungo now and then but could get nothing much out of him: he became too serious for that, whenever one mentioned Mungo, and of the dancing man in the temple I got barely a word; indeed I never even knew his name. He read divinity still, but not with the old zest, so far as I could gather whenever I went to see him, and I think that his thoughts were far away with Mungo.

"And as soon as May came round he was back at cricket; and sure enough, as you know, he played for Cambridge. That was the year he played first; and you have only to look at old score books to see that he never made less than forty-six all that year. He always got very shy when he neared fifty: he was too afraid of a four if he passed forty-six, and that was why he always approached it so gingerly, often stopping at forty-seven, though what he liked to do was to get to forty-six and then to hit a four and hear them applauding his fifty. For he was very fond of the good opinion of Englishmen, though the whole of our civilisation was really as nothing to him, compared with the fear of Mungo.

"Well, his average was magnificent; considering how often he was not out, it must have been nearly eighty. And then next year was the year he played against Surrey. All through May and June he went on with his forty-seven, forty-eight, forty-nine and fifty; and Cambridge played Surrey early in July. I needn't tell you of that match; after Oxford v. Cambridge in 1870, and Eton v. Harrow in 1910, I suppose it's the best-remembered match in history. You remember how Cambridge had two runs to win and Jembu was in with Halket, the last wicket. Halket was their wicket-keeper and hardly able to deal with this situation; at least Jembu thought not, for he had obviously been getting

212

the bowling all to himself for some time. But now he had made fifty.
With the whole ground roaring applause at Jembu's fifty, and two runs
still to win I laid a pretty large bet at two to one against Cambridge.
Most of them knew his peculiarity of not passing fifty, but I was the
only man on the ground that knew of his fear of Mungo. I alone had seen
his face when the dancing man went round him, I alone knew the terms.
The bet was a good deal more than I could afford. A good deal more.
Well, Jembu had the bowling, two to win, and the first ball he stopped
very carefully; and then one came a little outside the off stump; and
Jembu put his leg across the wicket and played the ball neatly through
the slips with his knee. They ran two, and the game was over. Jembu's
score of course stayed at fifty, no leg-byes could affect that, as anyone
knows who has ever heard of cricket. How could anyone think otherwise? But that damned African spirit knew nothing of cricket. How
should he know, if you come to think of it? Born probably ages ago in
some tropical marsh, from which he had risen to hang over African
villages, haunting old women and travellers lost in the forest, or
blessing or cursing the crops with moods that changed with each wind,
what should he know of the feelings or rules of a sportsman? Spirits like
that keep their word as far as I've known: it was nothing but honest
ignorance; and he had credited poor Jembu with fifty-two though not a
ball that had touched his bat that day had had any share in more than
fifty runs.

"And I've learned this of life, that you must abide by the mistakes of
your superiors. Your own you may sometimes atone for, but with the
mistakes of your superiors, so far as they affect you, there is nothing to
do but to suffer for them.

"There was no appeal for Jembu against Mungo's mistake. Who
would have listened to him? Certainly no one here: certainly no one in
Africa. Jembu went back to see what Mungo had done, as soon as he
found out the view that Mungo had taken. He found out that soon
enough, by dropping back to his old score of one and nothing in three
consecutive innings. The Cambridge captain assured him that that
might happen to anybody, and that he mustn't think of giving up
cricket. But Jembu knew. And he went back to his forest beyond Mount
Kenya, to see what Mungo had done.

"And only a few years later I came on Jembu again, in a small hotel in
Marseilles, where they give you excellent fish. They have them in a

little tank of water, swimming about alive, and you choose your fish and they cook it. I went there only three or four years after that match against Surrey, being in Marseilles for a day; and a black waiter led me to the glass tank, and I looked up from the fishes, and it was Jembu. And we had a long talk, and he told me all that had happened because of those two leg-byes that had never been near his bat.

"It seems that a tribe that had never liked Jembu's people had broken into his forest and raided his honey-pots. They had taken his ivory, and burnt his cathedral of thatch, and driven off all his slaves. I knew from speeches that he had made at Cambridge that Jembu in principle was entirely opposed to slavery; but it is altogether another matter to have one's slaves driven away, and not know where they have gone to or whether they will be well cared for. It was that that broke his heart as much as the loss of his honey-pots; and they got his wives too. His people were scattered, and all his cattle gone; there was nothing after that raid left for Jembu in Africa.

"He wandered down to the coast; he tried many jobs; but Mungo was always against him. He drifted to Port Said as a stowaway, to Marseilles as a sailor, and there deserted, and was many things more, before he rose to the position of waiter; and I question if Mungo had even done with him then. A certain fatalistic feeling he had, which he called resignation, seemed to bear him up and to comfort him. The word resignation, I think, came out of his books of divinity; but the feeling came from far back, out of old dark forests of Africa. And, wherever it came from, it cheered him awhile at his work in that inn of Marseilles, and caused him to leave gravy just where it fell, on the starched shirt-front that he wore all day. He was not unhappy, but he looked for nothing better; after all, he had won that match for Cambridge against Surrey, I don't see what more he could want, and many a man has less. But when I said good-bye to him I felt sure that Mungo would never alter his mind, either to understand, or to pardon, those two leg-byes."

"Did you ask him," said Terbut, "how Mungo knew that he got those two leg-byes?"

"No," said Jorkens, "I didn't ask him that."

Though the marvellous humorist Sir Alan Herbert (1890–1971) – 'A.P.H.' to his friends – was a great admirer of cricket, he could not bear the almost religious fervour with which it was treated by some people. 'I am all for cricket,' he once said, 'as long as it is not represented to be a superior branch of religion. I cannot accept that it is the nurse of noble character, and the school for saints. It is a tough and terrible, rough, unscrupulous, and ruthless game.' He did, though, still love it, and in pieces like 'Bitter Sweet: or Not Cricket' and 'The Fathers' Match' he mixed his affection with a certain leavening of gentle sarcasm. He even spoke about his own achievements on the field in the same manner. 'I was first bowler for my private school,' he wrote a few years ago, 'and time and again I used to get my 7 wickets. I bowled very slowly and cunningly in the style afterwards adopted by Laker and Lock. But in my young days things were very different. We did not have all this ritual nonsense about the New Ball. We got along with the old ball till someone hit it over the railway!' A.P.H.'s finest cricketing moment probably came during his time as an MP when he played for the Commons against the Lords at the Oval and scored 13. 'I remember to this day,' he said many years later, 'the dashing stroke that ended the innings, a drive through the covers that was caught by third man. I also once made 53, top score, in a literary match, and to my great surprise hit a 6 over the screen.' From 1924, Sir Alan was, in fact, a member of the Punch *staff, and apart from creating essays and poems for the magazine, also wrote a series of novels and several comic operas for the theatre. He was never happier in his writing – or more amusing – than when making fun of the news or of public affairs. I have taken just such an instance for inclusion here. In 1936 he composed the following story for* Punch *which was introduced with this remark: 'We hear that a film is now in preparation in Hollywood which depicts a cricket match in England. More remarkable still, we present below the story of a cricket match in Russia. It is based upon a well-known play by Vlov or somebody, brought up to date by a member of the OGPU and translated by our Mr. Haddock.'*

Cricket in the Caucasus
Or, The Volga Batman
by A. P. Herbert

I

'I tell you what it is, Andrey Andreyevitch,' said Stepan Papushkin impatiently, 'if the cricket competition does not soon begin it will be dark before it is finished. And then, you know, we shall be hampered by the wolves.'

'What is the hurry?' replied the old man, chewing grass. 'I am too drunk to umpire yet. Natalya Popova cannot find the bats. And, besides, the young men have not yet settled the dispute about the teams.'

'Sometimes,' replied the other passionately, 'I think I see the stars in your old eyes, Andrey Andreyevitch; and sometimes I do not understand you.'

Stepan Pepushkin was a poet. He wore a peaked cap and black knickerbockers. He was eager for the new game, which would bring

217

back poetry to the village, the Commissar had said. 'How can there be a dispute among brothers?' he cried.

'Well, you see, it is perfectly simple,' said the old umpire. 'I think I can stand now. I will get up. What a disgusting creature I am to be drunk on Wednesday! And Olga Merinin says the harvest will be late. What was I saying, Stepan Stepanovitch?'

'You were raving quietly,' replied the young man. 'There is Natalya, carrying the two bats like torches over her shoulders. How beautiful she is!'

'The young men are quarrelling. Boris Borisovitch has emptied the whitewash pail over Lopakhin; and now we shall have no crease. But all this is highly intelligible when you come to think of it.'

'If I were to kill Maria Andreyevna,' said the poet dreamily, 'would you marry again?'

'Excuse me, the trouble is that our village has been collectivized under the Decree. Everything is in common. We are all in common. We are all brothers. Naturally, therefore, say the young men, we cannot have two teams of brothers playing against each other, for there can be nothing brotherly in trying to get the better of one another. But the Commissar has a paper from Moscow. He says there must be two teams of eleven, each with a captain; but the young men will not have captains. It is all rather unpleasant. I think I shall lie down again.'

'Eleven is a beautiful number,' said the poet. 'Two ones. Two ones— two captains—two bats of forest wood. Some day, Andrey Andreyevitch, I shall go to London where this beautiful game was thought of.'

But the old man was asleep.

Stepan Pepushkin walked over to the debate of the young men. He went straight up to Natalya Popova and kissed her. 'Will you marry me?' he said loudly, because of the noise of the speakers, many of whom were talking in common. She had very brown eyes, like a small cow in springtime. She wore a Tartar skirt and knee-pads for the wicket.

'I think I am engaged to some of the others,' she said. 'Besides, you are a poet, Stepan, and there is no place for poetry now. We should have no food.'

'If I were to write in prose,' said the young man, 'would you love me?'

'Prose is more respectable, to be sure,' said Natalya Popova, 'but, excuse me, every one is active and vigorous now, ploughing and making grain for the State or combating the counter-revolutionaries. You are only a dreamer; Olga Merinin told me she found you feeding nightingales in the wood. What is the use of that when Russia is starving, Stepan Pepushkin? To-day, to take an example, the Committee will not let you take part in the batting. They have appointed you to count the runs. I tell you what is in my mind, Stepan; I am sorry I let you kiss me.'

Stepan smiled dumbly and listened to the speakers.

'Comrades,' shouted Serge Obolensky, the humane slaughterer, 'the solution is evident. We cannot have two hostile teams competing against each other, for this would be to play into the hands of the Capitalist Governments, which seek to divide the workers. But we can all play on the same side.'

'*Pravda!*' 'Well spoken, Serge!' '*Yashmak!*' cried the cricketers.

Big Lubov, the bearded schoolmaster, came to the rostrum carrying a stump. 'I have a proposition.'

'*Nitchevo!*' '*Chuchuk!*' 'A proposition!'

'My proposition is that all runs should be shared in common.

'*Pravda!*' '*Yashmak!*' 'All runs to be shared in common!'

But Bortsov, the Commissar, stepped forward. 'I have a paper from Moscow. At Moscow they say that you are idle; the grain lies unreaped, the bins are empty.'

'*Tchai!*' '*Merovestia!*' cried the angry villagers.

'Moscow says that the will to compete and act energetically must be born again in you. Therefore they have given you this cricket which the English workers play. Therefore you must have two teams striving for victory, and therefore each worker shall keep his own runs, striving to gain more than his comrade.'

'Kill the Commissar!' cried every one. 'Capitalism!' 'The counter-revolution!'

'I will kill the Commissar!' yelled Big Lubov the schoolmaster. 'Give me a bat, Natalya Popova,' he said in a softer voice; for Big Lubov loved Natalya.

'There are only two bats,' said the girl, 'and they must be restored to the Government after the game. It would be a pity to break them.'

'*Pravda!*' said Lubov; and he drove the sharp stump which he carried through the Commissar's heart.

'And now let us begin the game,' said the schoolmaster.

219

II

'Now that we have killed the Commissar,' Serge Obolensky was saying, 'we have no one who can explain the rules of cricket. But Russia is like that.'

'Who wants rules?' said young Nicolai Nicolaievitch. 'Rules were made for the bourgeois.'

'*Pravda*. True. But, excuse me, it would be convenient if we could come to some agreement about the method of our proceedings. To take an example, Nicolai Nicolaievitch, we know that there are two sets of stumps, for the Commissar told us so much; but where in the world are we to put them?

'It is simple enough, Serge Obolensky. We will put one set here and the other over there.'

'Yes, Nicolai,' replied the older man patiently; 'but where?'

'There.'

'I recognize the energy of your mind, Nicolai—but how far away?'

'Give me the Commissar's paper. Twenty-two yards—that is versts. *Cuculin!*' said the young revolutionary in triumph.

'No one in the village can throw a leather ball so far. I tell you what, we will let each man bowl according to his capacity. The strong man shall throw from a great way off and the weak from a little distance. Thus we shall establish equality. Big Lubov, to take an example, must throw at the batsmen from the next field, and I shall throw from here.'

'But,' said the young cynical clerk of the bank, 'suppose that the strong man pretends to be weak, then he will have an advantage.'

'Then,' said Serge Obolensky simply, 'we shall kill him.'

III

Big Lubov and Natalya Popova were still batting. All the village had bowled the round ball at them, some from this place and some from that. None of the peasants had hit them. Big Lubov defended his body nimbly with his great bat. But the young men did not like to throw the ball at pretty Natalya. They threw it away from her, so that she could not strike it with her bat. So it came about that Lubov had gained seven runs, but pretty Natalya had made none.

Old Volodja's best cow lay in the shade watching the game. Dreamily, sitting on the cow, Stepan Pepushkin wrote the runs in his book. He thought that Natalya was like a tulip.

'Ho, Stepan!' Big Lubov cries, 'how goes the count?'

'Lubov—9 runs,' answers the poet; 'Natalya Popova—7 runs.'

'*Nitchevo!* How is this? Not once has Natalya struck the ball.'

'From time to time I give her a run,' said the poet, 'because she is so beautiful.'

'*Yashmak!*' At first Big Lubov was angry. But he loved Natalya and he shrugged with good temper. When Big Lubov shrugged it was like a storm on the hills. Trees fell down.

'Besides,' said Serge Obolensky cunningly, 'since all the runs are to be shared in common, Lubov Lubovinsky, the question has no significance. Strictly speaking, the count is Lubov—8; Natalya—8.'

'*Botsch!*' shouted the schoolmaster angrily. 'No man or woman shall take *my* runs!' For Lubov had begun to enjoy the cricket, and the will to win was in his great heart, which was shaped like a pear.

'You are a *molak*, Lubov!' cried Nicolai Nicolaievitch. 'Run-hog! *Menshevik!*'

'Bowl, thou,' replied the big man with a threatening motion, 'or I will bat thee.'

Presently Lubov had made 13. Stepan gave Natalya two more runs because of the pretty curve of her waist, which was like the prow of a small ship. Natalya Popova was 9.

Then Alexis the blacksmith took the ball.

Lubov cries out: 'Ho! blacksmith, you come too close! Stand yonder by Obolensky in the farther field!'

But Alexis throws the ball strong and low and strikes the school-master in the stomach.

'*Yashmak!*' 'Hit!' 'Lubov is out!' cry the peasants.

'The blow was irregular,' cries the batsman angrily. 'He came too near. What is the verdict, Andrey Andreyevitch?'

All eyes turned to the aged umpire. But the umpire was still asleep.

'He is drunk,' said Serge Obolensky.

'I tell you what,' said Lubov, 'is it not a very extraordinary thing that all the time, while we have been playing this game, the umpire was lying drunk at the place called square-leg, and none of us perceived it?'

'Russia is like that,' said Serge Obolensky. 'My father's sister kept beetles in her bedroom and fed them on sunflower seeds. Nobody knew.'

'Practically speaking,' the schoolmaster remarked logically, 'the game, so far, has not been happening, for the official, in a manner of speaking, was not present. It follows therefore that I am still batting.'

'In that case,' said the cunning Nicolai, 'you have not made 13 runs, but no runs.'

'*Pravda!*'

Lubov weakened. He thought that none of the peasants would make so many as 13 runs.

'Besides, as you will be the first to appreciate, Lubov Lubovinsky, this umpire is only a mouthpiece for the voice of the people. Indubitably he is incapable; but what of that? The voice of the people has said that you are out.'

'Out!' 'Out!' '*Slava!*'

Lubov with a bad grace gave up the bat, saying, 'As for you, Andrey Andreyevitch, to-night I will give you to the wolves'.

The old man woke. 'The queer thing is, brother,' he said, 'that I have forgotten your name.'

'Russia is like that,' said Serge Obolensky.

'I have just remembered,' said Big Lubov unpleasantly, 'that I have a pistol in my breeches pocket. If any brother or comrade makes more than 13 I will shoot him through the head.'

IV

All the peasants batted in turn and were thrown out. Boris Polunin was stunned. Michael Andrid ran away. Only Natalya Popova remained always at the stumps. Natalya had 11 runs; but Stepan would not give her any more now for fear of Big Lubov's pistol. Alexis the blacksmith had made 7. The others had made nothing. Meanwhile Big Lubov had become exceedingly dogmatic and unpopular. When the last man was out he said, 'Well, it must be evident to all of you that Lubov Lubovinski has gained the victory'.

The angry shouts of the villagers drowned his speech; and Alexis the blacksmith said, 'Excuse me, the affair is not concluded. Stepan Pepushkin has not yet tried his skill.'

'*Pravda!*' 'Stepan!' 'Pepushkin the poet will put the schoolmaster down.'

They summoned Stepan to the stumps, and gave the ball to Nicolai

Nicolaievitch. The young poet was overjoyed to be batting with Natalya. On his way to the stumps he took her in his arms and kissed her.

'Your hair is like the wild jasmine which grows in the Caucasus,' he said. 'Now, Natalya, if I am not mistaken, you are going to see that I am not a dreamer only.'

Nicolai prepared to throw, but the poet stepped forward, lifting his hand. 'Excuse me, Nicolai Nicolaievitch,' he said, 'but, do you know, this is a highly significant moment? Here am I, a young man who never in his whole life has played with bat and ball before. I have never been clever with my hands. At carpentry and needlework I was the duffer of my school. I never could knit or tie up parcels. Truly, I don't know any one so clumsy with his fingers. I am always dropping my tea-cup, upsetting things, pushing things over. As you see, Nicolai, I am quite unable to tie my cravat in a presentable bow. The only tool I was ever able to use was a lead pencil. And yet——'

'Pardon my abruptness, Stepan Pepushkin,' said Nicolai, 'but if you are going to relate to us the history of your life it seems to me that the fieldsmen had better sit down.'

'That is as you please, Nicolai Nicolaievitch.' And all the peasants sat down on the grass.

'As I was saying,' the batsman continued, 'the extraordinary thing is that here I am with this really most unfamiliar instrument in my hands, and, do you know, I am superbly confident? I am absolutely convinced that I am going to succeed in the game, and gain more runs than this blustering schoolmaster. Is it not remarkable?'

'*Pravda*,' said the bowler, yawning slightly.

'The reason for all this is, I think, perfectly evident. It is Natalya—Natalya Popova, standing there with her Government bat like a torch of a new truth. Now that the Union of Soviet Republics has inscribed cricket upon its advancing banners I think you will agree that we shall conquer the world. Cricket was the one thing that Holy Russia lacked. Cricket will save Russia. Cricket——'

'Excuse me,' said Serge Obolensky, rising to his feet at mid-off; 'night is falling, Stepan Pepushkin; the grass is wet with dew, and I perceive that wolves are gathering at the borders of the field. It would be convenient to most of us if we could continue the game.'

'By all means,' answered the poet. 'But do you know, in spite of my confidence it has now occurred to me that men are but mortal and the future is uncertain? It is just possible that Nicolai Nicolaievitch will kill me with the ball. Permit me therefore to embrace Natalya Popova before we begin.'

'Naturally, Stepan Pepushkin.'

This ceremony concluded, the poet prepared to defend himself. Nicolaievitch threw the ball very hard at his head. Stepan put his bat before his face, and the ball, touching it, flew into the forest, scattering the wolves.

'Run, Natalya Popova!' cried the poet, and they ran.

Old Volodja, the long-stop, was fat and slow. They ran nine runs.

The ball was carried back at length, and Stepan, panting, faced Nicolaievitch again.

Big Lubov stepped forward. 'I tell you what,' he bellowed, 'I have just realized that all this business is simply a waste of time. When you come to think of it, there are crops to be garnered, cattle to be tended, cows to be milked. The moon is rising, and here we all are throwing a leather ball at Stepan Pepushkin. Is it not preposterous? What in the world does it matter, I ask myself, whether Stepan gains more runs than Lubov or not? Naturally it is most unlikely that he will overcome me; but will the State be any the better for it if he does? Andrey Andreyevitch is asleep again. Let us all go to the village and drink *tchai*.'

'What you say is extremely reasonable,' said Serge Obolensky, 'but, excuse me, you should have said it before. It is evident that Stepan Pepushkin has a talent for the game, and it would not surprise me if he were to overcome you.'

'*Pravda!*' '*Yashmak!*' cried the peasants, who hated the school-master.

Nicolaievitch threw the ball at Pepushkin's face a second time. The poet struck the ball towards the wood.

'Run, Natalya!'

'I run, Stepan. Do thou run also!'

A big wolf runs out of the wood and takes the ball in its mouth.

'Run, Volodja! The wolf has the ball. Follow and help him, Boris Borisovitch!'

The wolf runs into the wood. Volodja runs after the wolf. Boris Borisovitch runs after Volodja. Serge Obolensky runs after Borisovitch. Alexis the blacksmith runs after Obolensky. Olga Merinin runs after Alexis. Nicolai Nicolaievitch runs after Olga Merinin. The other peasants follow; and last of all, Andrey Andreyevitch, waking up, totters into the wood, where the wolves devour him with the others.

Only Big Lubov remains in the field, watching with a sour smile while Stepan and Natalya run up and down, hand-in-hand, between the stumps. Stepan has made two-hundred-and-ninety-four. Out of breath, he pauses; Natalya folds her strong arms about him.

'You are a true man, Stepan Pepushkin,' she whispers. 'We will go to Moscow together and make fly-papers for the Government.'

But Big Lubov has picked up the Commissar's paper.

'It is all very well,' he says spitefully, 'but, do you know, Pepushkin, we were playing without the bails? Moscow says that without the bails the game does not exist.'

Natalya wept.

'After all, then, Stepan, I find that I do not love you.'

'Russia is like that,' said Stepan Pepushkin.

For many people the funniest account of a village cricket match is that which occurs in A. G. Macdonell's famous book, England, their England, *published in 1933 and a delight to anthologists ever since. I debated seriously for some time about including the match in these pages – because it is a classic of its kind – but decided against it finally because it is so readily available and probably familiar to many of my readers. And also because I had something else of A. G. Macdonell's up my sleeve – an absolutely delightful retelling of Charles Dickens' classic story of the match between Dingley Dell and All-Muggleton which he wrote especially in 1936 to commemorate the one-hundredth anniversary of the publication of* Pickwick Papers. *It has never been reprinted and I think you may well find it almost as funny as the original, though certainly a great deal less well-known! Archibald Gordon Macdonell (1895–1941) was, in fact, a Scot having been born in Aberdeen, though it is likely he came to understand and depict the English character so well as a result of his education at Winchester and subsequent life in the South of England where he watched cricket regularly and played it occasionally. He was described as a player 'who might not make many runs, but would chase the ball with vigour and would certainly heighten any team's morale.' It was as a result of his experiences with a team of authors that he wrote the story of that match in* England, their England, *featuring several of his friends, thinly disguised, as the cricketers. Here, in not dissimilar fashion, he gives another innings to Dickens' redoubtable players. (As a matter of interest, there was a Pickwick Cricket Club in Birmingham in the 1880s which played on a field near Pershore Road and had a team of 'some note' according to one account. The side also boasted a fast bowler named, appropriately, Sam Tallboys, who was 'a rather diminutive, fat man who could, however, sling a wicket right when equipped with a ball' to quote the same report!)*

Dingley Dell v. All-Muggleton

by A. G. Macdonell

It was a fortunate circumstance that, on the occasion of the grand match between the cricket team of the corporate town of Muggleton and the representatives of the hamlet of Dingley Dell, there should have been present on the ground, by pure chance, at least one person who understood the game of the cricket both in its subtleties and in its noble essentials. For, with the exception of this one fortuitous spectator, and possibly, just possibly, one other, there does not seem to have been anyone else on the Muggleton ground that day, either bowler or batsman, umpire, captain, fieldsman, or onlooker, who understood more than the rudiments of the pastime. I say it is just possible that there was one other who may have appreciated the finer points, at any rate of village cricket, and, as he can be discussed and dismissed in a moment, I will get him out of the way without more ado.

Mr. Snodgrass, in order to make conversation at the breakfast-table after the unfortunate shooting-accident to Mr. Tupman—and making conversation at that table after that accident was no light matter, for Mr. Pickwick, with doubt and distrust exhibited in his countenance, was silent and reserved—inquired of Mr. Wardle whether he was a cricketer.

"I was once upon a time," replied the host; "but I have given it up now. I subscribe to the club here, but I don't play."

Now it cannot be pure chance that Mr. Wardle should have compressed into four short sentences the whole duty of the country landlord towards the sport of his tenantry and of his farmering neighbours. Mr. Wardle must have known, instinctively, through centuries of inherited squiredom, that every squire must have a legendary fame for prodigious feats on the pitches of long-ago, must on no account hazard that fame among a generation that was unborn when he was laying on the wood, and must subscribe to the Club.

Let us allow, then, to Mr. Wardle at least a knowledge of rural etiquette, and also a legendary fame. For whenever a squire is known to have been a cricketer in the days before the memory of all except a few greybeards, it is an axiom that he was an exceptionally fine player.

But the real expert upon the Muggletonian ground was, of course, Mr. Alfred Jingle. Mr. Jingle had a remarkably wide experience of cricket. Not only had he played the game, on his own admission, some thousands of times, but he appears to have been many years ahead of Lord Hawke in popularising the game in the West Indies. He also was responsible for the introduction of several interesting innovations into the rules, especially of the single-wicket game, a variation of cricket which has been unhappily allowed to sink into comparative desuetude in our times. For instance, it was Mr. Jingle who introduced the idea of starting a match at the cool hour of 7 a.m., an example which, if it had been followed during that unfortunate season not so long ago when some very distinguished players discovered, apparently for the first time, that cricket is played with a hard ball, might have averted much imperial bad temper.

It was Mr. Jingle, again, who first organised relays of fieldsmen—six at a time—to replace casualties. It is a pity that this magnificent conception should have been whittled down in a modern cricket to the provision of an occasional substitute, but I have no doubt in my own mind that it has been directly responsible for some of the manlier aspects of American football, a game in which the quick succeed to the dead in bewildering succession. Nor was Mr. Jingle parochially-minded. There was no narrow snobbery about him. Realising, long before his time, the immense value of organised games in welding together this heritage of ours into a happy empire, Mr. Jingle encouraged the West Indian natives not only to play cricket, but even to participate in matches with the ruling classes, including Colonel Sahibs, and it is hardly an exaggeration to say that Constantine and Headley are spiritual descendants of that great-hearted Quanko Samba who literally bowled himself to death. As for Mr. Jingle's own personal skill, I have searched all the records in vain for a score which exceeds his famous West Indian record of five hundred and seventy runs in one completed innings, mostly compiled with a seriously-blistered bat, and so far as I know it still holds the field for the single-wicket game. Indeed, it held the field for all classes of cricket including Matches against Odds, Smokers *v.* Non-Smokers, and Ladies *v.* Gentlemen (with broomsticks), until it was finally surpassed in 1899 by A. E. J. Collins at Clifton College with his 628 not out for Clarke's House *v.* North Town.

This, then, was the redoubtable cricketer who happened, by a lucky chance, to be present at the Muggleton ground on the day of the grand match.

Of course, from the outset Mr. Jingle had no illusions about the class of performance he was about to witness. It was not exactly the sort of thing he was accustomed to, but there is something in the very soul of cricket which creates an atmosphere of gentle, genial tolerance, and the greatest of players can be happy upon the humblest of greens. Thus Mr. Jingle saw at a glance that this was to be no desperate encounter such as the match between the Parish of Farnham (with Felix given) and All-England, but an occasion of social festivity regardless of the final markings of the scorers. Unerringly, therefore, he cast his eye over the luncheon arrangements (he had previously done the same office for the dinner to be held at the Blue Lion after the match), knowing well that if they were defective the social basis of the match would disintegrate. A gloom has been cast over more than one pleasant game by the presence of beef but absence of mustard, or vice versa. But here everything was in order, with rounds of the one and cartloads of the other, and the rigour of the play and the appearance of the players were at once relegated in his mind to a status of minor importance. The latter, indeed, must have appeared unusual to an experienced eye. The holder of the single-wicket record of the Empire could seldom have played his big matches against opponents who looked like amateur-stonemasons, or who were so prodigiously stout that they looked like gigantic rolls of flannel elevated on a couple of inflated pillowcases. Nevertheless Mr. Jingle's comments were wise and illuminating. He first summed up the game itself in six profound words. "Capital game"—for those who have the art to play it as a game of skill; "Smart sport," even for those who, sons of a sporting race, are compelled by the tenuity of their resources to look like amateur stonemasons; and, because your true cricketer's charity is inexhaustible, there are two words of kindly encouragement for those who look like the gigantic rolls of flannel and have neither skill at the game nor smartness at the sport, "Fine exercise."

From this brilliant, generous, and epigrammatic description of the pastime, Mr. Jingle at once turns to the players. He has only just formed their acquaintance; he feels instinctively that by his standards they are not expert cricketers; their clothes are unlike the clothes of Lord's. But they are cricketers and that is enough for him. "Splendid fellows—glorious," he cries, and one feels that any man, "be he ne'er so vile," so long as he is a devotee of cricket, is to Mr. Jingle a splendid and glorious fellow.

It need hardly be supposed that the one-sided nature of the grand match escaped such an expert eye. Mr. Jingle had not yet visited Dingley Dell, but he was not likely to be misled into thinking that it was a corporate town like its opponent, with mayor, burgesses, and freemen, taking a zealous part in high affairs, now petitioning the High Court of Parliament against the continuance of this, now against any interference with that, possessing corn-factors and fire-agencies, and, although sometimes addicted to torpor, at others nevertheless holding the strongest views on Simony and Sunday-trading. Mr. Jingle was hardly such a simpleton as to believe any such thing, and it is more than likely that he admired the Davidian courage of the tiny hamlet as much as he must have secretly deplored the slightly—shall we say—unsporting action of Muggleton in still further weighting the scales against its tiny adversary by recruiting its forces not only from the corporate town proper, but from the outlying districts, suburbs, and surrounding farms as well. (At least, that is how I read the circumstance that the team was called, not simply Muggleton, but All-Muggleton.)

But whatever Mr. Jingle felt on these matters, as on certain others that arose during the course of the match, he very wisely held his peace.

The spin was made for choice of innings, and Fortune, favouring as usual the big battalions, came down on the side of All-Muggleton, who very naturally elected to bat first. The wicket was hard, for there had been no rain for some time, and the Muggletonians, though mere townees, were sufficiently versed in weather lore to know that the sun, darting his bright beams since early morning, would long since have dried up the dew, which otherwise, had it still been glistening on every leaf as it trembled in the gentle air, might have made the fast bowling fly awkwardly.

The opening pair of batsmen were a Mr. Podder, known throughout the entire district as a pretty warm man in anything connected with Real Estate, and a Mr. Dumkins, both citizens born and bred of the town. And before we go any further, a word about this latter gentleman might not be out of place. Mr. Dumkins was a remarkable character. Still young enough to be one of the two best batsmen in the town, he was old enough to be regarded by his fellow-citizens as an authentic village, or rather town, Hampden. No generous cause ever appealed to him in vain; no defence of liberty, right, or privilege ever found Mr. Dumkins shirking from the barricades; and once he had set his hand to a task, he carried it through to the end with such inflexible determination that the word passed into general currency, and Dumkins for Determination became a famous tag. There were many citizens of Muggleton who could have told you that in their hour of misgiving and despair, the name of Dumkins, or, better still, a word of encouragement from his lips, had given them fresh inspiration and fire with which to resume the fight. I make no doubt whatever that five years after this cricket-match, Mr. Dumkins was carrying the torch of Reform with all the bulldog tenacity with which he carried his bat.

This, then, was the redoubtable pair which made its way to the wickets, and the grand match began.

It was fortunate indeed that the famous stranger was so imbued with the broad charity of cricket, for outwardly he showed no sort of astonishment at the proceedings which now unrolled themselves before him.

No sooner had the All-Muggleton pair taken up their positions at the wickets, than the Dingley Dell captain issued the strangest instructions. For he deputed his champion player, a Mr. Luffey, to bowl to Mr. Dumkins, and his second bowler, a Mr. Struggles, to bowl to Mr. Podder. Now this can only mean that the Dingley Dellers were not accustomed to deliver the ball in sequences of four, five, six, or even eight balls from the same end (each sequence forming what is called an "over"), and that, furthermore, they did not anticipate that their opponents would score in anything but twos, fours, or sixes. For imagine the confusion that would ensue if a stroke was played by which an odd number of runs was notched. If Podder scored a single off Struggles, the run would bring him to the wicket that faced Luffey. But Luffey's task was to bowl to Dumkins. Luffey would, therefore, have to cross over and change places with Struggles. But, then, whose turn would it be to bowl? This was confusion bad enough at the very beginning. Worse was to follow. The umpires, whether they were vague about their duties or whether they were bewildered by the bowling tactics of the Dingley Dellers, instead of taking post one at the bowler's end and the other at square-leg, both stood behind the wickets.

Now Mr. Jingle, veteran of thousands of matches, knew as well as his neighbour that an umpire behind the wickets at the bowler's end is admirably placed for a clear view of the proceedings over which he is to preside, but that an umpire standing behind the wickets at the batsman's end is not only in grave physical danger, but must seriously incommode the wicket-keeper in the execution of his duties. Mr. Jingle, to his great credit, preferred to make no comment upon these arrangements, but rather to concentrate, as a connoisseur should, upon the virtuosity of the play itself.

The fieldsmen were stationed at their several posts, the scorers sat alertly with knife and stick in one of the two marquees, the best place in the whole field, and Mr. Luffey polished the ball ominously against his right eyelid. Then, without waiting for the umpire at the bowler's wicket to open the match with his ceremonious "Play!" Mr. Luffey suddenly performed that office himself and simultaneously delivered a fast, dead-straight yorker or low full-pitch—the point will be argued in a moment—as nasty a ball as any batsman could hope for at the very beginning of an innings. I must hasten to add that I am not for one moment ascribing to Mr. Luffey's account any sort of sharp practice in this explosive opening. I am merely recording the facts. In any case it mattered little either way so far as the actual game was concerned, for Mr. Dumkins, wary and alert, was no more to be caught napping by a cricket-ball than by an illegal blocking of a right-of-way or the enclosure of a piece of common land.

Now as to that first ball. It was fast and straight, and Mr. Dumkins was only able to hit it with the very end of his bat. That sounds as if it must have been a yorker. On the other hand, the ball flew off the bat upwards and travelled for a considerable distance, an occurrence that is extremely rare off a yorker, if not almost unprecedented. It is more likely, then, that the ball was a low full-pitch, and that Mr. Dumkins mishit it off the end of his bat over the heads of the slips—the slips being, I think, the only group of fieldsmen which fits the narrative. For it will be observed that the ball flew over the heads of more than one man, and that it was moving so fast that they had not time to spring up from their professional crouch in order to intercept it. (I dismiss with scorn the suggestion that Mr. Luffey was bowling to a leg-side field, with four short-legs clustering round the batsman's elbow, the only other formation which would fit the text.) Let us conclude, therefore, that the stroke was a snick over the slips which a little more activity by those gentlemen might well have converted into a catch, and that Mr. Dumkins was very lucky not to be out first ball, either clean-bowled or caught. Two runs were notched by this indifferent shot, and the prudent batsmen were in no way flustered by the conflicting shouts and useless advice of their supporters.

A few minutes later it was the turn of Mr. Struggles to try to succeed where all other neighbouring bowlers had failed that year, and bring to an end the remarkable series of not-out innings wherewith Mr. Podder had garnished the laurels of himself and of Muggleton's season. For it is clear that when a batsman is chronicled in the description of a match as "hitherto unconquered" before he has received so much as a single ball, the phrase can only refer to the earlier matches of the year (for I think we may dismiss as pedantry the suggestion that the chronicler contemplated that Mr. Podder might be run out off the first ball that Mr. Dumkins received. Indeed it is more than pedantry. It is out of character. The champion of liberal causes would never allow a partner to be involved in a catastrophe which he himself did not share, nor would the cautious man of property have accepted such a risk).

Mr. Struggles advanced to the attack, and soon found that Mr. Podder was a very irritating customer. It was not that he was especially dexterous as a batsman. Quite the reverse. But he had developed to an extraordinary degree of efficacy the peculiarly unorthodox style which is almost universal upon the village grounds of to-day. That is to say, whenever a ball was bowled to him about which he was doubtful—or as the modern phrase has it, by which he was caught in two minds—he blocked it, either by chopping sharply down upon it, I imagine, or simply by not moving his bat at all. On the other hand, when Mr. Struggles tempted him with a bad ball, with a long-hop, perhaps, for a snick to the wicket-keeper, or with a full-pitch to leg for a catch on the boundary, Mr. Podder's repertory of strokes was so limited that, try as he might, he could not get his bat close enough to the ball even to snick it. But when it came to a good ball, a ball turning, let us suppose, sharply from the off-stump to the leg-stump or one that swung outwards and late, Mr. Podder took it and sent it flying to all parts of the field. We all know those batsmen who send the good balls flying to all parts of the field. On the offside, the execution is done with the edge of the bat, mostly through the slips and past third-man, with an occasional hit that pitches to the right of cover-point's right hand and spins very suddenly and obliquely across his front and past his left hand. On the leg-side, the deadly work is pursued by converting the bat into a scythe and sweeping every ball round to leg, with the right knee on the ground. Many a match has been won or lost in a very few minutes by a batsman of this calibre, and Mr. Podder, hitherto unconquered throughout the season, mind you, was no mean exponent of this style.

Nor was this all that the bowlers had to contend with. The ground-fielding was slovenly and at least one (not counting the possible chance off the first ball of the day) comparatively simple catch was missed. The ball was travelling hard, it is true, but it was head-high and straight to the fieldsman, and the bowler was entitled to expect that the fieldsman at least would get a hand to it. Instead of which he never even touched it, and he thoroughly deserved the indignant "Now, butterfingers," with which the august spectator stigmatised his incompetence.

For although Mr. Jingle had courteously refrained from commenting upon some of the arrangements and strategy of the rustic play, he did not feel himself similarly debarred from a discussion of the points of the game as it proceeded. (This habit of maintaining a running commentary upon a cricket-match in progress is very popular, I understand, in the outlying portions of our Empire, and it is certain that Mr. Jingle must have picked it up in the Antilles.) Hence his exclamation of "Now, butterfingers" when the slim fieldsman allowed the catch to strike him on the nose and bound pleasantly off with redoubled violence. But although Mr. Jingle's high standards did not allow him to pass unblamed bad attempts to catch the ball or failures to stop it, still less did his generous nature allow him to pass unpraised any piece of work which might even remotely be described as a good stroke, and his applause rang out frequently. Needless to say, his obvious satisfaction and approval on these latter occasions were highly gratifying to the parties concerned, coming as they did from such an excellent judge.

Meanwhile Mr. Dumkins and Mr. Podder were laying on vigorously, and the half-century had been passed for the first wicket, in spite of numerous changes of bowling, before the partnership was broken. Dumkins was the first to go, a catch being held at last, and then, shortly afterwards, a belated triumph fell to the Dingley Dell bowlers when the colours of the redoubtable Podder were hauled down on appeal to the umpire. For the man of property, flown with success, sprang out of his crease at a ball, probably one of Struggles's worst, missed it as usual, and was stumped.

But although the score was now fifty-four for two wickets, which is vastly better for the fielding-side than fifty for no wickets, it is not surprising that the Dingley Dellers wore a somewhat blank expression on their faces.[1] Any score over fifty is a good score on a village ground for a whole team, and there were still eight more All-Muggletons to be disposed of. Messrs. Luffey and Struggles refused to give up hope, and fought on eagerly and enthusiastically. But the advantage was too great to be recovered. Dingley Dell batted, were compelled to follow on, and, although they saved the innings defeat, nevertheless were beaten by a handsome margin very early in the fourth innings. But there is small doubt that the losers were consoled, as the winners were delighted, by Mr. Jingle's final verdict, "Capital game—well played." Then, as if to fill their cup to overflowing, the great and generous man added— perhaps with a silent prayer to Heaven for forgiveness: "Some strokes admirable."

1 By a curious error or misunderstanding, the chronicler records that at this point in the match the Dingley Dellers had failed to score. They had, of course, not yet batted.

The grand match was over. Stumps were drawn. The company straggled off in the evening sun to the Blue Lion Inn, where they sat down to a hearty cold supper, with the usual accompaniments of such occasions, speeches, toasts, and songs.

The party broke up at a late hour, and another cricket-match had gone to join the shades.

One last word. So little did Mr. Pickwick understand what was going forward on the green at Muggleton, that, many months later, when he befriended Mr. Alfred Jingle and paid his passage back to the West Indies, he actually advised him to give up cricket altogether. Mr. Jingle, although overcome with emotion at the moment, retained sufficient presence of mind to make no promises, and I have no doubt that his anxiety to earn money to repay the fifty pounds and more which Mr. Pickwick had laid out on his behalf was stronger than his regard for his benefactor's advice, and that, immediately on landing at Demerara, he turned professional.

During the years of the Second World War, the indominatable English still managed to continue playing cricket despite the efforts of Herr Hitler to put a stop to such activities. Often, though, they had to play in very difficult conditions, and occasionally in the most unlikely places – as the following story so amusingly illustrates. The author was Ian Hay (1876–1952), the masterful writer of comic novels and stage plays, who after a distinguished career in the First World War (in which he won the Military Cross) was appointed director of Public Relations at the War Office from 1938 to 1941. Hay became a keen all-round cricketer while at Fettes and Cambridge, and when he returned to his old school as a language master played a considerable part in coaching a successful School XI. This love of the game came through in several of his stories including Pip *(1907) and* Housemaster *(1936). He apparently played less and watched more when, later, he became a full-time writer. The story here, 'French Cricket', written in 1940, amusingly recounts how one group of cricket enthusiasts in war-torn France manage to satisfy their craving for a game – albeit in the most unusual circumstances!*

French Cricket

by Ian Hay

"*C'est un jeu fort difficile à comprendre,*" was Madame's comment to the Colonel, who stood with his Adjutant on a slope overlooking the ground.

The terrain was limited by slag-heaps which hemmed it in on three sides, the fourth being the bank of a canal, into which the ball was occasionally driven.

It was, however, the only open space available in the near neighbourhood and, in spite of tall grass concealing frequent rocks, the smoothest.

The Colonel agreed with Madame, not only because it has been ordained that our troops should try to sink their insularity and learn the language of the country, but because she was the owner of the local estaminet and of that one plot of land where cricket—of a kind—could be played. He compiled a careful sentence.

"*C'est un jeu tout à fait anglais,*" he explained.

"*Sans doute,*" replied Madame tersely, adding, possibly with sympathetic intention: "*enfin, il faut s'occuper de quelquechose.*"

Turning towards the house, she admonished Henri, who had

advanced his nine-year-old person, as she considered, too close to a danger zone.

"'Owzat!" he remarked in reluctant retreat, "roull out ze barrel!"

His mother, uncertain of the meaning of these quotations but suspicious of their moral tone, sent him indoors.

Meanwhile "A" Company, despite difficulties, had replied creditably to "C" Company's formidable 52 with 38 for six.

In case these figures seem to challenge the adverb and adjective employed, certain details must be pointed out: firstly, that much of the ground was covered with tall grass; secondly, that the pitch so discouraged pad-play that "A" Company's one county batsman had been carried off on a stretcher for his orthodoxy; thirdly, that the vegetation covered small boulders which, while tripping up the fieldsmen, were themselves no mean opposition to anything that did not clear the carpet.

One such obstruction, situated in a particularly dense patch of grass at mid-on, had earned quite a reputation as twelfth man.

Muscular drives bounded back from the impact with a rocky echo, till the oaths of the batting side were only equalled by the applause of the field.

Seldom had the rustic policy of "bloomin' 'ard, bloomin' 'igh, and bloomin' hoften" been better vindicated than on that nameless pasture.

Stylists, applying the lessons of the text-book, were utterly lost.

Their drives were checked a few feet from the bat; their forward defensive strokes ended in futility, their back-play in fatality.

But the adaptable Philistine flourished.

His cross-bat scored magnificently over the heads of the slips, his ballooners were missed by floundering fieldsmen, and his innings when it ended was quite probably worth a triumphant dozen or so.

Prominent in this school was Company-Quartermaster-Sergeant Blinder, who survived while three of his partners fell to the bumpers of Corporal Plugg.

Nerves and fortune failed them, but the Q.M.S. contrived, by thrice lifting a ball on his leg-stump over cover-point, to raise the score to fifty when the last man came in.

"Touch and go," remarked the Colonel.

"More go than touch," replied the Adjutant, "if Wyndham gets the bowling."

"Well, he hasn't—yet," said the Colonel; "it's the last ball of the over."

"And three to win," said the Adjutant. "I expect Blinder will take a chance."

As that player had been doing nothing else since he first came to the crease, it seemed a fairly safe conjecture. And it proved correct.

Removing himself as far as possible from the threatened line of the ball, and closing both eyes, possibly in prayer, the hope of "A" Company struck a violent blow for victory.

He hit the ball (a miracle in itself) with the middle of the bat, but somewhat early—"a premature," as the Colonel put it—so that, instead of leaving the neighbourhood for the enemy's trenches, it soared a stupendous height over mid-on.

"Run it!" roared "A" Company. And they ran.

Two fieldsmen started for the catch, but neither of them succeeded in keeping his feet over those execrable contours, and the batsmen had started for a second run before the ball came to earth.

Its manner of doing so was dramatic.

With a resounding crack it struck the centre of the obstructive clump and, rebounding on to the pitch, was gathered by the wicket-keeper, who whipped off the bails with both men half-way across.

"C" Company's astounding triumph roused the vocal efforts of both sides. Madame recognised the psychological moment and came out to see whether there might be a sale for *vin blanc*, while Henri took advantage of the occasion to escape from the house and mingle with the crowd.

"It was twelfth man who did it," said the Adjutant, nodding at the spot.

"It must be a regular mountain," said the Colonel, moving across to inspect.

Madame passed him with a full tray.

"*Ça, monsieur?*" she queried, "*mais c'est là depuis trois mois. C'est un obus qui n'a pas éclaté.*"

"What!" exlaimed the Colonel. "Be careful," he added, as the Adjutant parted the grass, disclosing an enormous dud shell.

Both men looked at *la patronne*.

"*Mais pourquoi, Madame,*" began the Adjutant, "*pourquoi . . .*"

His French failed him.

243

Madame understood, however. "*Pourquoi n'ai-je rien dit? A quoi bon, monsieur? Votre jeu de Cricket est plus dangereux que mille obus. Je ne le comprends pas, mais je vois bien que vous avez le sang-froid anglais. Un obus pour vous alors—c'est une bagatelle!*"

And she moved away with that expressive shrug which indicates a logical woman's inability to understand school-boys.

No such problems appeared to exist for Henri.

"'Owzat!" he was yelling to victors and vanquished alike, "roull out ze barrel!"

The Second World War provided an introduction to cricket for many American and Canadian servicemen who were posted 'over here'. And doubtless it puzzled a great many of them as much as American Football does English viewers. Several of our literary cricketers have made determined efforts over the years to introduce their transatlantic cousins to the game, and it is an abiding sadness to me that James Thurber, who was taken to a game at Lord's in 1938 by Francis Meynell, did not write about his experience. All we do know is that he found the game (a thrilling test match between England and Australia) 'very amusing' and drew a parallel between cricket and 'the match game I once played at Bleeck's with Wolcott Gibbs and John O'Hara'. Asked to elaborate by his host, Thurber explained that Bleeck's was a small bar in New York and the match game was 'a complicated and expensive form of gambling on the contents of a matchbox'! Francis Meynell also commented, 'I think Thurber enjoyed himself, but there was one thing I couldn't get him to see – that in cricket a draw is a result!' A Canadian humorist who did develop a passion for the game was Stephen Leacock (1869–1944) who considered he had something of a mission to explain cricket to North Americans! This fact comes as less of a surprise when one learns that Leacock's mother was a member of the Butler family of Hampshire and one of her forebears had lived at Hambledon and been intimately involved in the beginnings of the game on Broadhalfpenny Down. Leacock, who wrote of Hambledon as being 'to people who love the game, as Mecca is to a Mohammedan', actually possessed copies of some of the earliest scoresheets from games played on the Down. His inspiration – and qualifications – for writing the following amusing piece in 1942 are therefore clearly established. (Other examples of Leacock on cricket, incidentally, are to be found in his books, Our British Empire and My Discovery of England, and an anthology edited by that great cricket enthusiast, Ben Travers, called simply The Leacock Book.)

Cricket for Americans

by Stephen Leacock

At the present hour all of us who are British are anxious to cultivate cordial relations with the United States. It has occurred to me that something could be done here with cricket. Americans, I fear, do not understand our national British game, and lack sympathy with it. I remember a few years ago attending a county match in England with an American friend, and I said to him at noon on Wednesday (the match had begun on Monday), 'I'm afraid that if it keeps on raining they'll have to draw stumps.' 'Draw what?' he said. 'Draw out the wickets,' I answered, 'and call the game ended.' 'Thank God!' he answered. Yet this was a really big game, a county match—Notts against Hamps, I think, but perhaps, Bucks against Yorks. Anyway it was a tense, exciting game, Notts (or Bucks) with 600 runs, leading by 350, four wickets down and only another six hours to play.

Ever since that day I meant to try to put the game in a better light, so that people in America could understand how wonderful it is.

Perhaps I should explain that, all modesty apart, when I speak of cricket I speak of what I know. I played cricket for years and years. I still have a bat. Once I played in an All-Canada match at Ottawa before the Governor-General. I went in first in the first innings, and was bowled out by the first ball; but in the second innings, I went in last, and by 'playing back' quickly on the first ball, I knocked down the wickets before the ball could reach them. Lord Minto told me afterwards that he had never seen batting like mine before, except, perhaps, in India where the natives are notoriously quick.

Let me begin with a few simple explanations. Cricket is played with eleven men on a side—provided you can get eleven. It isn't always easy to get a cricket team, and sometimes you have to be content with ten or nine, or even less. This difficulty of getting men for a side really arises from the fact that cricketers are not paid to play. They wouldn't take it, or rather, they *do* take it when they can get it, but then they are professionals. This makes a distinction in English cricket as between players and gentlemen, although, as a matter of fact, a great many gentlemen are first-class players, and nowadays, at any rate, a good many of the players are gentlemen, and contrawise quite a number of the gentlemen are not quite what you would call gentlemen. I am afraid I haven't brought out the distinction very clearly. Perhaps I may add when we play cricket in Canada there is no question of gentlemen.

So, as I say, although cricket is properly played with eleven on a side, it is often difficult to get enough. You have to be content with what you can bring and pick up one or two others when you get there. When I played in an All-Canada game at Ottawa we had nine at the start, but we got one more in the hotel and one in the barber shop. When the All-England team goes to Australia they easily get eleven men because that is different. That's twelve thousand miles. But when it's only from one village to the next it's hard to get more than seven.

But let me explain the game. Cricket is played by bowling a ball up and down a 'pitch' of twenty-two yards (roughly sixty-six feet, approximately), at each end of which are set three upright sticks called wickets. A batsman stands just in front of each set of wickets, a little at the side, and with his bat stops the ball from hitting the wickets. If the ball hits the wickets he is out, but otherwise not. Thus if he begins on Monday and his wickets are not hit on Monday, he begins again on Tuesday; and so on; play stops all Sunday.

Of course, when you are looking on at a cricket match, you are not supposed to shout and yell the way we do over baseball on our side of the water in Canada and in the States. All you do is to say, every now and then, 'Oh, very pretty, sir, very pretty!' You are speaking to the batsman who is about two hundred yards away and can't hear you. But that doesn't matter; you keep right on, 'Oh, well done, sir, well done.' ... That day of the county match in England that I spoke of, my American friend heard an Englishman on the other side of him say, 'Oh, very pretty! very pretty, sir.' And he asked the Englishman, 'What was very pretty?' But, of course, the Englishman had no way of telling him. He didn't know him. So he turned to me and asked. 'What did he do?' And I explained it wasn't what he did, it was what he didn't do. A great many things in good cricket turn on that—what you *don't* do. You let the ball go past you, for instance, instead of hitting it, and the experts say, 'Oh, well let alone, sir.' There are lots more balls coming; you've three days to wait for one.

In the game of which I speak the really superb piece of play was this: The bowler sent a fast ball through the air right straight towards the batsman's face. He moved his face aside and let it pass, and they called, 'Well, let alone, sir.' You see if it had hit him on the side of his face, he'd have been out. How out? Why, by what is called L.B.W. Perhaps I'd better explain what L.B.W. is. I forget what the letters exactly stand for, but we use them just as in the States you use things like P.W.A., A.A.C. and S.C.E. and R.I.P. You know what they stand for. Well, L.B.W. is a way of getting out in cricket. It means that if you stand in front of the ball and it hits you—not your bat, but you—you are out. Suppose, for instance, you deliberately turn your back on the ball and it rises up and hits you right behind in the middle of your body—out! L.B.W.

There was a terrible row over this a few years ago in connection with one of the great Test Matches between England and Australia. These, of course, are the great events, the big thing every year in the cricket world. An All-England team goes out once a year to play Test Matches in Australia, and an All-Australian team comes once a year for Test Matches in England. So far they only play Test Matches, but as soon as they know which is really best they can have a real match. Meantime they keep testing it out. Well, a few years ago, the Australians started the idea of bowling the ball terribly fast, and right straight at the batsman, not at the wickets, so as to hit him on purpose. Even if he started to run away from the wickets, they'd get him, even if he was half way to the home-tent. I didn't see it myself, but I understand that was the idea of it. So there was a tremendous row about it, and bad feeling, with talk of Australia leaving the British Empire. However, outsiders intervened, and it was suggested (the Archbishop of Canterbury, I think) that the rule should be that if the bowler meant to hit the man and put him out, then he wasn't out, but that if he didn't mean to hit and he hit him then he was out. Naturally the bowler had to be put on his honour whether he meant it. But that didn't bother the Australians; they were willing to go on their honour. They're used to it. In fact the English agreed, too, that when they got the ball in their turn they'd go on their honour in throwing it at an Australian.

That, of course, is the nice thing about cricket—the spirit of it, the sense of honour. When we talk of cricket we always say that such and such a thing 'isn't cricket,' meaning that it's not a thing you would do. You could, of course. There'd be nothing to stop you, except that, you see you couldn't. At a cricket game, for example, you never steal any of the other fellows' things out of the marquee tent where you come and go. You ask why not? Well, simply that it 'isn't cricket.' Or take an example in the field and you'll understand it better. Let me quote with a little more detail the case to which I referred earlier in the book. We'll say that you're fielding at 'square leg.' That means that you are fielding straight behind the batter's back and only about twenty-five feet from him. Well, suppose you happen to be day-dreaming a little—cricket is a dreamy game—and the batter happens to swing round hard on a passing ball and pastes it right into the middle of your stomach. As soon as you are able to speak you are supposed to call to the bowler, 'Awfully sorry, old man'; not sorry you got hit in the stomach, sorry you missed the chance he gave you; because from the bowler's point of view you had a great opportunity, when you got hit in the stomach, of holding the ball against your stomach—which puts the batter out.

So you see when you play cricket there comes in all the time this delicate idea of the cricket spirit. A good deal of English government is carried on this way. You remember a few years ago that very popular Prime Minister who used to come to the House of Commons—and say, 'I'm afraid, gentlemen, I've made another mess again with this business of Italy and Ethiopia; damned if I can keep track of them; that's the third mess I've made this year.' And the House wouldn't vote him out of office. It wouldn't have been cricket. Instead, they went wild with applause because the Prime Minister had shown the true cricket spirit by acknowledging that he was beaten, though, of course, he didn't know when he had been licked. And, for the matter of that, he'd come all the way down from Scotland just for the purpose at the very height of the grouse season—or the fly season—anyway, one of those insect seasons that keep starting in Scotland when the heather is bright with the gillies all out full.

Looking back over what I have written above, I am afraid I may have given a wrong impression here and there. When I implied that the two batsmen stand at the wicket and stop the ball, I forgot to say that every now and then they get impatient, or indignant, and not only stop it but hit it. And do they hit it! A cricket ball is half as heavy again as a baseball and travels farther. I've seen Don Bradman, the Australian, playing in our McGill University stadium, drive the ball clear over the seats of the stadium and then over the top of the trees on the side of Mount Royal, and from there on. They had to stop the game and drink shandygaff while they sent a boy to get the ball. They almost thought of getting a new one.

And when I talked of hitting a cricketer in the stomach with the ball, I forgot to explain how awfully difficult it is to do it. Not that they've no stomach—no, indeed, plenty! You don't train *down* for cricket, you fill *up*. But the point is that the cricketer will catch any kind of ball before you can hit him. And can they catch! You'll see a fellow playing cover-point—that's north-east half a point east from the bat, distance twenty yards—and a ball is driven hard and fast above his head, and he'll leap in the air with one hand up, and, *while still in the air*, leap up a little farther still and smack goes the ball into his one hand. Can you wonder that the spectators all murmur, 'Oh, very pretty, sir.' . . .

And in point of excitement! You think cricket slow, but can't you see how the excitement slowly gathers and all piles up at the end—two totals coming closer and closer together—fifty to tie, fifty-one to win—then twenty to tie, twenty-one to win—then three to tie, four to win—one smashing hit will do it now!—Ah! there she goes!—high above the pavilion, a boundary hit for four! Oh, very nice, sir, very nice!!

Oh yes, cricket's all right. Let's have a shandygaff.

Punch *magazine has continued to maintain its love-hate relationship with cricket, and hardly a year passes without an amusing article or two on the game. This was particularly noticeable during the editorship of Bernard Hollowood (1910–) who was in charge from 1957 to 1968. Not surprisingly, for Bernard had experience of cricket at all levels – having played county cricket for Staffordshire, league cricket for Burslem in the North Staffordshire League, and afterwards both club and village cricket. Of them all, he said, he preferred league cricket, because it was 'a better game to watch'. This experience had also given him a unique insight into the game at all levels, and his many and varied essays on the topic which he wrote for* Punch *– both as a contributor from 1945 onwards and as editor – are spiced with authentic and amusing anecdotes. Some of his most pungent work is preserved in* Cricket On The Brain *(1970), but a piece which seems to encapsulate a number of his views on the game is the following item written in March 1963. It still makes me laugh over twenty years on and a dozen or so readings later . . .*

The Seasonable Twinge

by Bernard Hollowood

Financially and in its playing record the Whiteheath Cricket Club (1889) incorporating Whiteheath FC (defunct) and Whiteheath Hockey Club (defunct) has never enjoyed a more successful season than 1962. According to the annual accounts the balance in hand as at February 28 was £7 3s. 9d. or £120 17s. if money outstanding on the 1959 Derby Sweepstake is included. The match fee has been raised to eightpence, officials half-price, so that in terms of hard cash the club's future seems assured. And the win against Noddersthorpe must be accounted an exceptional feat for two reasons—first because it represents the only *real* victory enjoyed for several seasons (in other years drawn matches in which Whiteheath were thought to hold some advantage have been credited as wins), and second because the team representing the club at Noddersthorpe was strangely unrepresentative, as will be revealed.

As a lifelong member and player I suppose I should share in the aura of euphoria investing the AGM last week. But my pride in the club is clouded by many reservations.

Take first the ground itself. Any club in membership of the Southern Club Cricket Conference would, one might think, have a "square" large enough to enable the groundsman to vary the site of the playing strip from week to week. The argument at Whiteheath is that any wicket should be good enough for at least four hundred runs, and that it is senseless and uneconomical to move the stumps until this aggregate has been achieved. As a result at least half the fixtures are completed in an average season before the pitch is changed. Last year the four hundredth run was hit in the Mottersley game on July 12—as follows:

Whiteheath v. Tenbury	— aggregate 51
Whiteheath v. Lower Biddstone	— aggregate 23
Whiteheath v. All Comers	— aggregate 39
Whiteheath v. Old Crows	— aggregate 71
Whiteheath v. Mottersley	— aggregate 54

Five matches! During this period of about ten weeks the stump sockets had become so roomy that it was impossible to set a firm wicket; the bails trembled and tumbled at the lightest tread, and batsmen were given out (bowled or hit wicket) whenever the ball passed the bat. Obviously the precarious balance of the woodwork behind them did nothing to encourage footwork. Most batsmen, sensing the danger of playing back, lunged forward a-tiptoe even at long-hops. And as they lunged they committed the cardinal error of watching the stumps instead of the ball, and suffered accordingly.

The communal blockhole became deeper and wider—so much so that short batsmen were visible to the bowler only from the pads up, and had no space to attempt anything more adventurous than a tentative prod towards the foremost rampart of the excavation.

Where was this pitch located? Not, as you may think, at the centre of the playing area, but a mere twenty-five yards from the pavilion. This kind of thing would not happen if the groundsman and the captain enjoyed separate identities. For many years now Skipper MacReith has bowled his tweakers from the "Three Hearts" end and takes most of his wickets through catches at very deep square-leg. He has therefore a direct interest in an arrangement that makes the leg boundary one hundred yards or more from stumps to gorse bushes.

Lord's was content with one ridge: Whiteheath has two. They are politely supposed to be tumuli marking the presence of old land drains, but everyone in the know is aware that they record a wild detour made by MacReith's Vauxhall after a particularly prolonged session of the Fixtures Committee at the "Three Hearts" in December '57. I have heard it said that whenever the mower is used on the wicket, which is not very often, the depressions flanking the ridges can be clearly identified by the zig-zag treadmarks of Goodyear tyres.

I mention these matters without animus. After all, why should I care? I am retiring again this season and have no wish to end my days as twelfth man. Last season I was not selected until late August in spite of the fact that I was the first to pay the previous year's subscription in full, and continued as an active member of the group that polishes old balls and annually saves the club as much as £6 15s., the equivalent of two new grade three-star Pakistani hand-sewn "Oval" Specials.

It was on Bank Holiday Monday that I mentioned my availability to the secretary, Tuyers, a young fellow who joined the club as recently as 1954 and already fields at slip. We were standing by the nets at the time, our eyes peeled for balls escaping from a gaping hole behind the wicket and threatening to disappear in the dense undergrowth of the heath.

He feigned surprise. "Didn't know you were still keen," he said. "Didn't you pack it in last season?"

"I have attended practice three nights a week since April," I cut back. "Some of us take our responsibilities seriously."

"We thought you were just doing it for the exercise," he said. "But, by golly, this *is* good news. Delighted to have you back, delighted. How about Sunday? Biddleton away. Don't forget to bring your pads."

But my name wasn't on the notice board the next day. "You see, old boy," said MacReith, when I told him there had been some mistake, "we're definitely going all out for the quick scoring lark this season. The game's been in the hands of the academicians, like Barrington and you, far too long. Technical excellence isn't enough: we want chappies who'll get a move on."

There was nothing I could say to this. In a sense my cricket *is* like Barrington's—solid rather than flashy, determined rather than explosive. I don't like throwing my wicket away. Never have.

"You were grateful for my three not out against Minden a few years ago," I said.

However I *was* selected two weeks later—for the Noddersthorpe game. The call came late on the Saturday morning when I was settling down to watch "Summer Grandstand," and in the interests of the club I switched off immediately, packed my bag and got out the car. It turned out that MacReith had gone off to Lord's, taking his car with him and so leaving the team without transport for the Noddersthorpe game. I had to pick up three players at the "Feathers," two more at Whiteheath crossroad and another, the secretary, at his home, "Saltburn," Lea Garden Crescent.

Tuyers apart, they were all *boys*. Not one of them could have been more than fifteen, though they all in the ludicrous fashion of the day wore long trousers. Not one of them was on time. We arrived very late.

Fortunately we won the toss and batted, so that Tuyers (acting captain) was able to arrange the order according to the amount of changing—from civvies into flannels—needed. The boys, being instantly ready for the fray, went in early: I was down for number ten.

But I didn't bat. The boys, secondary modern types and utterly unschooled in the game, enjoyed incredible luck. They wafted their bats at everything and snicked fours and sixes everywhere. After half an hour the score was sixty-seven for three and the time five forty-five. At this point, the tea interval, we very properly declared, leaving our opponents an hour and a quarter to get the runs.

They went for them bald-headed and in no time at all were thirty-odd for one. Then it rained, torrentially. It was still raining at 7.05 pm by which time the older fielders and the umpires had retired dripping to the pavilion. The boys however continued to bowl and field with amazing zest. Deep pools dotted the Noddersthorpe square, the soggy heaps of sawdust behind the bowler's marks were submerged. Then, with the score at sixty-one for one, the batsmen too called it a day.

In the steaming pavilion the boys were furious, insisting that they could have, *would* have won. In their view our opponents had funked it, used the weather as an excuse for avoiding certain defeat. This display of youthful enthusiasm was much to the liking of the Noddersthorpe captain, a retired bookmaker and lay preacher.

"Very well," he said, emptying his boots through the dressing-room window, "we concede you victory."

And so it was that Whiteheath enjoyed their most successful playing season for years. I am proud that I shared in that success. But I shall continue to retire during the coming season. I want to go out with colours flying.

Bernard Hollowood's amusingly ambivalent attitude towards village cricket is also shared by TV personality and writer, Michael Parkinson (1935–). Michael, who has been described as 'Yorkshire's favourite son', was born in Barnsley, and after working as a reporter on a local paper, graduated to Fleet Street and successive jobs on The Guardian, Daily Express *and as a columnist for the* Sunday Times. *His typical Yorkshire sense of humour mingled with a very real affection for, not to mention understanding of, cricket has resulted in books such as* Cricket Mad *(1969) and* Bats In The Pavilion *(1977) as well as innumerable essays for newspapers and magazines. How this affection began, he now explains in as funny an item as you will find in this entire collection.*

Tripping O'Er the Greensward

by Michael Parkinson

When I was at school, our art master asked us to draw The Village Cricket Match. We all did the same drawing, depicting a scene of rural tranquillity with a Norman church at one corner of the ground and a thatched pub at another. Outside the pub sat rustics in smocks quaffing pints of foaming ale and at the wicket the local vicar batted against the village blacksmith. So what? Well, nothing really, except the school was in a pit village in Yorkshire and it was to be many years before any of the artists were to see a thatched roof, never mind a cricket ground anything like the one they drew.

The fact is, of course, that English village cricket is *the* most deeply enjoyed myth in British folklore. It symbolises a kind of rural paradise; the land we would all love to live in. The village cricket ground is the cliché image of the British countryside. Similarly, the village cricket match has become a favourite topic for succeeding generations of cricket writers, all of whom perpetuate the dream of jolly, jovial, nice people untouched by the real world, tripping o'er the greensward with many a joke and a jape.

The truth is less endearing but much more interesting. It took me more than 20 years on this planet before I found the cricket ground I drew at school in Yorkshire. At the time I was doing my National Service and was stationed in Salisbury. One Sunday our cricket team went deep into the countryside of Wiltshire or it might have been Somerset. Similarly I cannot remember the name of the village we played against except it must have been called Chipping Wallop or Nether Sudbury or some such.

When we arrived I had the immediate sense that I had been there before. And so I had in that it was the cricket ground I had drawn all those years ago. There was the Norman church at the far side surrounded by oak and yew and in the other corner the pub with a thatched roof.

But it was better than I had imagined. It was one of those days of English summer when you wouldn't be dead for quids. There was birdsong and woodsmoke in the distant hills and the smell of newly mown grass.

I stroke to the wicket convinced I was indeed a part of the rich tapestry of English life, a player in the pageant of our heritage. The umpire, a tubby yeoman, bade me a cheerful good-morning before I took my guard. As I looked about the field before settling into my stance I knew I was perusing paradise. What is more, I was determined to make the most of it and bat as long as possible.

I was fortified in this ambition by an inspection of the opposition which revealed not an awful lot to worry about. The first ball I received from their opening bowler was going so far down the leg side that I disdained a shot and in derisory manner let it hit my pads and bounce away. Immediately, the entire team yelled "Owzat" and to my horror, the umpire raised his finger. To make it even more ridiculous, he said in a loud voice, "That's out sir!"

It was always my policy to be nice to umpires but on this occasion I was compelled to break a lifetime's habit.

"What?" I said, in a loud voice.

"That's out sir," he shouted.

"Never," I said.

The umpire considered this for a minute and then said slowly, almost judicially: "Maybe not where you come from, sir, but down here it is." It's the old story; no matter how hard nature tries, humans will invent a way to louse it up. As with life, so with village cricket.

The simple fact is that village cricket, no matter where the setting, brings out our capacity to lie and cheat in a civilised manner. It also provides a means whereby seemingly ordinary folk can display their fantasies without being arrested. It is not that village cricket breeds "characters", it simply attracts them.

The first village team I played for was in a pit community in Yorkshire. It was as far removed from the rustic as was possible to imagine. The view from the wicket was the pit top and slag heaps and rows of red-bricked houses. The wicket itself was of the "sporting" variety which meant you had a fair chance of serious injury if you played enough innings on it.

Our two most successful players were George and Norman whose approach to cricket made Botham and Richards seem like stonewallers. George had a tin leg so only wore one pad. When struck on his false limbs the ball made a noise like a gong. "One o'clock and all's well," George would say cheerfully before he tried to hit the next ball into distant and hostile Lancashire.

When I was a kid, me and my mates would hero-worship the two big hitters. Our job every Saturday was to find the balls they were attempting to lose. While searching for a ball one day in a nearby cornfield, I came across two people I knew in intimate and loving embrace. Thus cricket became involved with my sex education.

I watched until I thought I'd seen enough. Looking back, I now think that I left before the end, if you know what I mean. I had to get back because Norman was batting.

He had a bat bound in a dark brown hide. "Kangaroo skin" he used to tell me "Tha' sees that's what makes t'ball fly like it does!" I believed him until the day I asked for a kangaroo skin bat in a sports shop and the man said he'd run out of them but he could sell me a left-handed spanner if I wanted one.

Our wicket-keeper looked like Kojak and was called Minty. He had a wonderful way with words and loved inventing conversation with the opposition which seemed innocent enough but always contained a trip wire. This best occurred while he was wicket-keeping to a newly discovered quick bowler. The first two balls were decidedly rapid and whistled past the batsman's chin. The batsman looked nervous and was no doubt reassured when Minty engaged him in friendly conversation.

"Quick, isn't he," said Minty with a smile.

"Very," said the batsman.

Minty nodded sympathetically, "Mind you," he said, "if tha' reckons he's fast now tha' should have faced him before he got gassed."

Minty umpired after he finished playing and sometimes, when he was pushed, he'd arrive at the ground in his pit muck. Thus begrimed he once asked an incoming batsman:

"What's tha' want lad?"

"Can tha' sing 'Mammy'?" the lad said.

Needless to say, he was given out the first time we appealed.

Our other umpires were equally merciless. "O.T." was so called because he worked as a barman at the local boozer and as opening time approached he could be relied on to get rid of the opposition. His proud boast was that he had never been late for work, which meant he never had a game that lasted after five to six.

Big Jim Smith was my favourite umpire. Instead of answering an appeal with "Not Out" or a shake of the head, he would answer with a piece of advice to the bowler. Thus a typical Jim Smith rejoinder would be: "Get thi' bloody hair cut." "Tha' needs a shave" or "Why don't you get yer eyes tested."

Jim Smith rarely gave a batsman out. He worked on the theory that bowlers were a conniving bunch and that his job was to protect batsmen from them. His manner of granting the appeal was as unique as it was rare. After the "Owzat" he would look down the wicket at the batsman and say, in sorrow, "Goodbye, old lad."

Jim Baker was our fast bowler. He had the longest run I have ever seen. He had to knock a hole in the hedge at one end of our ground to accommodate it. The psychological effect on the batsman of watching Jim mark out a run, which meant him leaving the ground and disappearing from view, can only be imagined. By the time he burst through the hedge as if heading a cavalry charge, the batsman was a nervous wreck.

It was rumoured that his career came to an end when he was playing away from home in a ground where his run necessitated leaving the ground and crossing a main road. Apparently, as he was galloping towards the wicket, he was knocked down by a bus. I can't actually verify that because it was my old man who told me the story and he could be a bit of a romancer.

In fact, for many years my father captained the collection of crackpots, characters and odd bods who made up our village cricket team. To him village cricket was not simply a game, it was a religion, a way of life, a complete experience.

Anyone who did not share his utter passion for the game was dismissed as an oaf. His enthusiasm was such that he could turn any village cricket match into a battleground, and when we went on holidays he would transform a game of beach cricket into an experience something like the landings at Iwo Jima.

He was not to be messed with and yet he had a lovely if at times sinister sense of humour. I was at the other end one game when he took a severe battering from a young and raw quick bowler. One blow was so brutal that the bowler was moved to apologise. "Sorry, mate," he said. "Don't apologise lad," said my father. "It's my turn to bowl next and I won't apologise when I hit thee." And he was as good as his word.

Our groundsman was old Cheyney and he was an artist who believed that "pig muck" and "'oss manure" were the foundations of a good wicket. Thus he prepared the pitch with good dollops of both products which he would roll into the turf. When it rained the mixture was churned into an evil-smelling mess which accounted for anyone with a delicate disposition.

Old Cheyney also owned a vast and ancient Packard which he used to drive to away matches. Being something of a rarity in the Barnsley district, the American car attracted a lot of attention and Cheyney made the odd bob or two selling parts of it. We knew he had started selling off the engine when we were overtaken on a hill near Rotherham by an old woman pushing a pram. After the car was finally dispersed we started travelling in a coal lorry and would arrive at away fixtures looking like the Black and White Minstrels.

Now all this is a long way removed from the popular version of English village cricket, and yet I suspect it's much nearer the real truth of the matter. And looking back, although it might lack the thatched roof, rustics, woodsmoke and the smell of an English summer, it did have a certain kind of beauty.

John Arlott OBE (1914–) as the man who fostered my interest in the funny side of cricket is obviously an essential member of my team. His contribution to cricket itself has, of course, been enormous and marked by numerous awards, including several for his radio and television work (in 1980, for instance, he was Sports Presenter of the Year for TV and also Sports Personality on the radio), while he has also been President of the Cricketers' Association since 1968 and an Honorary Life Member of the MCC since 1980. A former clerk, police detective, BBC producer, writer and broadcaster, John's dual passions of cricket and wine have been reflected in many of his books, and among the relevant titles should be mentioned, How To Watch Cricket *(1949),* Jubilee History of Cricket *(1965), his joint volume with Sir Neville Cardus,* The Noblest Game *(1969), and his excellent biographies,* Fred: Portrait of a Fast Bowler *(1971) and* Jack Hobbs: A Profile of the Master *(1981). Despite his huge output in newspapers and magazines, it is a fact that John has only ever written one piece of fiction, 'Ain't half a Bloody Game' produced twenty years ago for the now defunct magazine,* Lilliput, *and never published in book form. It is therefore, as John said when offering it for this anthology, 'almost as good as new!' I think this story makes the book worth the price on its own, and I know I am very pleased and privileged to have the chance to return it to print in the pages which follow . . .*

Ain't Half a Bloody Game

by John Arlott

The half-hit drive lobbed slowly up, seemed to hover a moment before mid-off caught it, and the first innings of the match was over: Hampshire 256 all out. Before the fieldsman's hands had closed on the ball, long leg, whose name was Kennett, began to walk briskly towards the pavilion.

Ten minutes is not long: it is not long enough. He had been reconciled to that fact for many years, but today it added heavily to the weight of his irritation. "Give us yer autograph, mister." He waved the boy aside. They ought not to let kids pester the players like this. He walked faster. Ten minutes seems even shorter when it comes at half-past-five. No one—none of the reporters or the committee members—ever cared that

271

you had gone out to bat after five hours in the field, with only ten minutes to do everything. He smeared the sweat across his forehead with his arm and pushed past several spectators, out of the dry sunglare, into the dressing room. The day had seemed all the hotter and harder for being the first after a fortnight out with a split finger; he felt the nag of a blister forming on his right heel.

The little boy pocketed his autograph album philosophically. They never *did* sign as they came off the field anyway. They would later. Keep on at them, that was the thing.

"Who is he?" asked his neighbour.

"Kennett," said the autograph hunter authoritatively.

"Has he ever played for England?" The policeman ordered them off the ground, as usual, and as they dawdled away the enthusiast, rummaging in his satchel, pulled out the cricket *Who's Who*, crumbs from lunch-time sandwiches clinging stickily to its cover. He looked up George Kennett in that mild biographical and statistical immortality in which cricket registers its performers—

KENNETT, George (Norshire) *b. Leeds* 16.3.1918. *Right hand bat: leg break bowler. Debut* 1947: *County Cap* 1949. 1,000 *runs six times*: 1,732 (*av.* 35.34) 1951 *best. Highest score* 206 *v. Kent*, 1951: *best bowling performance, five for* 42 *v. Cambridge University*, 1949.

"No—see—it don't say anything about Test Matches: he's not much good and he must be too old now, anyway."

He felt old. There was an ache at the back of his eyes, a drawn, tender tightness in the skin around them: he could feel the lines of the dust. He looked for his jug of cold tea. Some people had a beer as soon as they came in. All right for bowlers, but not if you were going out to bat. Cold tea was safe; it had always refreshed him, ever since he first asked his mother to save a jug for him after games in the park at home. He knew before he felt the jug that it was lukewarm. "Damn it, young Hayter, why didn't you get the tea when I told you—sitting around signing your autograph, I suppose." Jimmy Hayter, whose importance declined to his official rank of twelfth man when the players came in, muttered something half-apologetic and bustled out to the score box for the bowling figures.

George Kennett ran some cold water into one of the wash basins and stood the jug in it. His shirt clung and twisted as he wriggled out of it. Then he slipped off his rubber-soled boots—the skipper was always making acid remarks about them, but they were the only rest for a cricketer's feet in five months of daily cricket. His flannels tugged at the knees as he kicked them off. Ah, the cold water; handfuls of it, over his face, his thin hair; gloriously over his chest, stomach, thighs. He paused. No: he knew it too well: there is not enough time in the ten minutes between innings for the extra luxury of putting your feet in cold water, powdering them and putting on fresh socks. You are still struggling after the fielding side is out if you try it. He towelled himself, tried to relax as he walked slowly to his place in the dressing room, took a cigarette out of his blazer pocket and lit it. He leant back against the varnished match-boarding, closed his eyes; two long, slow draws at the cigarette; the ritual was like a timetable. Up now: he dropped his towel and, as he moved to his bag, the skipper pinned up the batting order. Kennett looked quickly—almost nervously—at it.

Why? he wondered. For six years he had barely bothered to glance at it. He was Norshire's number one. It had made very little difference when, last year, Jim Stevens took first ball instead of himself: he preferred it really; what difference was there between number one and number two? Yet it seemed, in a way, to mark the beginning of the slide down the far side of the slope. Now he was half frightened to look until he had seen that no one but Jim Stevens, Jack Connor and himself was hurrying to get ready. There it was, in the skipper's half-neat, half slapdash hand (initials for the amateurs, even there, the blasted snob)—

> *Stevens*
> *Kennett*
> *Connor*
> *Wainwright*
> *Redding*
> *K. E. Tallis*
> *Pearce*
> *D. R. Bridges*
> *Adam*
> *Copp*
> *F. R. Lee*

At the bottom, the pompous initials—"K.E.T." Damn him.

273

As Tallis turned, his eye caught with quick surprise the taut line of Kennett's lean, spare body; naked, crouched as if he were going to spring, as he looked at the batting order. Curse the fellow, did he really think his captain the sort of man to change a player's place in the batting order just like that? The trouble with these fellows was that they could never appreciate the decent tradition in the game. Look at him now; gulping cold tea like a navvy: and why didn't the scruffy devil change his socks when he came in after a day's fielding? Why didn't he *say* something, instead of those blank looks? But why be annoyed by him? The man was a dull player and not a very good one, anyway. Of course, he was cricket mad in his grim Yorkshire way—but what right did that give him to look at his captain so contemptuously because, in an effort to liven up the game, he played a chancy stroke that cost him his wicket? In any case, Kennett would soon be gone: there was no room for sentiment in modern county cricket. The committee had agreed that the captain should have the final word on playing staff and he was going to use it to get a side that won matches—and won them handsomely. When Kennett went, the committee and the press would see that he meant business—and bright business—in building the new Norshire team.

George Kennett picked his strap out of his bag, stepped into it, reached for his thigh-pad and began, automatically, to tie it on. Perhaps he was not all that good a player; still, he had been unlucky—just this season, when he needed the breaks.

Although the players' contracts began and ended in March, the renewals were always fixed up in the previous August. He knew the others whose two-year periods finished next March had been approached a week ago. He had heard Tim Pearce and Bob Copp discussing it when he looked in on the dressing room during the Kent match. No one in the office had said anything to him about a contract when he reported at the County Ground to come to Portsmouth. Most significant of all, none of the players had mentioned the subject on the trip down. They knew what he was only just realizing—that he was going to be sacked.

He looked round the room. The bowlers had their boots off; Frank Copp already had his feet up and, stretched out on the seat, was starting to doze.

As he pulled a clean shirt over his head, his mind nibbled back into the grievance of the fixture list. That split finger had cost him the games against Leicester at Leicester, Sussex at Hove, and Kent at Norchester. Three of the best wickets of the season to bat on, too. There could have been a century—perhaps two—in that lot: say three hundred runs altogether; he would just about have scraped his thousand. The skipper's words at the pre-season meeting echoed back through his mind—not addressed to him by name, but meant for him—"You see, you chaps, it's not just a matter of a thousand runs or fifteen hundred runs; it's the way the runs are made; we've got to entertain the crowds or they won't come—and the committee have made it pretty clear to me that they expect me to get something done about it."

Well, something had been done. Next year, Frank Winter, the Australian, would be qualified: an opening bat who got on with it—a fair change-bowler and a great close field. One of the batsmen would have to go to make room for him: there was no doubt now that George Kennett was that "one of the batsmen." At the beginning of the season it was a toss up: it might have been Ellis Wainwright: but now Ellis had twelve hundred runs in the bag: a ton against Leicester at Leicester, just to rub it in. Kennett, the averages in *The Norchester Chronical* said last night, had made 526 runs at 16.96: and it was well into August. Four more games after this one: Derby at Chesterfield, Lancashire on that pig of a wicket at Norsea—it wasn't really fit to play on, but they gave it a fixture for the holiday crowds—then Surrey at the Oval and Northants at Rushden.

Again George Kennett cursed himself for being the sort of fool who takes to cricket. The greatest life in the world had seemed to open for him, twenty-three years ago, when they asked him—a sixteen-year-old office-boy—to play a game with the Club and Ground side, and afterwards offered him a job on the ground staff the next spring. That was in 1934 and, if the county had not stayed in the running for the Championship, he must have been given a couple of games with the first team in 1939. He pulled on his batting flannels, nearly as thin as his shirt from so many dry-cleanings as had washed out the line where the turn-ups used to be.

It would have been different if Geoff Thomas had kept the captaincy. They had both been at Salerno: not together, but it was something in common, even though they didn't talk about it. They had played together in a few Service matches out there, too, when things eased up. Tallis was different. Perhaps it had been silly to pull his leg in his first match after he "bought" George Tribe's googly; but any of the lads would have taken it and, after all, a capped pro should be able to pull a youngster's leg: it was meant friendly enough, anyway.

He was still buckling his pads as Jim Stevens picked up bat and gloves and walked to the door "Umps are out, George." The skipper, with a towel on his arm, was on his way to the shower. He looked back over his shoulder. "We don't want to lose a wicket tonight, but don't shut it up—this is a holiday crowd, remember—they want to see a few runs; if you get anything loose, hammer it." How much loose stuff did the blasted man think this side were going to serve up with the new ball? "O.K., skip," said Jim. George Kennett, average county cricketer, grunted and reached into his bag for his gloves.

"Come on, George." A tug at his shirt, a bend of the knees to ease his pads and, blinking in the sudden glare, he and Jim Stevens, each at his own gait and with no hurry, walked through the sputter of polite, unenthusiastic handclaps, out towards the middle.

As they went, David Bridges put the letter he was reading into his wallet, thought idly that Kennett was a poor devil and thanked God that he, for his very different part, could play this interestingly odd game for fun in the summer holidays from school teaching. Almost aloud, he thought "What a devil of a game this is for the chaps who aren't quite good enough—or does it find them something in the end, somehow?"

As the two batsmen walked out, Stevens broke off his habitual, soft, tuneless whistling to say, "256 will take enough getting on this, let alone trying to hit these chaps off; but, if he wants it, I suppose he must have it—a couple of fours early on would sweeten him enough."

Then they were in the middle, and walked to their opposite ends. Stevens fussed a little before he took his guard from Alec Skelding. The field gathered: four short legs and a wide mid-on: two slips, gully and a man between cover and mid-off: no long leg, no third man: an attacking setting. Shackleton was already waiting on his mark to bowl as Stevens turned towards him, almost upright, easy, bat barely touching the ground. It was all very quiet: a hard side, Hampshire: they rarely had many runs in the bag; were long conditioned to the struggle to allow even fewer to the other side. Always this tight opening: Shack and Vic—Shackleton and Cannings—peppering a rash on, and just short of, a length; moving the new ball late; in their element on this Portsmouth wicket where there was always enough "green" for the quickies to do something off the seam, with a foot or so of life.

276

Shackleton ran in, the wind from the sea at his back. The first ball came down on the line of the middle and, just before it pitched, dipped sharply in. Stevens had barely moved: his bat was still drawn warily back as the ball hit his pad. The fifteen people concerned—two batsmen, two umpires, eleven fieldsmen—those out of line as much as those in position to see, knew that it was missing the leg stump by five or six inches. Yet no appeal seemed almost more hostile than a "shout" would have been. Peter Sainsbury from backward short leg, moved in and, in two quick jerks, the ball had gone from him to Harrison, standing up close to the stumps, and back to Shackleton. Outside it all, round the ring, there was talk: inside the game, it was completely quiet. The next ball, too, was an in-ducker: Stevens was over it and, with the swing, he pushed it hard between Sainsbury and Horton. "Come" and they ran a safe single.

Kennett took his leg-stump guard from Alec Skelding and bent with a cramped determination over his bat. Suddenly it was all different: it was no longer the familiar daily routine, exhilarating yet grim, something which was there always. All at once it became vital and, in another way, precious: a thing to be fought against, yet defended. His senses seemed sharpened like those of a man who has lost someone dear to him. He heard the thump-brush of Shackleton's run-in; the creak of pads as Harrison bent down behind the stumps. Then the whole world was concentrated into a sharply red cricket ball, its seam a keen, slanted line, holding steady as it came down. His back-lift was no more than a gesture; bat and pad were near together as the ball "did" a couple of inches in at him, and hit his left pad. Shack, checking in his follow-through, peered down the line and, with a half shake of his head, decided not to appeal. Watch this chap, always likely to move one the other way off the pitch—the sixth ball did. Kennett was over it, wrists slack; the ball fell back off a dead bat. "Over". He leant on his bat, tried to look relaxed: he saw his hand was trembling.

The other umpire, Emrys Davies, walked in from square leg: a couple of good ones; at least there was little fear of a bad decision. Vic Cannings bowled: twice the ball moved away from the off stump as if it were tugged on a string: twice Stevens, well across, lifted his bat and let it go through to Harrison. The third ball was a little further up, moved late towards slips. Every cautious batting sense in George Kennett cried out, "Leave it, you fool," as Jim Stevens, with a full flow of the bat, went over and hit it, off the middle, through the empty covers. No need to run: there was a round of applause as Rayment jogged across to collect the bumbling throw-in from a small boy in the crowd on the boundary.

There was the difference between the two batsmen. Order George Kennet to go for that stroke in the first few minutes and he would be out—because he knew he would be out. Cannings kept short of driving length for the best of the over. A maiden from Shackleton to Kennett—two on the pad, four on the middle of a passive bat—another from Cannings to Stevens: yet another from Shackleton to Kennett.

A man down by the score board shouted, "Come on, Norshire, don't send us to sleep." Stevens took a two through mid-off, a single wide of cover point's right hand: Kennett soldiered out the over.

Still there was no fieldsman deep. Stevens was lifting his bat higher, feeling surer, but four balls of the over drove him on to the back foot; two he played, not very happily, on the half cock. Twenty minutes gone; Norshire eight for no wicket: Stevens 8; Kennett 0. By now the skipper would be out of his bath, watching. To have seen the brightest of the shine off against these two was something: but Tallis would not think so. Cannings started a ball outside the leg stump; Kennett half shaped to turn it—checked; it swung across him. Awkwardly, with a quick blackness in his belly, he snatched his bat away. Turning as it went by, he sucked in a quick breath: it missed his off stump by no more than a couple of inches; he had not known it was as close as that. Damn it, he had been all at sea with it, might as well have edged it as not.

He pushed forward to the next ball, played it to Cannings' left, looked for a run, but Jim Stevens was already shaking his head as he looked. The next ball began about middle stump; as it moved away, Kennett shuffled quickly across, jabbed it to cover. Even as he played the stroke, Rayment was racing to cut it off. "N—no," he said, restlessly. All right, what did it matter? He had not had a ball he could be expected to score from; not that Tallis would know. Tallis be damned. Give him six balls that could be hit for four and he would hit them for four; six good balls were six good balls, Tallis or no Tallis. As the field crossed he heard Desmond Eager say to Shackleton, "I want Malcolm to have a try at your end after this."

Malcolm Heath was faster than either of the other two, but not so devilishly, naggingly accurate: there might be the odd one down the leg side. Carefully now: see Shack off, that would be a point to the batsmen. Stevens flicked at Shackleton's inswinger and dragged it wide of Eagar at leg-slip: they ran one. There was a cold ache under Kennett's ribs as he took his stance. A quick back-lift—higher than usual—wait for the swing—no, it was going with his arm. George Kennett pushed his foot firmly down the wicket, his right hand, low on the handle, punched through; he felt the swell against the meat of the bat and, as he lifted his head, saw it racing away through the mid-off gap. The clapping rolled across the field and warmed him. Shackleton looked down the wicket at him; "Good shot," he said. He did not mean it, of course; no bowler could, but very civil of him. Still no word from anyone else; these Hampshire fieldsmen never talked any batsmen into confidence.

Better now, though; his shoulders seemed looser; he felt the sweat soft across his back; flexed his arms and dropped easily into his stance. Shackleton ran in again; the inswinger. As he sensed it would move outside his leg stump, Kennett turned to play it down through the short legs. It pitched—and angled back off the green. He had gone too far round; stranded he dropped his wrists as by second nature, but he felt the pluck of the ball on the outside edge of his bat, there was the shout—"Haaaat"—Harrison was holding the ball high in his right hand.

No need to look at Alec Skelding: but—just in case—the old umpire's finger was up and, as Kennett looked, he waggled it at him in humorous reproof. As he turned, bitter disappointment in his face, Leo Harrison grinned sympathetically. "It ain't half a bloody game, mate, is it?" he said. These chaps had had bad trots themselves; they knew what it meant, but they were not in the game for their health. As they crossed in the pavilion gateway, Jack Connor, going out to bat, gave him, from habit more than anything else, "Hard lines" and then, "Still moving?" "Yes; that ducked in and then left me off the track." "That'd be good enough for me, too." Kennett brushed through the formal sympathy in the dressing room, avoiding Tallis's eye as Tallis avoided his; went on to his corner, stripped and went into the shower. The water—hot, tepid, cold—was like a balm to his aching shoulders and feet.

A couple of pints in the bar afterwards was part of his day's cricket. It had probably always been like this; in a crowd of a dozen or more players from the two sides, no one was going to fall round a man's neck because he was off his game. Jim Stevens or Tim Pearce might have said something, but all the talk was general:—deliberately general?—or just his imagination? "Well bowled, Shack," he said. Derek Shackleton grinned, "Not a bad one was it?—I keep it up my sleeve for the awkward customers."

Supper at the hotel would raise too many problems he was not ready to face. If it had been a home game, now: Betty had never learnt anything about cricket. It was not that she disliked it, it simply had no meaning for her. If he made runs, then she was pleased with cricket, because he was happy. If he did not want to talk, she was content to make odd remarks he did not hear, expecting no reply. He bought an evening paper to read over supper in the little Italian restaurant. There it was, in the Stop Press, "Kennett caught Harrison bowled Shackleton 4. Norshire 28 for one: close."

He saw a little group—Keith Adam, Bob Copp, Ellis Wainwright and Jim Stevens—in the hotel lounge as he went through the hall to the lift and up to bed. A good idea to have had those few beers on the way back; get to sleep easier: would not think. Hell—he would *have* to think about it pretty soon. Not a county cricketer any more; Not George Kennett the Norshire opening bat but "George Kennett—remember him?— used to play for Norshire."

All at once he became conscious of his clenched fists, clamped teeth and tensed arms. What is this? Pull yourself together, Kennett. It was always going to happen; it has only come a season or so sooner than you thought. Whenever it had come you would have felt it was too soon. There will be some sort of job: umpiring—that would keep him in the game—or coach at a school, making young players. He knew that would not do. He had too much playing still in him. The Leagues? He had thought of that before, but the League clubs wanted men who make their runs fast—star pros.

There would be work. At worst, some sort of labouring job. He would not starve; he had had his fun: and, in his heart, he knew it had been fun. If he had wanted to make money he would never have become a cricket pro. Now he had to pay for it. Only relax, man: go to sleep; there is nothing you can do about it. Tallis, luck; all right, that just makes a season's difference. One minute he was realising he could not get to sleep; the next, it was morning and he was waking. Morning tea; as he lifted his head, he felt the ache still in his stomach. But it was all settled now.

He savoured—as he had never quite savoured it before—the late morning of the cricketer, the comparative luxury of a middle-class hotel. It would not be like this next summer. He walked into the dining room to the usual away match breakfast scene. Round a group of tables, morning papers, propped against tea-pots, provided the basis for the county cricketer's stock conversation—county cricket. Each score of the other matches came in for analysis; without rancour, envy or delight but with professional interest. As he went to his table he heard Tim Pearce, the senior pro, saying to Tallis, "Either Hayter, or send back for Phillips, skipper—not much in it either way, I don't think. . . ." As he half-consciously waited for the conversation to go on, it ended, still in the air. With a drowning feeling, he realised that it had stopped because they had seen him. They were discussing which of the ground staff lads to play in his place in the next match. Dropped; somehow, he had not thought of that. To finish at the end of the season, that was how these things happened. No, they didn't; they happened just like this. "Kennett stands down to allow young Hayter, one of the county's promising young players, to gain first-class experience." He himself had first come in for old Ted Jelfs in the August games. He recalled, for the first time since it happened, Ted wishing him luck that day; Ted's face; ten years ago.

As he sat down at the table opposite Keith Adam—"See what Don Sheppard did to Warwick, George?—eight for 32." "Must have had a bit of rain" he heard himself say. He reached out for the teapot and gradually the murmur of talk washed over him. Yorkshire were winning; good: so were Surrey—and after a bad start, too . . . the pattern of the previous day's play ticked into his mind from the talk.

It was an easy walk to the ground through the morning sun. Once there, with nine more Norshire wickets to go down, his was the clearest day of all. Time for a couple of cups of coffee and then idle watching as Stevens, Connor, Wainwright and Reddings gave the innings a steady grounding: 130 for three at lunch. No need to hurry over the invariable cold meat, salad, biscuits and cheese of the county cricketer's midday, that constant summer diet which the player eats almost without noticing it.

The sun had gone behind dark clouds and, sitting back on the verandah, Kennett watched Redding edge Cannings for Barnard, at slip, to make a full length dive look casual and catch him no more than an inch off the grass. As Tallis walked confidently out, one member turned to another in the pavilion seats with "Ah, Tallis; he'll liven things up—a real stroke-player." Kennett, behind them, grinned sourly; if they did not know the difference between a stroke-maker and a Flash Harry, how did they understand what they were watching? Tallis followed his first ball from Cannings—deliberately pitched a foot outside the off stump—and hit it magnificently through the covers for four. The first member turned to his neighbour—"What did I tell you—fine stuff."

While Wainwright went steadily, Tallis drove: twice he hit across the line of the ball from Shackleton with such eye and timing as to reach the long-on boundary. Wainwright, trying to hook Heath, dragged the ball into his stumps. With Pearce as his partner, Tallis reached 45, went for another stroke across the line and the ball steepled up so high that the batsmen had crossed before Shackleton caught it: 195 for five. Bridges, the incoming batsman, passed him with a smile "Well hit." "Thanks—keep it going, will you—I'd like to declare at tea." "I'll do my best."

Pearce hooked Heath for a solid enough four; he followed the next ball round and Harrison, standing back, dived and caught him: 199 for six. Before Adam could reach the wicket a stinging shower came down; five minutes of it, not heavy enough to delay play at all after it cleared, but enough to put another yard of lift in the always well-grassed Portsmouth wicket. A four to Bridges and then another shower drove the players in. When they came out, Hampshire took the new ball. Eagar himself caught Bridges, after a few forcing strokes, diving at leg-slip off Cannings. Shackleton bowled Adam and had Lee caught by Marshall in the gully off a spinning mishit. Norshire were all out, almost exactly at tea time, for 221. As they came in, another heavy scud drove briefly over the ground.

"What do you think of it, Pearce?"

"She'll do quite a bit, skipper; it always lifts a lot here when it's wet on top and hard underneath, like this. I expect they'll have the heavy on it, but it will wear off after four or five overs and then it'll give the quickies everything."

Kennett was already in his place at long leg when Roy Marshall and Jimmy Gray came out to start the Hampshire second innings with a lead of 35, only a slight reassurance with such a lively wicket in prospect. Eagar had, indeed, ordered the heavy roller and, when Lee dropped his first ball short, it rose only a little more than hip-high. Marshall, most militant of opening bats, swung round viciously at it, hit a little late and sent it, curling and spinning, towards long leg. Kennett, already walking in as the stroke was played, began to run, but then he saw it would drop well short of him. No point in playing to the gallery: a running forward dive would still leave him short of it. He moved back and round, judged the bounce and spin carefully, took it chest high on the first bounce and dropped his throw accurately into Pearce's hands by the stumps as Gray made his ground for the single. He caught Tallis looking at him as he turned to walk back and heard the clap of his hands as he said, "Come on, now, fellows, come on." As he trotted in at the end of the over, the captain was waiting for him. "What the devil— weren't you watching?—if you had been in the game, that was a catch, Kennett: no side can afford to give this chap Marshall a life and I see that as a catch missed—you must try these chances." For a second he was more surprised than angry; Tallis had turned his back on him before he could speak. As the anger swelled up into his throat, Jim Stevens walked across in front of him, "Think we are in for more rain, George?' He almost smiled "Thanks, Jim."

Gray took a smart single and Marshall, twisting on to the back foot, forced two fours through the off side field in Copp's over. As Lee began to bowl again, Kennett caught Tallis's signal to move round square. He cantered away to his left but, before he had even reached his new position, Gray glanced the first ball fine. Checking, Kennett dug his toes in to turn back: as he did so, he felt the damp grass slide under him; flat on his chest, he lifted his head to see the ball going over the fine leg boundary. A man near the sight screen threw it into to the wicket and, as Kennett brushed the grass and mud off his flannels, he sensed—and then saw—Tallis coming out to him from short-leg.

"Get into the pavilion and put spikes on, Kennett: those blasted creepers could cost us this match."

"But these *are* spikes—I wouldn't wear rubbers after a shower."

"Then the spikes must be in bloody poor shape—see they are fixed."

He bit back the words he wanted to say; all that came out was a husky "Right". He ran quickly to his place; his chest was tight; his eyes were stinging—heavens, he was a grown man; was this tears? Forget it: hadn't he decided with himself last night that it was all over?

The old hands were right. In Lee's third over a ball stood up and cracked Jimmy Gray on the elbow. Even Bob Copp, a yard less pacey, brushed a couple past Marshall's chest. Then it was "on". It had to be pace now: seam straight between the fingers, arm high, plenty of wrist and dig it in, short of a length. Tallis plastered men up close to the bat. Gray, determined and watchful, began to take a beating: allowing three or even four balls of the over to hit his body rather than push his bat into the danger of the lifter. Marshall, at the other end, tilted at the windmills. One great soaring hook passed high above Kennett's head into the crowd. Once, young Lee, eager to bowl, sent one too far up and Marshall, whipping his bat into the half volley, drove it over the sight screen. 50 for none. This was bad business for Norshire; there should have been four Hampshire wickets down by now. Only Wainwright, apart from Copp and Lee, bowled at the pace to use this wicket. Hampshire, of course, always took three main seamers—Cannings, Shackleton and Heath—into their games at Portsmouth, as well as Gray and Barnard as medium-pace changes. Norshire's three spinners were a sheer waste here. A credit mark, over and above his batting, to Wainwright if he did anything. Kennett thought ruefully of his own bowling. Once he fancied himself as a leg-spinner—a roller really, but steady. He had in fact had one or two good sets of figures. He remembered the spell, on a batsman's wicket at Fenners, which had its place in his record in the cricket annuals. Old Phil Ashmore, the county coach, had warned him against it in 1949. "You want to forget this bowling, young Kennett: they'll always be using you on good tracks, and you don't want to go out to bat straight away after ten or a dozen overs." The county had plenty of spinners, anyway; so he had turned it in. Tallis knew about it: "You gave up bowling, Kennett, didn't you?" "Yes, skipper, I did: I was too fast off the bat." Of course he should have sounded keener: it wasn't that he was too lazy to bowl: he would have liked it well enough but, if he talked himself on now, he could easily get a lot of stick: you have to bowl leg-breaks regularly to bowl them well.

A brief word between Tallis and Tim Pearce, and Wainwright came on for Lee who pulled on his second sweater and walked off to third man, muttering at his failure. Then the wickets began to fall. Copp made one leave Jim Gray off the pitch, it touched the edge of his high back stroke and hit his chest on the way to Tim Pearce's gloves. Henry Horton, after trying his steady, straight, defensive bat against bowling that spat off the pitch, began to drive. One rounded stroke ran through mid-on, another flew off the edge through slips; but soon he found himself playing off his face and Tallis, at short leg, took an easy catch. Still Marshall threw his bat at the lifting ball, secure enough, in fact, from being bowled since any ball which came through low enough to hit the stumps would have to be a half-volley—and no one proposed to offer Marshall that invitation to a certain four.

Rayment set out to play strokes, made one or two and then, aiming a cover drive, saw the ball fly up to the splice and loft away so that David Bridges had to run in from cover to catch it. Tallis brought Lee back in place of Wainwright. Certainly he would be half-stiff and not properly rested from his earlier spell, but they must strike now. "Sorry, Frank, but there's only an hour to go—give it everything you've got." Marshall took 10 off his settling-down over and then was caught off his gloves by Adam, at forward short leg. Mike Barnard made a couple of spectacular drives on the rise: Desmond Eagar swept a bouncer from Lee down to long leg—one bounce into the crowd—but like Sainsbury who, head down, tried to battle it out, they went to Lee and Copp before the close at seven. Harrison and Shackleton lived out the last ten minutes, and Hampshire finished the day 120 for seven wickets.

Back in the dressing room, Tallis adopted the Napoleonic air which each of the pros, in his different way, resented. "We should be winning if we had got rid of Marshall at the start" (no one looked at Kennett) "but I think we can still beat them: this wicket will have dried out easy by the morning." No one said anything. "Eh; Pearce?" "If it can rain this afternoon, it can rain tomorrow, Mr. Tallis." "Ah, you're an old pessimist Pearce." "No, we must have a chance, but they are a hundred-and-fifty-five on, and this is never an easy one to bat on."

For the second time in his cricketing life, George Kennett spent a night at an away match alone. Something, which he supposed was pride, would not let him talk to any of his friends about packing up. To have been with them while he—and they—avoided the thing which filled him would have been even worse.

He had supper again in the Italian café and walked idly on the long promenade, all but emptied by the gusty wind. Old matches came back into his mind and, carefully avoiding any thought of practicalities, he soaked himself gently in nostalgia. When he woke next morning the wind was still rattling his window and there was rain on the panes. At breakfast, the communal newspaper-reading was punctuated with talk of the wicket. There had, it seemed, been steady light rain for three or four hours in the night (do cricketers stay awake timing the rainfall or, if not, how can they be so sure?) The general impression was that there had been just about enough to keep the wicket angry. At the ground, the groundsman, non-committally, thought that might be so. Eagar told him not to use the roller. Let it get worse.

Copp bowled from the pavilion end and Shackleton, swinging at his third ball, hit it over the top of mid-on. Trying to do it again, he was caught by Bridges. Cannings, to his comic annoyance, played a short ball down on to his wicket in the next over. Malcolm Heath watched Harrison hit a boundary and then a three off Lee and, as the wicket recovered its venom, take most of a maiden over from Copp on his body. Heath missed three lifters from Lee before he waved his bat at a straight half volley and was bowled. Harrison was left high and dry with 17: the three outstanding wickets had gone down in a quarter of an hour and Hampshire were all out, 131.

The few scattered spectators calculated on their score-cards that Norshire wanted 167 to win and, including the extra half hour to five o'clock, had five hours all but five minutes to get them in. "34 runs an hour," announced a small boy, after laborious calculation.

George Kennett looked at no one, spoke to no one, but began to get ready. Tallis picked up a batting-order sheet. Opposite the figure 1, he wrote "Stevens". Then he hesitated. What were the chances that, if he opened himself, he might hit a quick twenty or so before the effect of the heavy roller—for the second time in half an hour—wore off? He looked at Kennett, who was putting on his batting flannels, and shook his head with irritation. "Kennett," he wrote, at number 2.

George Kennett had never felt quite like this before: certainly not when sober. There was a lightness in his chest, his face was warm, as if he was blushing; he felt as if he wanted to sing and he grinned at himself. Tallis's voice cut through his mood. "There is only one thing to do, fellows—we have got to hit our way out of this: if we go down, at least let's go down with our flags flying and all our guns firing." David Bridges wished Tallis was not so embarrassingly grand with his clichés: "Corny" was the word; no wonder the pros had nothing to say.

The opening pair walked to the door. "Get on with it before the rolling wears off." "All right, skipper," from Jim Stevens. Kennett looked at his captain, but did not see him or think of him.

Derek Shackleton's first ball to Stevens left on the pitch the ominous black bruise which marks the "green 'un." Stevens hooked him chancily, but mightily, for four. Kennett edged Cannings' outswinger; whipping round, he saw Barnard sprawling as the ball passed wide of him; they took two. It should not happen again. He dug in.

Tallis turned angrily to David Bridges, "Damn that bloody Kennett: why doesn't he go for runs while there's a chance?—I should never have sent him in." Bridges looked him in the face. "Poor devil: he only lives for this silly game, and that is how he plays it."

Minute by minute the grass sprung back to its true plim. Stevens twice hooked Shackleton off his chest; made a hectic 32 before, playing in front of his face, he saw Sainsbury dive forward to take the catch. Kennett, flexing and tensing his finger to make sure that the lifter from Cannings had not broken it, saw Keith Adam coming out to bat—sent in to swing for quick runs. As he went by Adam jerked at him, "Skipper says to hit." Kennett did not answer: he watched Adam flail at his first ball: yorked by Shackleton. He barely noticed Jack Connor coming in to get his head down at the other end. There were the minutes of silver, bought with pain which, oddly, did not hurt. There was nothing outside this leather ball, the friend and enemy of all his fears and hopes ever since his father first bowled under-arm to him in their little backyard, with the clothes line overhead to mark the straightness of the bowling. Heath had come on, his arm as high as a lamp-post: get the bat out of the line: again the ball thudded against his ribs. Don't rub it: that only encourages the bowler. There was the harsh drag of the seam across his chest: was the wetness sweat or blood? He looked: just a little sweat. He thought idly that, if only he were fatter—as fat as Tim Pearce—the ball would thud on him instead of cracking. Just now and again, if you were behind the line, one 'did it' soon enough and short enough to be pushed for a single. One from Heath leapt at his face and he hooked it from before his eyes for six. Back into the groove. Connor was gone: caught Barnard, bowled Cannings; 16. It was Wainwright who walked in to lunch with him. They had been lads on the staff together. Only, "Well played, George." He did not answer.

He sat through lunch in the dressing room: not too lazy to take off his pads, but wanting to feel them there. Jimmy Hayter brought him a jug of cold tea. Ellis Wainwright; beaten by the pace ball after ball, but hanging on until Cannings, at short third man to Heath, caught him, head-high, off the shoulder of the bat. Then young Bill Redding: going

287

to be a good player; watches it well. Barnard coming on?—why? His first ball was on a length and leapt, spitefully; drop the wrists; it ground into his solar plexus. So that was why: watch his pace off the wicket; safe enough if you do, he's mot moving it. Play or leave. If you play, be sure of middling it. Redding's ten runs were worth fifty; but he was not quite to the pitch of one from Heath he tried to drive: Henry Horton took the lobbed catch easily: 106 for five. Kennett walked away from the wicket, looked neither towards the pavilion nor the opposite end until he saw Heath moving in to bowl at Tallis. The first ball was over-pitched and Tallis drove it magnificently through mid-off. The next—the last ball of the over—reared from short of a length: short—hookable. Tallis pulled back as it whined past his head: pulled too far back and Kennett saw his face suddenly white. Eagar brought on Jimmy Gray. Damn it—he had forgotten how much this chap swung even a worn ball: he was just in time to play the big inswinger, awkwardly, half behind his pad and drop his bat on it as it rolled on. A single off the next ball. Tallis middled the sixth towards the gap between the bowler and wide mid-off: "No," he said. Why? There was an easy single in it. Kennett looked down the wicket at his captain and knew; the man was frightened, trying to keep away from Malcolm Heath. Tallis looked back defiantly, knowing that he knew.

Again Kennett hooked Heath over the short legs. In Gray's next over, Tallis, pushing with the swing, missed; Harrison took the ball wide of the leg stump and, as the batsman lifted his back foot, stumped him. 115 for six: 52 to get.

Tim Pearce, a touch of comedy in his half-waddling walk, but his weathered face solemn, passed him with a nod and "Plenty of time before five." Shackleton for Heath: Kennett pushed him for one, wide of cover point's right hand.

The applause crackled round the ground: Shackleton was clapping. Kennett looked at the score board: under the figure 2 were the figures 50. He touched his cap: the applause went on; he pulled off his cap; the sun had bleached its original blue to a faded purple; the thought occurred to him that it would have been a waste of money to have bought a new one for this season. Shackleton pushed on at his leg stump: and it angled back off the seam: he was in line all right, but not ready for so much lift: too late to leave it now: get your body behind it. There was an agony of lights as it drove his split finger against the bat handle. Yet, after the first stab, it was clear and cool, like water. "All right, George?" It was Harrison from behind the stumps. He must have staggered—or cursed—"Yes, right as rain."

"Well, if you're all right, I must be better than I feel." Nod.

Wait, wait, wait: the runs will come. Never mind the applause for the maiden overs; laugh at that bloody fool trying to start a slow handclap. Tim Pearce was old in this game; content to wait for that one down the leg side and slap it gratefully for four.

Another? It cut back and bowled the senior pro—leg stump—through the middle of his glance. 143 for seven. Bridges to come; then nothing: Bob Copp and young Lee were not worth a light. But Bridges was an amateur; he would not fancy this stuff. David Bridges was almost respectful. "Take what you can, Kennett: I'll do my damnedest, but I'm out of my class." They plugged on. Bridges played and missed, played and missed, but always his body was behind it: he cursed and rubbed, but did not flinch. Heath came back. Keep Bridges away from this: keep him away from Shackleton, too. A single off Heath left Bridges the last ball of the over: he chased it outside the off stump, edged it: grinned half-shamefacedly as it beat the field and went for four. Carry on. It grew no easier: damn it he did not want it easier. As Heath bowled, Kennett saw his body shake with effort: the bouncer: he hooked, but late, swung round behind the ball; half-hit it and, as he turned, saw Eagar throw himself into the line of it, but below it. Horton at long leg was not bothering to run in for it. "Well played." They were there. He looked again at the scoreboard as it ticked up to 167 and—under Batsman 2—72.

It seemed very dark in the dressing room. "Thanks," he said, "thanks." In the shower, alone, he body cold with tiredness, he caught sight of himself in the mirror, his flesh grey under the electric light and pied with the marks of the ball, the red circles purpled on the line of the seam. "Have a drink, Kennett." It was David Bridges. "I'll be out in the bar in a minute—thank you." Slowly back to his seat; his clothes were the last left on any hook; the bags round him ready packed and strapped for the next match. He looked incuriously at the letter on the corner of the table. "Mr. George Kennett." He turned it disinterestedly; the flap bore the stamp "Thomas & Sons." Geoff Thomas—his old skipper— must be the family business he went to manage—a factory or something. He pushed a bruised finger under the flap.

Dear Kennett,

I wonder if you would be interested in the post of groundsman at our works ground? Pethick has just retired on pension and it occurred to me that you would soon be looking for a permanent job. If you feel like striking out now, and if the county can release you, it could be worth while. The pay would be about the same as you are getting now, and the house and sports goods shop go with the job.

Your only fixed duties would be the ground and some coaching. You would, however, be an asset to the works team. My father is President of this county club, which plays in the Minor Counties competition: they badly need an opener of your experience and we would make you free to play regularly for them if you cared to do so.

You could take over in September and I hope you will—I for my part, should be very happy to renew our old association.

Yours sincerely,

Geoffrey Thomas.

Bridges and Tallis were near the door as Kennett made his way to the bar: he heard Bridges say, ". . . not the kind of thing Norshire can afford to lose."

Tim Pearce turned with a pint of beer for him. "Cheers"—the mugs were lifted. Then Tallis was at his elbow. "Well played, Kennett—give me just a moment and then the next one is on me."

"Yes, skipper."

"I don't mind telling you, I had not asked the committee to review your contract—I believe in being frank—but that innings of yours today took a lot of guts: I can't promise you a regular place, with Winter coming in next season; but you would certainly start as first reserve batsman; you could be useful with the staff lads and I'll try to get you anyway a year's contract—with match money when you are in the first team, of course."

"Thanks, skipper, but I've made up my mind to retire at the end of the season"—he hesitated—"but I'd like to see the season out with the side." Tallis smiled—with some relief, as Kennett recognised—

"Well, you know your own business best; all right—now, have a drink—a jolly good innings."

As Kennett lifted his glass, the stiffening bruise on his elbow made him wince. Leo Harrison, beside him, caught his quick intake of breath and looked him half-solemnly in the eyes, "It ain't half a bloody game, is it?"

Leslie Thomas (1931–   ) as one of Britain's leading modern
writers, needs very little introduction, and indeed his novel,
The Virgin Soldiers *(1966), may just be the most comical*
book of recent times. Leslie, who was born in Newport,
Monmouthshire, and educated at Dr Barnardo's in
Kingston-upon-Thames, did not discover cricket until he was
in his teens, but as he explains in the following piece, it gripped
his heart immediately and is now listed as his favourite
recreation in Who's Who. *As a former local newspaper*
reporter and feature writer on the London Evening News *he*
frequently came into contact with the game and some of its
personalities, and cricket has a habit of intruding into his
novels. He also belongs to the Lord's Taverners. 'Daffodil
Summer' written in 1982 is as evocative a piece about one
man's unswerving support for a team as you will probably
ever read . . .

Daffodil Summer

by Leslie Thomas

In the fading August of 1948, on a day by the southern seaside, J. C. Clay, the gentleman of Glamorgan, bowled a measured off-break which struck Charlie Knott, of Hampshire, on the pad. The story has it that Dai Davies, the umpire, a brown, beaming man, raised a dramatic finger and, unable to contain himself, bellowed at Knott: "You're *OUT*—and *WE'VE* won!"

Glamorgan had indeed won. Not only a remarkable match, but the County Championship, and for the first time. On that dun afternoon in Bournemouth the pavilion trembled with Welsh singing, voices that floated over the English regular roses, causing raised eyebrows among the gardens and where the band was playing by the sea.

For Johnnie Clay, the lean, grey man, wise as a heron, the triumph had come in his fiftieth year and after seasons of failure, disappointment, even ridicule, for his beloved county. I remember that day, trotting on my trivial rounds as a junior reporter on a local newspaper in

Essex, hearing the wonderful news on the radio while I was cross-examining a lady about the thrills and spills of the Women's Institute flower arranging contest. "Why," she asked briskly, "are you grinning like that? Flower arranging is *no* laughing matter." "I'm sorry," I remember saying, knowing she would never understand. "I'm doing it because I'm happy."

Happy indeed I was, along with a throng of others. Of the four hundred telegrams sent to Arms Park, Cardiff, the next day was one from an exile in Paris. The news, he said, had made him decide to return home to Wales. What, after all, had Paris to offer?

For me the love affair was new. It is a confession I hesitate to make, even after these years, but, brought up in wartime Newport, I hardly knew of the *existence* of cricket, until I was gone twelve years. Then, after the war—after I had heard about it and was growing in love for it—one day in 1947, I went for the first time to Lord's and had scarcely had time to place my spam sandwiches and myself on one of the free seats (as they were loftily called) below the heads of the trees at the Nursery End, when I witnessed the most exquisite sight of my youthful life. Willie Jones, small as a button, batting against Middlesex, leaned back, folded his body like a spring, and square cut to the boundary. The ball hit the boards with an echo I can hear now. It was as though he had waited for my arrival, after all those unknowing years. From that moment—and although I had left the Land of my Father's and my birth—I had Glamorgan written on my heart.

*   *   *   *

The trials of the early days of Glamorgan County Cricket Club are nowhere better contained than in a tale told by Jack Mercer, eighty-odd now. He was a Glamorgan player when almost anyone who owned a bat could get a game. "We had six captains and five wicket-keepers in one season," he recalled. "The oddest people used to turn up and get in the side. A great big fellow was in the team one day and Johnnie Clay, being a gentleman, didn't like to ask him whether he was a batsman or a bowler. So John asked me and I didn't know either. 'Well,' said Johnnie, 'we'll put him in the slips. Even if he can't catch, he's a big chap—something might hit him'."

J. C. Clay, the dear man, the quiet cricketer, in the phrase of Wilfred Wooller, was a member of the side which first played in the County

Championship in 1921. The application for first-class status had been grudgingly approved. Cricket authority sniffed and intoned: "If you can get eight other clubs to play you, then you are accepted." Glamorgan got six and Lancashire and Yorkshire agreed at the last moment to join the list. Certainly the Roses Counties never overrated the urchin Welsh team. "Yorkshire only ever booked a hotel for two nights when they came to Cardiff or Swansea," sighed Wilfred Wooller.

The team amazed itself and everyone else by winning the opening match against thoroughbred Sussex. From then on it lost. *Wisden's* comment that Glamorgan's entry into first-class cricket "was not justified by results", was honestly echoed by the county's annual report which related sadly: ". . . Glamorgan were like no other side; some say it was not a side at all." The main bowlers were Harry Creber, who was forty-seven and Jack Nash who was forty-eight. In that first season Nash only just missed his hundred wickets.

The sickly infant years were slow to go. After two seasons in county cricket Glamorgan not only had a solitary specialist slip fielder, they were also £6,212 in the red at the bank. But John Clay believed and others joined him in his faith. Cricket had never been considered to be a "Welsh game" but now, from the valleys and the sandy seaside towns of the south, men who could play took tentative steps towards Cardiff. Dai Davies, the man who, as umpire, played his part in the fateful day many years later, Emrys Davies, a staunch opener, Arnold Dyson, a poetic batsman, and, momentously, a man called Maurice Turnbull.

Turnbull, as captain and secretary, pulled Glamorgan up by the laces in its cricket boots. He organised both the bowling and the finances, he made centuries and friends, he was as articulate in the chair as he was in the field. He was the first Glamorgan cricketer to play for England and then—outrageously—he was killed in the war before all his selfless work came to splendid justification.

In the final seasons before the war the county finished in positions of untold respectability—midway up the table. At that time Wilfred Wooller first walked out to bat, the rugby hero come to the summer game. A big man, combative, unyielding, some said, and still do, too forthright, but a leader born to lead. He was to be Glamorgan's man of destiny. But first he had to wait six years and a war.

*   *   *   *

They say that when Wilfred Wooller played his first match after his repatriation from a Japanese prison camp and went out to the wicket, tears were running down the cheeks of grown men.

"Like a big skeleton, he was," an uncle of mine told me. "And yellow."

But it would have taken more than the Japanese to daunt Wooller. We played a game at Changi prison camp in Singapore on Christmas Day," he remembers. "Somehow we found a ball and a bat and we made some stumps. We had an England versus Australia Test match right there in front of the Japanese guards. They looked puzzled."

Forty years on Wooller is still a big man, tall, unstooping, broad-shouldered, broad faced. He prowls rather than walks. A man like a large leopard. His was the sad but familiar story of a return from years of captivity and privation only to find that life had changed behind his back. His pre-war marriage was quickly over. "I remember getting in my car and driving from London up the Great North Road—anywhere," he said. "I had no idea where I was going." The road, oddly, led to Africa and a frightening adventure in a crash-landing airplane which made him, abruptly, realise that life was still precious. He decided to do something with his—and returned to Wales to become captain of a Glamorgan team that was to make history.

"At the beginning there was really only half a team," he recalled. "The remnants of what we had before the war. But there was a new generation of young cricketers wanting to play, boys like Phil Clift, Gilbert Parkhouse and Alun Watkins, all gifted, all eager. Then we took on some chaps from outside, players that their own counties had decided they did not want." Three of those cricketers, Len Muncer, Norman Hever and a lad called Eaglestone, were from the richly-endowed Middlesex team. With the rag-tag-and-bobtail already assembled in Cardiff they became, under the steely leadership of Wooller, a side of supermen.

It was Johnnie Clay that Wooller patently admired and still remembers with affection. "He was the most wonderful of men. Quiet, a true gentleman. He loved cricket and lived for it. All the winter he bowled on a practice wicket in his garden. But he was never so serious that his sense of humour would not come bubbling out. One day we were playing against Somerset and C. C. C. Case—'Box' as they used to call him—was batting. He was always a difficult man to get out, he would block ball after ball and never take risks, and on this day Johnnie Clay became so exasperated with the stone walling that he substituted a rubber ball for the cricket ball and bowled that. You should have seen Box's face when the thing took off vertically right in front of his nose."

Alun Watkins, a Plymouth Argyle footballer, a man built like an armchair, but not in the least static, came into the side. He was a pugnacious batsman (I once saw him hit a ball for four to leg—after it had passed the wicket-keeper), a good medium pace left-arm bowler. He was also a fine close-to-the-wicket fielder, one of the clutch which Wooller recruited, taught, inspired, and to whom he gave faith. Wooller says: "In the season we won the Championship there were plenty of county sides who had far better batting than us, and quite a number with better bowling. But not one had a more brilliant fielding side."

The county which, only a generation before, had only one man brave enough to call himself a slip fielder, and which had found it necessary to "hide" four old men in the field, now had a roost of men who were capable of the most miraculous catching feats. Wooller remembered how Ernie Toshack, the Australian, had bowled to a leg-side close field and he employed that in his Glamorgan team. Around the corner the Glamorgan fielders loitered like shop-lifters. "Our secret weapon," smiled Wooller. "In our championship season Watkins, Phil Clift and I took about 120 catches."

Emrys Davies and Arnold Dyson opened the batting, until the veteran Dyson went to take a coaching appointment at Oundle School, reappearing to play a notable part in the finale to the Championship. Both players from Glamorgan's days of struggle, acquainted with grief, they gave their sober experience to the younger players of the side. Emrys coached the elegant Gilbert Parkhouse and the dapper Phil Clift who became his opening partner. He would stare down the wicket at Clift like a minister in chapel. "Emrys was a good man, a sober, dedicated fellow, a great father-figure to the team," said Wooller. Arnold Dyson studied the game every moment, winter and summer. They used to say that he was such a perfectionist that if he touched a catch to slip he always walked even if it were dropped. Morally he was out.

Willie Jones, the bean-sized batsman, topped the county batting averages that summer of 1948, amazingly hitting *two* double centuries but no single centuries. Welsh-speaking Willie had to be encouraged, bolstered. After scoring two thousand runs in a season he was worried in case his contract was not renewed. He never went to the wicket without trembling, scarcely believing that he was capable of doing the things he did. Jones played his favoured square cut like a man prodding a bear. At Gravesend, against Kent, in June he scored 207. "When he came in after batting," remembers his captain, "his hand was shaking so much he could hardly hold a glass of orange squash. 'I'll never be able to do that again, skipper,' he mumbled." A week later he *did* it again—212 not out against Essex, with Emrys Davies getting 215 in a total of 586 for five declared.

They used to call Haydn Davies, the wicket-keeper, The Panda. He was large and dark of head and eye and adopted the stance of that curious, benign and powerful creature. For all his heaviness, both in body and aspect, he was the lively one, the joker, the charmer, the boy for a night out, even when the stern Wooller disapproved. "He telephoned me one day and said, 'Skipper, I've got a broken finger'," said Wooller. "I asked him what he intended to do about it and he said, 'I'll go on playing. I'll try to keep it out of the way'."

There were others who came in and out of the side as the summer progressed, George Lavis, Jim Pleas, and an absorbing spin bowler from Swansea eponymously named Stan Trick. "He worked in his father-in-law's garage and he couldn't always get away to play," smiled Wooller slowly shaking his head. "But the Swansea wicket was made for him. There he was just about unplayable." In his first match at the St Helen's ground against Somerset, he took six wickets for 77 in the first innings and six for 29 in the second. But only at Swansea could he do it. They said his sort of bowling didn't travel well.

Of the three imported players, all from Middlesex, the most significant was Len Muncer, a beaming, oval-faced spin bowler, approaching his final seasons. He got through twice as many overs as anyone else, apart from Wooller, and took 156 wickets in the season at an average of 17.12. He was also only just short of a thousand runs. Young Eaglestone batted soundly when he was needed and Norman Hever, the fast bowler, topped the first-class averages for some weeks. At Lord's against Middlesex, the county which had rejected him, he took five wickets for 34. With relish.

*   *   *   *

But Glamorgan were never players of mere matches. They had the fun and charm and good companionship of a touring repertory company. J. B. G. Thomas, the legendary sports editor of the *Western Mail*, travelled around with them that Daffodil Summer. "They had an old mangle, the sort your mam used to have at home, and this was transported on the back of a little lorry, together with a pile of tattered, suspicious-looking blankets," he remembers. "If Glamorgan arrived at a ground and there had been overnight rain then everybody would set-to spreading the blankets and putting them through the mangle to get the pitch fit for play."

"They were a lovely bunch of boys. I don't think they quite knew what was happening to them when they won the Championship that summer." Bryn Thomas would travel by train with the team, sometimes taking his infant son along also. "We used to be crowded into the compartment, talking cricket, laughing, a whole bunch of us, and little Craig would be up in the luggage rack, staring over the top, taking it all in." Such an exotic childhood, travelling suspended above those gods, no doubt gave Craig Thomas the seed he needed to become the successful novelist he is today.

The first match of the 1948 season told nothing of the amazements that were to follow over the sunny early weeks. Glamorgan played a friendly game against Thomas Owen's XI, an occasion which, however, was not without its oddities. The year was scarcely out of winter and the conditions were chill, indeed so inclement that Maurice Leyland "retired hurt" in the visitors' first innings. He had cramp. Emrys Davies, grey as the weather, assembled a painstaking 31 before being dismissed by Len Hutton, a thoughtful bowler in those days, who took two further wickets in the Glamorgan innings at a cost of 22 runs. Sporting declarations in the weather-washed game resulted in Thomas Owen's team being required to score 85 in 45 minutes to win. They were four runs short at the end. One of the umpires was Douglas Jardine. I wish I had seen him. And Hutton bowling.

Another friendly, against Somerset, was played at Newport where once, it was gossiped, the wicket was prepared with more than a touch of witchcraft. Certainly, before the war, the Glamorgan groundsman, was rumoured to have prepared a strip of mystic components including silt from the River Taff, coal dust from the River Ebbw and mud from the River Usk "all boiled up in a Welsh cauldron". It was forecast that the potion would help the Glamorgan spinners against Gloucester in the summer of 1938. Gloucester made 581 of which Hammond got 302. He liked batting on coal dust.

The 1948 match against Somerset at Newport went better for the Welshmen. Somerset crumpled to the diminutive spin of Willie Jones (who also got 93) and lost by 98 runs.

Essex next were defeated at Cardiff (where the cricket ground was behind the Arms Park rugby stand) by five wickets; then Somerset again at Swansea with Stan Trick from the garage, taking his famous twelve wickets. At Derby, at the end of May, against a strong bowling side, came defeat by the not inconsiderable margin of 301 runs. But there followed three successive triumphs—against Kent at Gravesend (Willie Jones's nervous double hundred) and versus Hampshire at Cardiff, where Hampshire scored a hundred in an hour, going for victory, and were then summarily dismissed in the next hour, mostly by the flighted left-arm bowling of, once again Willie Jones. "He made the ball 'ang in the air, aye like a grape," my old uncle said.

Kent were humbled at Swansea in June, Stan Trick, having more time off from the grease pit, taking ten wickets and Len Muncer eight. More than 30,000 people watched this match over the three days, the multitude that were to follow Glamorgan throughout the season. Wooller, the rugby man, the winter hero, was bringing Welshmen out of the valleys to see a different game, but one which they embraced with hardly less heart and, naturally, with as much singing. It was the first time choral works had been heard at first-class matches.

The uplift was needed, not only in Wales but throughout a Britain bled grey by a war that had finished three years before. Clothes and food were still rationed, there were shortages of almost everything. But the pundits were unimpressed. "It was not a vintage year," decided a cricket aristocrat. He was one of many who refused to believe that this unfashionable, even *foreign*, county could actually win. Victory after victory was discounted even when the Welshmen led the table in June, and the setback period which followed in July was acknowledged by those who knew, or thought they did, as only right and to be expected. Lesser counties simply did not ascend like larks. At the end there was a multitude who were not so much surprised as shocked. It was as though the prize had been taken by stealth.

That same season up and down England, in the Test matches and through the counties, went the conquering Australians on their first post-war tour. They scored seven hundred runs *in one day* against Essex at Southend.

At the Oval, England were briskly dealt with: all out for 52. Don Bradman walked out for his farewell innings. He was cheered and applauded all the way to the middle, only to return minutes later in the silence of disbelief—bowled by Hollies for no score. I was there in that throng. I had never seen him bat and now I never would.

On that day Alun Watkins played his first match for England, and received such a battering from Lindwall, that he was too bruised to play in the historic game at Bournemouth which took the Championship.

*   *   *   *

Meanwhile Glamorgan appeared to have lost their way. They fell to Middlesex and to Leicestershire and there came a faltering series of drawn games, partly through the summer weather turning sour. The game with the Australians never came to any flourish, although with lumpy rain clouds hanging on the Bristol Channel and not an inch of room in the ground, Keith Miller made 84 in the only innings, which came to a stop in a downpour with the tourists at 215 for three. In another July game Gunner G. A. R. Lock, playing for Combined Services, the only squaddie in the parade of Lieutenant Colonels, Squadron Leaders and Commanders, took six wickets for 43, a taste of the great days that were to come for him with Surrey and with England.

A victory against Warwickshire, at Neath, kept Glamorgan's nose near the top of the table and then came, in mid-August, with the Welsh weather mending, a wonderful and crucial victory against Surrey at Cardiff. Wilfred Wooller's brave batting, driving and hammering square cuts, ensured a Glamorgan total of 239. Wooller scored 89, his best of the season. Then Johnnie Clay, coming into the team in the absence of Watkins, having reached the age of fifty, bowled out one of the strongest counties in England for fifty runs. Clay took five wickets and when Surrey followed on took another five. The long, frail, silver man was almost bowled over himself as the Arms Park Welshmen charged across the pitch at the end to acclaim him and the Glamorgan team. The smell of success was in the Cardiff air and very sweet it was.

And so to the final match against Hampshire, at Bournemouth—not the *last* match of the season but the one that had to be won. "It needed to be then," remembered Wilfred Wooller laconically. "Because the last game was at Leicester." Jack Walsh, the Australian-born spin bowler, played for Leicester and Wooller's team knew they would be pressed to scrape even a draw on the home side's wicket. (So it proved for, having secured the Championship, Glamorgan went to Leicester and were soundly beaten by an innings—the second time that the Midlands county had defeated them that season.)

The habitual champions, Yorkshire, who might have finally overtaken Glamorgan, were engaged against Somerset at Taunton, on the other side of Dorset, and Glamorgan began their innings at Bournemouth with conspiratorial clouds on the sea. Arnold Dyson, on holiday from his school coaching, was asked to play because Phil Clift was injured. Johnnie Clay came into the side instead of the Test-match-bruised Alun Watkins. Both replacements played crucial roles in the events of the next two days.

Emrys Davies and Dyson went forth to bat. Emrys's wife went off to walk around the town. As she shopped she listened for sounds from the ground.

Only ten minutes after the innings had begun dull summer raindrops sent the players to the pavilion and there they remained for the rest of the day, staring out at that most glum of views, the English seaside in the wet.

Sunday was spent wondering. On Monday the skies appeared kinder and once more Emrys and Arnold went to the middle. There now remained eleven and a half hours to win the match. The pair batted steadily as the clock turned, but knowing that the time would come for acceleration. Dyson was out for 51, trying to force the tempo, and at lunch Glamorgan were 99 for one wicket. Willie Jones emerged (tentatively) and, locking up his dashing shots, stared low and anxiously down the wicket at the fiercely advancing Shackleton, one of England's finest pace bowlers.

In mid-afternoon Emrys stroked (yes, *stroked*) a six, an extravagance greeted with almost chapel-like pursed lips from the Welshmen present. Emrys smiled apologetically. Willie sidled his way past his fifty, and when Emrys was eventually out for the most important 74 he had ever accumulated, the unassuming little man from the valleys assumed the mantle, stitched his way patiently through the whole innings while Wooller and Len Muncer and Norman Hever, at the tail, threw their bats. The side were all out for 315, Jones returning, smiling unsurely, with 78 not out.

It was still only early evening and the Hampshire openers, Arnold and Rogers, went out with over an hour left for play. Wooller and Hever bowled. In the captain's second over Rogers played a true leg glance and Gilbert Parkhouse, who had failed with the bat, swooped like a local gull to catch the ball an inch from the ground and no more than three yards from the bat. It was the catch that made Glamorgan really *believe* they could do it. Before the end of play on that brief evening six Hampshire batsmen were back in the pavilion. Glamorgan went to bed looking forward to the morning.

There seemed hardly room or time to breathe on that ground the next day. Not long ago I played in a match there and I sat after the game, in the lemon sun of the evening, years later, trying to imagine how it had been. Wooller, seriously, sent a telegram to Somerset playing Yorkshire at Taunton. The two counties, having for so long been treated lightly, disdainfully, had a mutual bond, and the message "Hold on to Yorkshire. We're beating Hants" was received and understood. "Don't worry," came the reply. "We're beating Yorkshire."

With that assurance Glamorgan set about the Hampshire second innings. Every so often a whisper would go from the pavilion around the crowd that Somerset were keeping their word.

John Clay had been out early to sniff the salty air. He pressed his finger tips into the wicket and knew everything would be all right. The information he kept private. He and the oval-faced Len Muncer finished Hampshire for 84. There were now four hours during which to get them out a second time.

Arnold and Rogers batted without any crisis for twenty minutes and four hours began to look a short time indeed. Then young Hever got one under Rogers' bat, pitched right up and moving a shade. Clean bowled. Hope rekindled.

Desmond Eagar, a fine player, charged the Glamorgan bowlers, hitting Willie Jones for a six that came near to disturbing people on the beach. But Muncer and Clay came back and that was enough. Muncer curled one around Eagar's feet to bowl him. The next man Bailey was promptly run out and the two spinners, so disparate in physique and style, whittled their way through the tail. Muncer had claimed five wickets in the first Hampshire innings and Clay three. Now it was the tall Johnnie's turn. The man who had played in Glamorgan's first county match in 1921, bowled as he had never bowled before. By the time he had Knott lbw, and had received the historical affirmative from Dai Davies (Knott swears to this day that the umpire appealed as well!), he had taken six for 48. It was still only mid-afternoon.

So there it was. The miracle at last. They still talk about it in Wales and wherever one Welshman meets another. It was wonderful that time long ago. That Daffodil Summer.

In my estimation, the funniest cricket books of recent years have been the two volumes of Tales from a Long Room *published in 1981 and 1982 and written by self-confessed cricket fanatic Peter Tinniswood (1936–   ). These dotty and often prejudiced reflections of 'the Brigadier' from Witney Scrotum about what cricket is – and isn't! – were given a tremendous reception when first published, and then became something of a cult when adapted for a television series in the spring of 1985. The success of the series was due in no small measure to the performances of Robin Bailey as 'the Brigadier'. It was a part for which he felt ideally suited, for as he said later, 'I was never particularly good at playing the game, but I'm a great fan and love watching.' (He is, in fact, a member of both the MCC and Surrey CC.) And such has been Robin's success, that he is now constantly being invited to speak at cricket clubs all over the country, and when he turned up at a recent test match at Old Trafford, Brian Johnston talked on the air for some time about the fact 'the Brigadier' was present! Peter Tinniswood who grew up in the Yorkshire cricket heartland of Sheffield and worked on local papers there and in Liverpool and Bristol before breaking into writing books and plays, has a rich store of anecdotes about cricket from which to draw his material. He maintains all the stories are based on 'the real thing – even if they do develop it to the ridiculous.' Of 'the Brigadier' Peter adds, 'He is a stalwart of all that is noblest and finest in the English way of life. Traditional country virtues such as after-hours drinking and wife-swapping.' He also acknowledges the debt he owes the old man. 'I can shelter behind "the Brigadier",' he says, 'but it has certainly given me the opportunity to meet some of my heroes. I went to some Test matches in Australia and was able to meet the players. It was marvellous.' Whether those same players might feel the same about Peter after reading the following piece specially written in June 1985, I would not like to venture an opinion . . .*

The Test in Witney Scrotum

by Peter Tinniswood

Just as I expected—the scum did not turn up.

Yes, the Australian tourists failed to appear to play the One Day Test against Witney Scrotum.

Their excuse? Feeble in the extreme.

The vermin had had the profound impertinence to inform us that on the day arranged for the great game they had been compelled by the Authorities at Lord's to play a Test Match at Old Trafford against Ian Botham.

Good God, do these hairy-nosed Colonials think we are total nincompoops to swallow that load of of balderdash?

I happen to know for certain that on that very day Mr Ian Botham was in Cheltenham addressing a Meeting of The Ladies Guild of Nude Autocyclists.

309

I am not a prejudiced man, but . . . No I must contain my anger.

The village had been hard at it for weeks preparing for our visitors.

For three days Miss Roebuck from the Dog Biscuit Shop had been mucking out Farmer Emburey's Stable to provide overnight accommodation.

The Cricket bag repository had donated sacking and sawdust for bedding and the fire brigade had installed a static tank in the unlikely event of our guests wishing to wash themselves.

The village Elders, Arlott, Mosey and Johnston, had been freshly scrubbed in neat gin and turpentine, and with breathless anticipation we awaited the arrival of our friends from the Land of Weak Beer and short-sighted Umpires.

Sure enough, dead on the dot of eight, the Motorised Mobile Charabanc drew up outside the Baxter Arms.

A great cheer went up from the crowd only for it to be stifled in their throat when from the coach stepped a most curious figure dressed in shocking pink silk, pantaloons, and black-laced double-breasted blazer.

"Gosh, it's Joan Collins." exclaimed Miss Roebuck from the Dog Biscuit Shop.

"No, it's not," said the village blacksmith and Toad Circumcizer, Gooch, "it's Richie Benaud."

Indeed it was.

The villagers crowded round him fearfully fingering his coiffure and timidly tugging at the lower lips of his 13 mouths.

And then a howl of terror and rage went up.

Remember they were poor simple folks who had never seen such a vision before.

In awed silence they conducted him to the village stocks. A great bonfire was constructed and lit.

I turned my gaze away. I could not bear to witness the ghastly sight. What happened to him I do not know.

And so dear readers next time you look at the pictures on your moving television screen, think to yourselves: "Who is the real Richie?"

It is my opinion that he is currently appearing as the frightful stinker Blake Carrington—either that or he's making a guest appearance as Miss Ellie.

Dear, dear Richie—what will the summer be without him.

In view of the outcome of the most recent test series against Australia, it is perhaps only cricket to give an Aussie the last word. And who more suitable to have a final say than Professor Terror Tomkins, the former test fast bowler turned university lecturer, who represents to the likes of 'the Brigadier' the totally unacceptable face of cricket. Terror is, of course, the creation of one of today's finest sportswriters, Ian Wooldridge (1932–), and the man from Oz's occasional virulent diatribes in the pages of the Daily Mail *are certainly a highlight of any cricket reading for me and, I am sure, thousands of others. One reader enthused after the appearance in August 1985 of the item I am reprinting here, 'Best piece of literary writing I have read for ages. Okay the spelling is histerical, but it's hilariously funny, and potently true are his observations. Let's have more of this Wizzerd of Oz!' Such generous tributes are not unknown to Ian Wooldridge who has been named 'Sportswriter of the Year' on no less than three occasions, and has authored some highly successful cricket books including* Cricket, Lovely Cricket *(1963) and* MCC: The Autobiography of a Cricketer *with* Colin Cowdrey *(1976). His fascination with the game was begun at Brockenhurst Grammar School, increased as a reporter on such newspapers as the* Bournemouth Times, News Chronicle *and* Sunday Dispatch, *and has now been shaped by years of observation of matches, into a profound understanding that can be turned to serious or comic effect with equal agility. I agree with that* Daily Mail *reader who found Professor Tomkins' observations so hilarious: they provide an ideal climax for me to draw stumps and leave the field of laughter, still chuckling heartily as I go. And I trust that you, too, have shared some amusement through these pages . . .*

The Wizzerd of Oz

by Ian Wooldridge

'*Professor Terror Tomkins, now senior wrangler in anthropomorphic didactics at the University of Woomera, is better known to readers as a great ex-Test fast bowler for Australia and occasional writer. Though now mellowed by academic responsibility and domestic contentment – his first wife, Gloreen, eventually ran off with an Indian jockey – we have flown the professor to Britain to comment exclusively on the dramatic climax to one of the most glittering Test series ever played.*'

Lissen, who rites these bleedin interductry bits? For a start Gloreen ran off with some born-agin Chrischun tennis woofter wot kept saying 'love-six, love-six' which she misherd as usual.

And as fer this bein the most glitterin Test serious ever plaid, well, blokes like me and Dennis and Fred Trueman are falling about with hillarity.

I mean, did you clock that shot (note to editer: pleese be careful about how that word's spelt bekauz I'm in enuff shot already) to which Andrew Hilditch got out in Orstralier's second innins? I mean, if he wasn't Bobby Simpson's daughter's husband I don't reckon they'd ever let him back into Oz.

Pleese note, Poms, that I'm bendin over backwards to be ingenuous. Yore definitly the best of two teams wot wouldn't have got inter the Ugandan Army XXII in my day. That said, its bleeding hard to come here and stomick the way the good shepherd always sticks up for the lamb when its been hit on the foot.

Histerical incident, that. Could never have happined in the days before cricketers starting cheatin one another like Armenian horse deelers.

In the old days the batsman wood have said: 'Lissen, did that bleedin shot strike you on the poxy instep before bein caught by Mr Gower?'

On the reply 'Yes' he would have felt as sick as a dingo and hoofed it to the paverlion without so much as a dirty look at the umpire. On the reply 'No' he wood have staid just where he was.

Cricket's never bin the same since the Bishop of Liverpool went into polerticks. There's so much cash now flyin around for winnin that the poor bleedin umpires don't stand a chance.

I didn't aktually see the incerdent myself. I was still flyin to England for this currant litray assinment with Sportsmail, not a happy journey, I can tell you, now that Orstralian airplains have been fitted with this new-fangled radio.

On the flite deck they'd been hooked up to the BBC radio commentry which ment they had to wait about two hours for the latest score while this new comidy team of Honkers, Bonkers and Wonkers tried out wot sounded like an Oxfam appeal to old ladies in the English outback to send them some cake.

Apparently the silly old bats do it so regularly, just to get menshuned, that whenever Alan McGillivers is about to say somthin sensible, either Honkers or Wonkers stuffs a merang in his orriface.

This did not please Captain Bruce Kernaghan up on the flite deck. After dodgin a few helicopters on the Heathrow runway he addressed us thus over the intercome:

'Lissen, none of you is allowed to even unfasen yore seat-belts until we've polished off every drop of duty-free on board. Disasterous news

314

awaits us. If Professor Tomkins is on board, will he please indemnify himself with a member of the cabin crew.'

Gingerly stepping over the prostate stewards I found this hostie at the back. She was rebuttoning a blouse with koalas and kangeroos all over it.

Wossup,' I arsked. 'Wossup?' she expectorated, 'we've lost the bleedin Test Match, that's wossup and I'm Jugoslavian by birth.'

Well, we was ardly off the bleedin plain before the gloatin started. 'Bit bleedin late. Terror, ain't you?' said this bloke with gold rings up to his elbows and a turban. 'They could definitely have done with you at Edgbastin.'

'Who are you?' I questioned. 'The Mayor of Calcutta?'

'None of yor Orstralian allegorical allusions,' he replied. 'I'm a senior immergrashun officer at Heathrow with two kids at Millfield, a charge account at Harrods, several newsagents shops in the London suberbs, a chaufer, a four-day week and an index-linked penshun.'

Anyway, he got the last word. He made me stand in this line of 2,000 prospective Ethiopian refugies while he waved former Nazi air aces and some Eyetie arms salesmen through an empty channel marked EEC.

'Everyone except old Comrades, I see,' I yelled nastily.

I was plannin to go strait up to Birmingham to deliver this personul letter from our Prime Minister to Allan Border but it was not to be.

'No chance, Terror, I'm afraid,' said this bloke at the railway station. 'Times has changed since you was last hear. Now that we've got some cole to put in the train we ain't got no trains to carry the cole, let alone human beans.'

'Bleedin good advertisements for Birmingham and the 1992 Olympic Games,' I said. 'Don't worry, Terror,' he replied. 'We may even have a skelerton service runnin by then.'

You Poms hasn't changed a bit. You celebrated VJ-Day by litin thousands of candels for Hiroshima. You are kicked out of world football and I can still sit there watchin a TV program implyin that the grotty little hooligans are deprived citizens. You give your trade union leeders more airtime than Terry Wogin.

Some of us Oz aktually love yore bleedin country. The funny thing is, as the sun sinks slowly over the Ashes, that some of us aktually seem to love it more than you do.